Child Pornography

THE UNIVERSITY OF
WINCHESTER

Martial Rose Library
Tel: 01962 827306

To be returned on or before the day marked above, subject to recall.

Child Pornography
Crime, computers and society

Ian O'Donnell and Claire Milner

Routledge
Taylor & Francis Group

LONDON AND NEW YORK

First published 2007 by Willan Publishing

This edition published 2012 by Routledge
2 Park Square, Milton Park, Abingdon, Oxon, OX14 4RN
711 Third Avenue, New York, NY 10017

Routledge is an imprint of the Taylor & Francis Group, an informa business

ISBN 978-1-84392-356-5 paperback
        978-1-84392-357-2 hardback

British Library Cataloguing-in-Publication Data

A catalogue record for this book is available from the British Library

Project managed by Deer Park Productions, Tavistock, Devon
Typeset by GCS, Leighton Buzzard, Bedfordshire

Contents

List of tables and figures

Tables

Figures

List of boxes

Acknowledgements

Part II of this book has its origins in a study funded by Ireland's Department of Justice, Equality and Law Reform, whose financial support is acknowledged. An unprecedented level of cooperation, especially from police and prosecutors, allowed an unusually wide-ranging inquiry to be conducted into how child pornographers are investigated and brought to justice. In addition, a number of judges spoke candidly about how they exercised their discretion when dealing with a category of offender that excites a high level of public interest and revulsion. While the empirical focus is on a single jurisdiction the arguments raised are of more general relevance.

We have a number of debts to record.

From An Garda Síochána we are grateful to Chief Superintendent John O'Mahony, Detective Garda Philip Ryan, Detective Garda Séamus Duffy, Superintendent John Shanahan and the Crime Policy and Administration Unit. Special thanks go to those members of the force who took time out of their busy days to fill in our questionnaire.

The Director of Public Prosecutions, James Hamilton, and his legal research officer, Clara Connolly, were generous with their time and expertise.

The study was facilitated by Esmond Smith, former President of the Circuit Court, and Peter Smithwick, former President of the District Court, together with his colleague Dolores Moore. We are very grateful to all of the judges who shared their experiences with us.

Jim Mitchell from the Irish Prison Service, Pat Walsh and Niall Muldoon from the Granada Institute, and Peggy Garvey from the

Censorship of Publications Office gave us valuable perspectives on the issues at hand. We are also obliged to Tom O'Malley of the Law Faculty in NUI Galway who shared with us some of his ongoing work in the fields of sentencing and sex crime. Cormac Behan and Eoin O'Sullivan were kind enough to read, and comment upon, a full draft of this manuscript.

The production and consumption of child pornography are viewed with particular abhorrence. We hope that we have managed to deal with this emotive topic in a way that does justice to victims and perpetrators as well as contributing to a better understanding of an issue that is placing criminal justice agencies under increasing strain.

Part I
Understanding the Context

Chapter I

The enduring appeal of child pornography

The history of child pornography is difficult to write. While the academic literature might be modest in size and of recent origin, the same cannot be said for the phenomenon it describes. Paintings depicting adult men engaging in sexual activities with young boys have been discovered among the remains of ancient Greek civilisation (Dover 1978) and the Romans were famously tolerant of pederasty (Veyne 1987). This indicates that the origins of such activity, and the desire to record it for future viewing pleasure, date back at least to Antiquity. The invention of the printing press in the middle of the fifteenth century meant that large-scale reproduction became possible. The first pages to be stamped with hot metal and ink were the books of the Bible. But erotic material soon followed and by the middle of the sixteenth century the amount of obscene literature in circulation caused such alarm that Pope Paul IV established the *Index Librorum Prohibitorum*, a list of books forbidden by the church that was added to until 1966 (Lane 2001: 8, 98).

Examples of written pornography detailing sexual acts with children have survived from seventeenth-century France and England. One of the most successful erotic novels ever, John Cleland's *Fanny Hill, or the Memoirs of a Woman of Pleasure*, was first published in 1749 and has been in print ever since, an edition appearing as a Penguin Classic in 2005. Part of the novel's enduring appeal may lie in the fact that the eponymous heroine was just past her fifteenth birthday when she began life as a prostitute. Tate (1990: 33–4) put it well when he observed that: 'Almost since man discovered the ability to write or draw he has recorded the sexual abuse of children'.

The pornography industry did not really take off until the early nineteenth century when the introduction of the camera, and improved printing processes, allowed pornography to be produced in a volume capable of satisfying a mass audience. By the late 1800s pornography was widely available in England (Pearsall 1969: 364-392). For example, in 1874 London police raided the studio of Henry Hayler and confiscated over 130,000 indecent photographs. Hayler was a good businessman and the catalogues that illustrated his wares were widely circulated. This was a family concern with Hayler, his wife and two sons working on both sides of the camera. He was also well connected and managed to flee the country before his home was raided, probably on the basis of a tip-off (Hebditch and Anning 1988: 4–5).

In Victorian England, establishing a studio, making and marketing obscene photographs and avoiding scandal required money, a degree of common sense and good connections. This was a middle-class pursuit and the price of the product meant that purchasers were likely to be men of reasonable means. Looking at the early industry, Jenkins (2001: 31) observed that: 'Often, these images sought a kind of respectability by portraying their subjects in classical and artistic poses, but the prominent display of the genitalia leaves little doubt about the erotic purpose of the works'. The case of Charles Lutwidge Dodgson (whose pen name was Lewis Carroll) is often cited in this context. He photographed young girls naked or in various states of undress, though never in any sexual act. Some of his photographs found their way into late twentieth-century magazines and a number of paedophile organisations (e.g. the Wønderland Club, see Box 2.1 pp. 38–9) have used his name or the titles of his stories to indicate the kind of fantasies that appeal to their members.

Liberalisation and mass production

Child pornography production and consumption in Europe in the twentieth century were at first closely tied to the adult pornography industry. Due to rudimentary production processes, the trade was amateurish in the forties and fifties and appears to have been focused more on written material than photographs. However, the publication of naturist magazines, which carried pictures of unclothed children in everyday (non-pornographic) situations, quickly gained a paedophile following (Tate 1990). Probably the best-known naturist publication, *Health and Efficiency*, which began publication in the USA in 1900 and in London in 1956, is still widely available (now as *H&E Naturist*) but no longer shows naked minors. Another example of this genre was *Sunshine and Health* which began publication in the USA in 1931 and unselfconsciously described itself as the 'official organ' of the American Sunbathing Association. According to Lane (2001: 45) it made more nude photographs available than any other source, and cost less.

The sexual revolution of the mid-1960s, marked by the availability of effective methods of birth control and an openness to sexual expression and variation, heralded a burgeoning demand for pornography, with adult bookstores springing up in many European and American cities. Reflecting this change in attitude, most Western European countries relaxed their censorship laws and there was a narrowing of what was perceived to be obscene.

Denmark led the way in this regard. Encouraged by professional opinion in favour of decriminalising pornography, and difficulties convicting those brought before the courts on obscenity charges, the Danish government legalised the production of all forms of pornography in 1969. This included child pornography. Sweden followed suit in 1971. By failing to introduce relevant legislation or enforce existing legislation, it could be argued that other Western governments allowed child pornography to be produced or distributed by default. In an enlightening account, Tate (1990: 33) described the period from 1969 to 1979 as a 'ten year madness', during which time the circulation of child pornography became a global industry.

The speed with which the earliest producers were able to offload material indicated a strong latent demand. As Willy Strauss, a major Danish child pornographer, bragged:

Most dealers in Copenhagen showed one kind of pornography. I saw very early that there was only one thing better than normal pornography and that was bizarre pornography, speciality pornography ... In 1971 I was the first to produce children magazines, at least with pictures ... We printed the first 10,000 copies. It was the first child-sex magazine in the whole world: *Bambina Sex*. I sold those 10,000 copies on the telephone to other porn dealers in two hours and ordered another printing. By the end of the week I'd sold 19,000. (Cited in Hebditch and Anning 1988: 317–18)

The operation run by Strauss and his wife Leila soon became one of the world's biggest sources of commercial child pornography. Their initial involvement was opportunistic. A customer of their adult shop offered photographs of a man and a young girl having sex. Strauss took the pictures and put them in his desk drawer. Several weeks later he was offered a special price on a job lot of paper which had become available because another of his customers, a magazine publisher, could not pay his bills. Strauss decided to use the free photographs and the cheap paper to make a magazine. Readers responded by sending in their own photographs and by Strauss's estimation he promptly made another 40 or 50 magazines with the material sent in by enthusiastic amateur photographers from all over the world. In his view this was a 'normal kind of business' and because it was legally acceptable it was morally unproblematic (Hebditch and Anning 1988: 317–19).

The Danish company, Rodox/Color Climax Corporation, established by the Theander brothers, Peter and Jens, also capitalised on this new market. They created a huge pornography production camp on the outskirts of Copenhagen in 1975. Over the next two decades it is estimated that they produced nearly 100 million magazines and 10 million films (ibid: 53). While most of the content was adult, the company also produced a large number of child pornography magazines with varying degrees of explicitness and 36 hard-core child pornography films, the *Lolita* series. These were sordid and brutal affairs, which according to Taylor and Quayle (2003: 44), 'exclusively involved pictures of young girls being sexually abused, primarily by men, but sometimes involving women or other children. The girls were mainly in the age range 7–11, but with some younger'. These films were around ten minutes long and the marketing strategy left nothing to the imagination. The series included such titles as: *Sucking Daddy*, *Fucking Children* and *Little Girl Sex*. More than a decade later, Tate (1990) claimed that US Customs identified the *Lolita* series as still the most widely traded of all commercial child pornography films. The Theanders rapidly became, and have remained, multi-millionaires. They had come a long way from the second-hand bookstore they opened in Copenhagen as ambitious twenty-somethings.

In addition to legalising pornography, Denmark's liberalisation repudiated the 1923 *United Nations International Convention for the Suppression of the Circulation and Traffic in Obscene Publications*. As such, little effort was made to stop the exportation of any form of pornography (Tate 1990). While both adult and child pornography were actually illegal there, Amsterdam became the primary distribution centre for child pornography exported from Denmark and other European and American cities throughout the 1970s. Dutch tolerance of the pornography trade provided an environment that allowed it to become highly profitable. The Netherlands also had its own producers, most notably perhaps Joop Wilhelmus who continued, unchallenged by the authorities, to publish *Lolita* magazine for seventeen years. As Tate (1990: 59) observed, the content was unashamedly explicit:

> *Lolita* frequently included editorial pleas for new child pornography to publish: 'This magazine can only exist if you help us! Send us photos from your collection.' 'We desperately need more photos from private files.' Those requests amounted to an incitement by Wilhelmus for the magazine's readers to abuse more children and mail him the evidence. Lolita also provided a contact service for its readers, enabling them to advertise both for child pornography and for new children to abuse.

One advert read: 'English gentleman, 37, paedophile, wishes to meet a mother with Lolita daughter or lady with paedophile feelings with view to marriage'. The authorities eventually closed the magazine by charging Wilhelmus with unlawfully procuring young boys for sex, but not before it had reached issue 55 in 1984 (Hebditch and Anning 1988: 326). Like the *Lolita* film series, Wilhelmus's *Lolita* magazine became an almost universal brand name for child pornography images.

The pornography industry developed a market earlier in America than in Europe, as evidenced by the publication of Hugh Hefner's *Playboy* magazine in December 1953, featuring a full-colour photograph of a nude woman in every issue. In parallel with European developments, a commercial interest in the production and distribution of child pornography soon emerged. Once again, liberal views on pornography, combined with lax law enforcement, enabled the trade to flourish. After lengthy deliberations, President Johnson's Commission on Pornography and Obscenity concluded in 1970 that the national interest would be best served by repealing all laws that restricted the distribution of obscene materials in the USA. Unsurprisingly, the Commission's findings were hugely controversial and overwhelmingly rejected by the Senate.

The case of *Miller v. California* in 1973 was significant in facilitating the growth of child pornography into an organised commercial activity. Marvin Miller, operator of one of the West coast's largest mail order businesses dealing in sexually explicit material, was prosecuted on foot of complaints from unwilling recipients of one of his mail shots. He was convicted under Californian law of distributing obscene material. Miller appealed to the US Supreme court on the grounds that the sale and distribution of obscene materials by mail was protected under the First Amendment's freedom of speech guarantee. In a 5–to-4 decision the court found against him. The *Miller* judgment found that obscene material did not enjoy First Amendment protection and replaced existing definitions of obscenity with the following three-pronged test:

> (a) whether the average person, applying contemporary community standards would find that the work, taken as a whole, appeals to the prurient interest ... (b) whether the work depicts or describes, in a patently offensive way, sexual conduct specifically defined by the applicable state law; and (c) whether the work, taken as a whole, lacks serious literary, artistic, political, or scientific value.

The Supreme Court thereby indicated a narrow view of what constituted obscenity. It put the onus on state governments to legislate against obscene material. As the overwhelming majority of states did not have the relevant legislation in place at this time, child pornography soon became part of the commercial mainstream of pornography. According to *The Meese Commission Report* (Attorney General's Commission on Pornography 1986: 595): '... by 1977 [child pornography was] sold over the counter and in considerable quantities. While a substantial amount of such material was of foreign origin, much of it was made using American children'. Commenting on the ease with which such publications could be obtained, Jenkins (2001: 32) noted that:

> At least for a few years, it was easy to walk into a store in New York, Los Angeles, or London, and purchase what was frankly advertised as child porn. This might include pictures of, say, young girls performing oral sex on adult men or women or men performing anal sex on young boys, as well as countless pictures of eight- or ten-year-old girls in Penthouse-type cheesecake poses.

International collaborations also emerged, with photographs and films criss-crossing the Atlantic in an effort to 'launder' the products and conceal their origins (O'Brien 1983: 115–18). Healy (1996: 4) discovered that:

Most of the children depicted were Caucasian. Many who were featured in European child pornography magazines were photographed in the United States and the photos were published in magazines assembled abroad. Some of the material produced in Europe during the 70s, however, included children from India and Mexico and one series included black children from Africa.

These magazines and films also developed a following outside the paedophile community as society opened up to sexual experimentation and individual choice. Jenkins (2001: 32) described how, in the early 1970s, European and US avant-garde magazines, which were notionally devoted to rock music and radical politics, would 'throw in occasional images of pubescent nudes', thereby reaching an unprecedented audience.

Paedophiles start networking

The emergence of paedophile support organisations during the 1970s was a further sign of the lax attitude of the authorities towards adults expressing a sexual interest in children. The Paedophile Information Exchange (PIE) was founded in the United Kingdom in October 1974 in order to campaign for an acceptance and understanding of paedophilia. Its formally defined aims included giving advice and counsel and providing a means for paedophiles to contact one another. To this end it held regular meetings in London and produced magazines and a 'Contact Page', a bulletin in which members placed advertisements, giving their membership number, general location, and brief details of their sexual and other interests. Keith Hose, chairman of PIE, summed up the group's intentions in its 1975–1976 annual report:

> The only way for PIE to survive was to seek out as much publicity for the organisation as possible … If we got bad publicity we would not run into a corner but stand and fight. We felt that the only way to get more paedophiles joining PIE … was to seek out and try to get all kinds of publications to print our organization's name and address and to make paedophilia a real public issue.

PIE claimed that advertisements seeking erotica or contact with children were turned down, but Tate (1990: 134) reproduced a

f notices that give the lie to these assertions and argued
)aid paedophiles to provide it with non-obscene pictures
1 (usually boys) for its various publications. At one stage,
surveyed its members (numbering around 180) to identify
11 their preference was for boys or girls and which age range was
of particular interest (Wilson and Cox 1983). Among PIE's members
were an employee of MI6 (the British intelligence service) and the
author Tom O'Carroll, who managed to have a book on the subject
published in London in 1980. *Paedophilia: The Radical Case* advocates
a change in the law to allow for sexual relationships between adults
and children. O'Carroll has continued to be an activist in this area
despite serving a number of prison terms. In 2000 he addressed the
annual meeting of the International Academy of Sex Research in
Paris on the theme of sexual privacy for paedophiles and children.
His book remains easily available but, as is often the case in this
area, potential purchasers will pay a premium for their interest
with second-hand copies going for US$210 (€171) on Amazon.com
and STG£201 (€287) on Amazon.co.uk (Web sites accessed 5 April
2006). Ironically, the entire text is available free of charge on the
Internet.

While exposure led to intimidation and loss of employment for
PIE members, these groups received an unusual level of tolerance
compared to what they could expect in today's society. For example,
in May 1977 Tom Crabtree, a columnist with *The Guardian* newspaper,
wrote about PIE, saying they needed to 'come out into the open and
argue their case where everybody can hear it'. PIE complained about
the article to the UK Press Council, on the basis that they had not
been approached for a comment before the article appeared and
were denied a right of reply afterwards. They received a judgment in
their favour in December of the same year (O'Carroll 1980: Chapter
12). (For an account of the organisation's demise, written by a former
chairman, see Smith 1986).

PIE was one of several paedophile support groups in operation
during the 1970s and 1980s. This was a time when those with a
sexual interest in children became emboldened and assertive. Other
groups included Arbeitskreis Päderastie-Pädophilie (AKP; a German
group which was active in the early 1980s and catered mainly for
heterosexual paedophiles), Centre de Recherche et d'Information sur
l'Enfance et la Sexualité (CRIES; a Belgian group), Indianerkommune
(children's liberation commune; strongly identified as paedophile
and several independent local groups are apparently still active in
Germany today), and Norwegian Paedophile Group (NAFP; one of

the strongest and best established networks while it existed) (see http://www.paedosexualitaet.de/org).

The Danish Paedophile Association (DPA) was a relatively big, successful group which shut down its operations, including its Web site, in March 2004 while the public prosecutor investigated the group's activities. Within a month the Web site had been reopened by a faction within the DPA which felt unprepared to cave in to what it saw as 'unjust' and 'anti-democratic' pressure. The organisation itself however was not reconstituted; only a presence in Cyberspace continued. Between April 2004 and November 2005 the site received 42,179 visitors. In December 2005 the official investigation concluded that if the DPA were to re-establish itself it could not be legally shut down. The organisation claimed that it had been 'exonerated'.

Again mirroring the European situation, paedophile support groups emerged in the USA around the same time. The Childhood Sensuality Circle (CSC), founded in 1971 in San Diego, California, lobbied for the abolition of consent laws and promoted incest. The Rene Guyon Society (motto: 'Sex by year eight or else it's too late') was created in 1962 and encouraged its members to allow their own children to experiment sexually with adults. Both organisations were defunct by the mid-1980s (deYoung 1989).

Most infamous, and most enduring, the North American Man/Boy Love Association was formed in 1978. In the early 1980s, NAMBLA was reported to have over 300 members. For a while it had a public face. O'Brien (1983: 124) remarked that a conference on the sexual exploitation of children, held at Boston University in 1981, was disrupted by NAMBLA members and their legal representatives who felt that their side of the story was being ignored. The protest was supported by a group of 12 to 16-year-old boys whose placards read, 'Repeal Child Porno Laws'. More recently, the organisation has kept membership data private, but an undercover FBI investigation in 1995 discovered that there were 1,100 people on the rolls (*Union-Tribune*, 17 February 2005). While recent media reports suggest that the group no longer exists, NAMBLA continues to maintain a Web site that shows addresses in New York and San Francisco and a contact telephone number in New York. It offers publications for sale, including the *NAMBLA Bulletin*, a copy of which was brought to the attention of the Censorship of Publications Office in Ireland in December 1995 and banned as an obscene publication. Today the availability of the *Bulletin* online means that the censor is effectively bypassed. The office voicemail suggests a continuing level of activity and, despite the emphasis on rights and empowerment, callers are left in little doubt as to the organisation's intent (see Box 1.1).

> **Box 1.1: NAMBLA voicemail greeting (10 November 2005)**
>
> You have reached the voicemail of NAMBLA, the North American Man/ Boy Love Association. We're a political and educational organisation, well into our third decade. We believe that relationships should be evaluated on the basis of whether or not they are mutually consensual and desired. We have consistently spoken out against coercion and violence in any form and we support the right of young people to make choices free of state interference. We support legal changes in accordance with our views but the organisation does not break the law nor do we advocate that others do so.
>
> This is a voicemail system so there is never anyone here who can take your call live. Volunteers pick up and return calls at their discretion. If you need to be called back please state slowly, clearly and audibly your name, phone number and the best time to reach you. Include your area code even if you live in New York. It may take a few days to get back to you so please be patient. Our return calls block caller ID so if your phone rejects such anonymous calls we will be unable to reach you.
>
> For more information please send one dollar US and a self-addressed stamped envelope to P.O. Box [details omitted]. You can obtain a sample publication for an additional six dollars US. All mail sent by us will have only our return address as previously stated. An alternative and free source of information can be found on our Web site at [details omitted]. All change of address notifications and address corrections should also be sent in writing to our P.O. Box. If you would like to join an organisation that speaks out for the empowerment of young people and against the societal oppression of love, our yearly membership dues are thirty-five dollars US for residents of North America, fifty dollars US otherwise. Send them to the address previously mentioned. Thank you.
>
> At the tone begin recording.
>
> (*Source*: NAMBLA contact telephone number, New York.)

In the 1980s membership of NAMBLA was seen by some as a statement of support for civil liberties, akin to showing solidarity for those oppressed by society's prejudices. The American poet Allen Ginsberg (2000: 170–71) described his reasons for joining in the following terms:

NAMBLA's a forum for reform of those laws on you
sexuality which members deem oppressive, a discussion s
not a sex club. I joined NAMBLA in defense of free speech .
Most people like myself do not make carnal love to hairless
boys and girls. Yet such erotic inclinations or fantasies are
average ... An afternoon's walk through the Vatican Museum
will attest centuries of honorific appreciation of nude youths,
an acceptable pleasure in the quasi erotic contemplation of the
'naked human form divine.'

The terms of the debate have narrowed dramatically in recent years
and the political temperature has been increased. Any semblance
of a reasoned historical perspective on the love that adults exhibit
towards children has disappeared. In combination this means that
the prospects of a public figure attempting to return the focus to
matters of principle are slim indeed. This is an issue characterised
by monochromatic thinking; where a possibility of child abuse exists,
there is no room for nuance.

Nevertheless, a number of organisations have arrived on the
scene more recently. Based in the Netherlands, the significance of
Ipce (International Pedophile and Child Emancipation) is difficult
to gauge. According to the mission statement published on Ipce's
Web site, it is ostensibly dedicated to 'scholarly discussion about the
understanding and emancipation of mutual relationships between
children or adolescents and adults. In this context these relationships
are intended to be viewed from an unbiased, non-judgmental
perspective and in relation to the human rights of both the young
and adult partners'. Ipce believes that all individuals have the right
to contact and relationships with other humans, including minors.
It advocates breaking down age barriers, which are seen to place
artificial (and arbitrary) constraints on the development of meaningful
engagements between people, arguing that:

In any intergenerational relationship or contact, both partners,
the adult as well as the young person, should have it in their
power to regulate their own lives, their relationships and the
grade of intimacy. Each partner has the right to self-determination
and the responsibility to acknowledge this right in the other.
Therefore, both partners in open communication will at any
moment choose the grade of intimacy.

The group publishes a lengthy list of reference material on its Web
site. This contains work by known paedophiles and omits some of

the best-known critical work in this area. Many of the key texts upon which this book is based are not to be found among Ipce's extensive listings. Newsletters document details of annual meetings and progress reports provided by paedophile support groups from a number of countries. The *Newsletter* dated 2 October 1997 (No. 2) provided information from the eleventh Ipce meeting held in Munich in July 1997. There were, '... persons from Germany, the United Kingdom, Austria, New Zealand, USA, Greece and the Netherlands. The meeting regretted that DPA and NAMBLA had no delegates present at the meeting'. The report provided by the Canadian delegates surveyed recent developments as follows:

> The *Coalition Pédophile Quebecois* is still working quite effectively, whilst the *Fondation Nouvelle* (that tried to work for the whole of Canada) has apparently ended its work and existence. The Ipce members are asked not to mention the *Coalition* and its address in public, because this is hazardous for its members. Another message tells us that the legal age of consent for males and females is 14. The law however, treats sex with pre-teens very harshly. The gay press in Canada and even some of the mainstream press has been quite supportive towards pedophilia ... The child pornography law of Canada, which is very strict (even the *NAMBLA Bulletin* is forbidden), has been strongly criticized by almost all the Canadian media. There is a good possibility that this law will be abolished.

A later *Newsletter* (July 2005, No. 19) reported that Ipce had 79 members in 20 countries. Its annual accounts showed a total income in 2004/05 of €717. This demonstrates that its presence in Cyberspace is based on a very slender support base. There is no mailing address (a post box in the Netherlands was given in the early days before communication became exclusively electronic). Postings to the Web site are unsigned (as are Newsletter articles) and the entire edifice could result from the activities of a couple of determined individuals. The Web site claims to have around 100 visitors each day. Its *Newsletter* reports occasionally on developments in Ireland (for example, September 1998, No. 3; and January 1999, No. 4) suggesting the possibility of a local member. However, according to minutes of meetings available online, an Irish delegate has never attended.

In 1998 the organisation discussed changing its name by removing the 'P' as it was felt that the use of the term 'pedophile' was 'disastrous from a public relations/communications point of view' (*Newsletter*

No. 6, July 1999). A compromise was found. This was to keep the name, but as a noun (Ipce) rather than an abbreviation (IPCE), and not to explain the original meaning.

On 31 May 2006 a group of Dutch paedophiles launched a political party to lobby for a reduction in the age of consent from 16 to 12 (as a first step in getting rid of it completely) as well as the legalisation of child pornography and sex with animals. The Party for Neighbourly Love, Freedom and Diversity (PNVD) also advocated free rail travel, public nudity, the elimination of marriage and a prohibition on the consumption of meat and fish. The group felt that since the Dutroux case in neighbouring Belgium (see pp. 23–5) paedophilia had become a taboo subject and that it was time to reopen the discussion.

Recognising the problem

The heyday for those with a sexual interest in children was the 1970s. PIE and NAMBLA were at their peak, child pornography had been legalised in a number of countries and was tolerated in others, and child protection had not yet become a political priority. But the 'discovery' of child sexual abuse as a significant social problem towards the end of the same decade marked a point of departure. Long hidden away, this issue had been overlooked by professionals who were 'culturally blind to its existence' (Thomas 2005: 125). This was around the time when the phrase 'child abuse', which had hitherto referred to physical abuse or neglect, became inextricably intertwined with notions of sexual interference. Hacking (1991; 1995) noted that a major force behind this shift in meaning was the feminist movement's exposure of the crime of incest as a widespread problem. This brought public awareness to child sexual abuse in general and the prospect of paedophiles adopting a public profile diminished rapidly.

More specifically, decency campaigners successfully promoted the idea that there was a direct link between pornography and sexual misconduct, sparking a 'ferocious morality campaign' (Jenkins 2001: 32–3). With increasing recognition of its consequences, not only for individuals and their families but also for society as a whole, the sexual abuse of children emerged as an issue of international concern. It quickly became a major area of research and practical social welfare intervention, commanding intense government and media attention and fostering the growth of new sub-specialties of intervention, particularly around preventing the commercial sexual exploitation of children (Adler 2001a). Although recognised to be an age-old practice that had existed to some degree in every society, anxiety arose that child sexual exploitation was acquiring 'a new and disturbing dimension, owing to the link between international crime and pornography, prostitution and trafficking in children' (Council of Europe 1991). This resulted in increased governmental regulation both in Europe and the USA.

According to Tate (1990: 63), the first real public awareness of child pornography in America came in September 1975 in New York City. In preparation for the 1976 Democratic Convention the administration launched a clean-up campaign against sex shops, targeting four in particular that were known to sell child pornography. The media focus on the impending convention meant that the issue of child pornography became national news in America. The following year, NBC journalist Robin Lloyd published *For Money or Love: Boy Prostitution in America*, in which he claimed that a huge network of prostitution involving 300,000 boys existed (1976: 226). Lloyd wrote the book after his two teenage sons were picked up on vacation by a man who brought them to his home and took nude photographs of them. When Lloyd tracked the man down he discovered that he was a school football coach and had taken similar photographs of a number of other boys. This got Lloyd thinking about the extent to which his sons' experience was an isolated one.

Whatever about the precise scale of the problem, which was disputed, some of the small ads reproduced by Lloyd on the inside cover of his book show how open some people were in expressing their desires. Where they were not explicit, the code (for example, 'chicken' for child) was simple to decipher as the following examples show. It is inconceivable that such notices would appear in printed listings today.

CHICKEN LOVERS! If you crave a diet of scrumptious chicken, have a pocketbook to match your gourmet taste and don't look and act like Henry VIII, I have the recipe for you. Take your pick of everything, from springers to roosters. Details sent following dtld letter from you.

MOROCCO CHICKEN? Need exp companion for discreet but lively chicken tour of Morocco.

OHIO. Young boy, r u lonely? Need a friend? I'm 27, W male, brown hair, blue eyes, 5'9". I want to meet you if young, good looking, sincere. 13 to 16 only! Prefer Southern Mich or Ohio area but will answer all who send pic!

Schuijer and Rossen (1992) proposed that the notion the child pornography trade was big business was initiated in Lloyd's book. Despite there being no empirical basis to his claims, anti-child-pornography campaigners presented his figures as reliable estimates. Chief amongst these was Dr Judianne Densen-Gerber (director of the Odyssey Institute, a New York drug rehabilitation centre) who, along with Dr Frank Osanka (a Chicago-based private behavioural consultant), held a conference in February 1977 to attract media attention to what they saw as a growing problem and to demand specific child pornography legislation (Tate 1990: 64). Across the country, extensive press coverage was devoted to the campaign. As Schuijer and Rossen (1992: 56–7) recalled:

> The media followed the stories of child exploitation in detail. In the national periodicals during 1977 nine articles appeared. The *New York Times*, a paper known to avoid sensationalism, printed 27 articles that year compared to one in the two years before. When in May 1977 the highly popular television series *Sixty Minutes* devoted a program to child pornography, a tidal wave of letters to politicians resulted.

The media used extravagantly inflated (and unfounded) statistics to present child pornography as a pressing social menace. A 1977 report on NBC television news claimed that as many as two million American youths were involved in the burgeoning child pornography business. According to Jenkins (2001: 33): 'The 1977 campaign began a pattern that would dominate accounts over the next decade, when moralistic critics competed to assert the most excessive claims about the size and profitability of the trade'. Despite these charges being discredited, at the time they mobilised public opinion against child pornography and the pressure grew for governments to act.

By October 1977 a new federal statute, the Protection of Children Against Sexual Exploitation, was passed. For the first time, the use of children in the production of child pornography anywhere in the USA was clearly outlawed, as was the transportation of child pornography (and children to be used in sexual activity) across any interstate boundary.

The new statute should have sounded the death knell for the US commercial child pornography production industry. Before the law was introduced, Crewdson (1988: 243) claimed that it was possible to buy more than 250 different child pornography magazines in the USA (with titles like *Torrid Tots, Suckulant Youth* and *Incestuous Love*); afterwards the open sale of such materials ceased abruptly. Law enforcement agencies in the USA began to report two mutations of the domestic industry in the wake of the new law (Tate 1990: 67). First was a change from commercial to homemade child pornography, the latter being swapped rather than sold. Simultaneously, the remaining commercial producers opted to launder their material through European countries where child pornography was still legal.

In 1982, the US Supreme Court unanimously held that child pornography was not entitled to First Amendment protection. In the case of *New York v. Ferber* the court held that portraying minors engaged in sexually explicit activity could be criminalised even if it was not obscene according to the *Miller* test described above. The rationale was that children required as much protection as possible from this particularly damaging form of exploitation. In 1990, in the case of *Osborne v. Ohio*, the US Supreme Court extended the *Ferber* ruling to the effect that, unlike obscenity, a person could be convicted of mere possession of child pornography.

Around the same time as child pornography was being outlawed in America, voices in the Scandinavian countries began to call for legal prohibition (Schuijer and Rossen 1992). By 1980 Denmark and Sweden acknowledged the negative consequences of child pornography and banned it entirely. However, by the time the law was reformed many thousands of child pornography magazines and hundreds of hours of hard-core films had already been published and disseminated throughout the world. According to Jenkins (2001), this era has achieved legendary status among devotees of such material, and much of what was produced in the 1970s can still be obtained and lies at the centre of many child pornography collections. Police seizures of child pornography regularly include copies of this material, including the *Lolita* magazines and videos (Taylor and Quayle 2003).

Despite the ban, commercial production in Denmark and Sweden continued into the first half of the 1980s. More significantly, the government in the Netherlands failed to take adequate action against the trade and this country continued to act as the chief exporter of child pornography around the world, effectively making the new laws redundant. Schuijer and Rossen (1992: 55) described this unusual situation, and what changed it, in the following way: 'Child pornography was not a public issue in the Netherlands, even though photographs of children were openly for sale in most pornography shops. In the classified advertising section of *Vrij Nederland* [a left-leaning magazine] undisguised offers of child pornography regularly appeared. That changed in July 1984, when police raided a number of Amsterdam sex shops'. The ensuing media attention elevated child pornography to a prominent social issue.

Healy (1996) believed that an NBC documentary, *The Silent Shame*, broadcast in the USA during August 1984, exposed the international trade in pornography and was instrumental in pressurising governments to become stricter in their enforcement efforts. Influential also was the claim by US Postal Inspectors that 80 per cent of the child pornography collectors they investigated had abused children sexually. Healy claimed that US officials specifically credited this documentary with causing an immediate drop in foreign shipments during 1984. At that time, the USA emerged as the leading crusader in the fight against child pornography. It took on the role partly because it appeared that the bulk of all commercially produced child pornography ended up in the collections of American paedophiles, and partly because a vacuum existed: no other government seemed as willing to prioritise the eradication of child pornography (Tate 1990).

In November 1984, following a visit by a group of American Senators, Dutch law enforcement professionals began to address the problem in a more concerted way (Schuijer and Rossen 1992). There was a dramatic decrease in the number of shops in Amsterdam openly selling child pornography (cited in Tate 1990: 77). Willy Strauss, the Danish originator of commercial child pornography, reported how when the law changed an immediate consequence was that the trade went underground, the cover price of magazines increased tenfold, and his profits soared. The boom was temporary as police activity increased also and in 1983 Strauss was raided. More than 10,000 magazines, videotapes and playing cards involving child pornography were confiscated. This was not the end for Strauss. He stayed within the law by diversifying into hard-core child pornography stories illustrated with explicit drawings of children being violated. His first book, *Lolita Slavinder* (Lolita Slaves), appeared on the shelves in Denmark in 1986 (Hebditch and Anning 1988: 319–21).

In January 1985, another US visitation, this time involving a team from the State Department, toured the Netherlands, Denmark and Sweden in order to press for greater action. The Dutch drew up new legislation to outlaw the child pornography trade. Child pornography was included in the Criminal Code, with the legislation finally coming into effect on 26 July 1986. Thus, in Tate's words (1990: 78), '... the era of the overt dealers' was brought to an end.

A cottage industry emerges

Increased regulation by governments resulted in a significant decline in the commercial production and distribution of child pornography. Schuijer and Rossen (1992: 71) observed that: 'After 1984 the magazines and films virtually disappeared from sight'. By this stage, the business appeared to be on the verge of extinction and it seemed realistic to expect that a thorough suppression of the whole child pornography trade would have occurred given time (Jenkins 2001). It was simply too risky for any mainstream producer to continue to cater for a niche market that accounted for a small percentage of profits and jeopardised overall viability. Regardless of the moral or legal context, the production of child pornography no longer made financial sense. Kincaid (1998: 173) noted pithily that at a police seminar he attended in California in 1990 it was announced with pride that the only publications still being produced were made by the government for use in sting operations!

However, in tandem with these developments, society witnessed a technological revolution whereby inexpensive communication and recording devices started to become widely available. Most significantly, Healy (1996: 5) documents how the mid-1980s marked the advent of the camcorder and a dramatic increase in the production of non-commercial amateur pornographic home videos involving children. As she saw it:

> The development of new technology has made a tremendous impact on the international production and distribution of child pornography. The first important leap in technology was the video camera ... Because the recording media does not have to be commercially processed, and can be easily duplicated, individuals enjoy complete privacy. As a result, amateur pornographic videos have become increasingly common.

As a result of expanding access to these increasingly inexpensive technologies, child pornography quickly mutated into a 'sophisticated global cottage industry' (Healy 1996: 1) where material was produced in domestic settings and exchanged or bartered for personal rather than profit motives. Distribution was somewhat limited by the fact that the quality of videotapes deteriorates the more that they are copied. A fourth or fifth generation copy is almost unwatchable. The introduction of digital recording to the domestic market in the 1990s removed this limitation. Now copies were as good as the original as well as being quicker and easier to make.

A further source of material was created by sex tourists. These are individuals (usually from the wealthier countries of the world) who travel (usually to developing nations with inadequate legislation and child protection services) in order to sexually abuse children. McLachlan (2000: 21) observed that child sex tourism is a long-established practice as evidenced by two of the publications in circulation before it became a focal point for concern. *Mankoff's Lusty Europe* (Mankoff 1973) and *The Discreet Gentleman's Guide to the Pleasures of Europe* (Anon 1975) revealed where 'Lolita-eyed nymphets' and '10-year old prostitutes' could be found. The latter included contact addresses, telephone numbers and price lists. One member of PIE made the memorable observation that, 'paedophiles need a good travel agent rather than a psychiatrist' (Wilson and Cox 1983: 66).

Where The Young Ones Are, a guide to US amusement arcades, beaches, street corners and fast-food joints where young boys were said to be available, was reported to have sold 70,000 copies (Lloyd 1976: 226); impressive sales figures for any 'travel guide'. It listed a total of 378 places in 59 cities and 34 states where 'young action' could be found. It was claimed that all entries had been checked and verified, suggesting an extensive network of contributors (O'Brien 1983: 37–8). According to Carr (2001) the growth in child sex tourism in the 1980s and 1990s increasingly saw images of children from Asia and Eastern Europe being added to the stock of pornographic material. The Council of Europe (1991: 10) noted that:

> For some years, tourist agencies have been organising – mainly for a predominantly male clientele – trips whose particular attraction lies in the prospect of low-cost exotic sex. A few of these agencies are specialised ones making use of paedophile magazines for publishing their advertisements. Most of them, however, are highly respected businesses which insert more or less ambiguous references in their widely circulated brochures. The regions affected by 'sex tourism' are mainly to be found in Asia, Africa and Latin America. In view of the fact that the local authorities are not usually inclined to intervene in cases of child prostitution, paedophiles from rich countries, often well-informed by specialised magazines, profit.

Crewdson (1988: 33–4) made the further point that the income generated by these visitors was welcomed by the local economies, adding to the reluctance to take effective action. In this regard he singled out the revenues generated by Manila's Ermita district, the 'baby brothels' of Bombay and some sections of Bangkok. To combat this, a number of states have gone so far as to adopt extraterritorial criminal laws, to make it possible to initiate prosecutions at home for sexual offences committed against children in other countries.

International developments

In 1989, the United Nations drew up the most influential legal instrument in the history of child protection. The Convention on the Rights of the Child (UNCRC) provided a baseline international standard for the protection of children from sexual exploitation. The UNCRC is the most widely accepted human rights agreement having been ratified by every country in the world, except Somalia and the USA. Article 34 provides that state parties undertake to protect children from all forms of sexual exploitation and sexual abuse. For these purposes, they are required to take all appropriate national, bilateral and multilateral measures to prevent: (a) the inducement or coercion of a child to engage in any unlawful sexual activity; (b) the exploitative use of children in prostitution or other unlawful sexual practices; and (c) the exploitative use of children in pornographic performances and materials.

To reinforce the content of Article 34, an Optional Protocol to the UNCRC on the sale of children, child prostitution and child pornography was adopted by the General Assembly on 25 May 2000 and came into force on 18 January 2002.

While international awareness of the existence of child pornography mobilised some governments to take legislative action, few were prepared to admit a problem existed within their national boundaries. The Council of Europe (1991: 20) undertook a survey of 20 member states in 1988 and found that most claimed to have no significant child pornography production. Only Italy admitted a 'flourishing market' for child pornography but failed to provide precise figures. Some replies indicated that available material originated in Southern Asia, the USA and the Scandinavian countries. Furthermore, an apparent downplaying of the problem was observed:

> The Committee deplored the obvious shortage of data on the sexual exploitation of children and young adults as well as a certain trivialisation of the problem ... The effectiveness of specific action of this kind depends, at least in part, on the

acknowledgement by the general public of the seriousness of the problem of sexual exploitation. Combating the trivialisation of such exploitation presupposes a general awareness of the existence of commercialisation of sex and its damaging effects on the well being of young people (ibid: 2, 4).

In 1991, the Committee of Ministers of the Council of Europe adopted a Recommendation concerning sexual exploitation, pornography, prostitution of, and trafficking in, children and young adults. Defining sexual exploitation as 'the sexual use for economic purposes of a child or a young person, which violates, directly or indirectly, human dignity and sexual freedom and endangers his/her psychosocial development', the Committee argued that such exploitation constituted a major threat to future generations. This was the first international text to deal comprehensively with these issues, in response to the concern aroused by the rapid expansion of sex tourism in Africa, Asia, South America, and Eastern Europe. In its report, the Committee acknowledged the extent of the problem of child pornography and called on member states to review legislation and practice, provide appropriate sanctions (taking into account the gravity of production and distribution offences), improve international cooperation and raise public awareness.

The experience of international agencies working with child victims was that the commercial sexual exploitation of children was flourishing, facilitated by the growing mobility of people and goods and the rapid development of reliable and secure communication technologies. The agencies highlighted the strong link between child prostitution, child sex tourism and child pornography. In 1994, a campaigning organisation called End Child Prostitution in Asian Tourism (ECPAT) was launched in Thailand. In 1996 its name was changed to End Child Prostitution, Child Pornography and Trafficking of Children for Sexual Purposes, to reflect the organisation's geographical expansion and broader mandate and it became the prime force behind the growth of international pressure. ECPAT (the organisation retained its original acronym) began a sustained campaign, lobbying governments to address the problems of child sex tourism, child prostitution and child pornography and to legislate accordingly. This campaigning was given impetus by the shockwaves created by the Dutroux case in Belgium.

On 15 August 1996 Marc Dutroux was arrested in Charleroi and a career of vicious sexual abuse and murder was brought to an end. Dutroux had been convicted in 1989 of the rape and abuse of underage girls, but was granted early release from prison for good conduct, having served only three years of his thirteen year sentence. After his release, Dutroux abducted 8-year-olds Julie Lejeune and Melissa Russo in June 1995. They starved to death while he was in custody under investigation for stealing luxury cars. His wife testified that she had been unable to feed the girls as she had been too scared to go down into the basement cellar where they were imprisoned. The following year the bodies of An Marchal (17) and Eefje Lambrecks (19) were discovered near the chalet of Dutroux's accomplice, Bernard Weinstein. Both girls had been drugged and buried alive, just like Weinstein himself who was found next to the bodies of Julie and Melissa in Dutroux's garden. Dutroux claimed he had merely put the girls to sleep and that it was Weinstein who had murdered them. He also claimed to have no knowledge of Weinstein's murder.

On 28 May 1996, 12-year-old Sabine Dardenne was abducted by Dutroux and his accomplice, Michel Lelièvre, while on her way to school. For 80 days she was imprisoned in a specially constructed underground cellar in Dutroux's house. Dutroux also took pornographic photographs of her. This was not his first foray into photography as he had previously made videos of Julie and Melissa. In her memoir, *I Choose To Live*, Sabine described her initial incarceration and abuse and how this was captured on camera.

> There was only me and him now – a man without a name, in a ground-floor room of a house without a name … He said I was to get undressed, and to get into one of the bunk beds. So I did. I'd asked so many questions and cried so much during the journey that I had no more strength left other than to obey. I was probably paralysed with fear and my head all drugged … No sooner had I done what I was told than he put a chain around my neck which he then padlocked to the ladder leading to the top bunk. He put a chamber pot beside it. My chain was about three feet long, just enough to let me reach this pot.

> … On the second day my head was a bit clearer and, having removed the chain, the creep led me through to another bedroom next door, which appeared to be his, with a double bed, which I later named the Calvary room [Calvary in French also means agony]. It was there that I was forced to put up with this man doing things to me. I know that he also took some polaroids. Before or after, it's difficult to say as I only realised what he was doing after the second or third flash. It seemed so strange.

I mean, why did he need to photograph me naked and chained to this bed? ... I never stopped crying, and this really got to him. He seemed to think that I should've enjoyed it. Afterwards I'd be taken back to the other bedroom to be reattached to the bunk and told to go to sleep. (Dardenne 2004: 20–4)

Although Sabine does not provide graphic descriptions, the little detail she does give leaves no doubt about the physical, mental and emotional abuse inflicted on her. On 9 August 1996, 14-year-old Laetitia Delhez was abducted by Dutroux and kept in the underground cellar along with Sabine. Six days later both girls were found by the police following the arrest of Dutroux and his swift confession.

When the case finally came to trial eight years later, Dutroux minimised his involvement in the abductions, abuse and murders, claiming he was merely a pawn in a wide network of paedophiles and child traffickers. Sabine rejected the paedophile-network story, viewing it as an attempt to obscure Dutroux's personal culpability. She testified in court that throughout her incarceration she had never come across any evidence of a network, having only ever had contact with Dutroux himself. Her presence at the trial and her testimony did not go down well with supporters of the paedophile-ring theory. Sabine's legal team had to work tirelessly to convince the press and public that she had only been drugged during the first few days following her abduction and that her recollections were accurate. Although she had not spoken to the media since her release eight years previously, Sabine was forced to hold a press conference in order to prevent her evidence from being undermined through damaging insinuations. (A propensity to accept that child abuse is organised and ritualistic is not uncommon; it seems that the more grotesque and sadistic the purported activity, the greater the willingness to suspend disbelief. However, such stories are almost always without foundation as shown by La Fontaine (1998) with regard to the UK and by Nathan and Snedeker (1995) with regard to the USA.)

In June 2004, Dutroux was convicted of the kidnap and rape of six girls and the murders of two of them (An and Eefje). He was also found guilty of Weinstein's murder. No one has ever been charged with the killings of Julie and Melissa. The jury accepted Sabine's testimony and rejected any suggestion of a paedophile network. Dutroux was recognised as a lone sexual deviant and imprisoned for life. His wife got thirty years and Lelièvre, twenty-five.

The case caused such upset amongst Belgians that it prompted one of the largest peacetime demonstrations since World War II, the 'White March' of October 1996, and a shake-up of the Belgian government, leading to the resignation and dismissal of several government officials. A report into the affair by a parliamentary commission recognised the gross negligence and amateurism of police and government officials involved in the investigation (*The Irish Times*, 16 April 1997). It is said that one in three Belgians with the surname Dutroux applied for a name change between the time that the offences came to light and the trial.

The ramifications of the Dutroux case were the principal topic of an international conference organised by ECPAT, UNICEF (United Nation's Children's Fund) and a range of non-governmental organisations concerned with the UNCRC. The First World Congress against the Commercial Sexual Exploitation of Children was held in Sweden in August 1996 and attended by more than 500 accredited representatives of the world's media. The Congress Declaration recognised that:

> The commercial sexual exploitation of children is a fundamental violation of children's rights. It comprises sexual abuse by the adult and remuneration in cash or in kind to the child or to a third person or persons. The child is treated as a sexual object and as a commercial object. The commercial sexual exploitation of children constitutes a form of coercion and violence against children, and amounts to forced labour and a contemporary form of slavery.

What became known as the Stockholm Agenda for Action was unanimously adopted at this event by 122 nations. Building on the UNCRC, the Agenda called on governments and other relevant parties to work together to face the growing challenge of child prostitution, child pornography and the trafficking of children for sexual purposes (see http://www.ecpat.net). More specifically, Article 4B of the Agenda built on Article 34 of the UNCRC. It provided for the development, strengthening, and implementation of national laws to establish the criminal responsibility of service providers, customers and intermediaries in child prostitution, child trafficking and child pornography, including possession of child pornography. This gives some indication of how prominent the issue had become on the international political radar and of the pressure being exerted on all countries to implement effective legislation and policy.

Between July and December 1996, Ireland held the Presidency of the European Union, and child protection was declared a top priority.

In November, the Justice and Home Affairs Council approved a number of important measures to tackle the problem of trafficking in human beings and the sexual exploitation of children. One proposal saw the mandate given to Europol's Drugs Unit extended to include trafficking in human beings. This covered the activities of paedophiles and those who supplied children to them as well as trafficking in women for the purposes of sexual exploitation.

Another led to the creation of a multi-annual financial programme (known as STOP), establishing a framework for information, training, research and exchanges. The programme encouraged cooperation among the various professionals (for example, immigration officers, judges, police, social workers) responsible for action to combat human trafficking and sexual exploitation of children. Of relevance, the Child Studies Unit at University College Cork received funding under this programme to conduct research into the sexual exploitation of children on the Internet, specifically by means of pornography. As a result the COPINE Project (Combating Paedophile Information Networks in Europe) was founded in 1997 in the university's Department of Applied Psychology.

Most significant was the Council's approval of a Joint Action obliging all member states to undertake a major review of their laws. The EU Joint Action to Combat Trafficking in Human Beings and Sexual Exploitation of Children (adopted in February 1997) defined sexual exploitation as 'the inducement or coercion of a child to engage in any unlawful sexual activity; the exploitative use of a child in prostitution or other unlawful sexual practices; the exploitative use of children in pornographic performances and materials'. The Joint Action committed all member states to render trafficking in human beings and the sexual exploitation of children criminal offences and provide an adequate range of penalties. Of particular importance was a commitment by member states to ensure that all aspects of the use of children in pornography were criminalised including production, sale, distribution and possession.

The Joint Action was superseded by an EU Council Framework Decision of December 2003 on Combating the Sexual Exploitation of Children and Child Pornography. The preamble to this Framework Decision recognised that:

> Child pornography, a particularly serious form of sexual exploitation of children, is increasing and spreading through the use of new technologies and the Internet ... It is necessary that serious criminal offences such as the sexual exploitation of

children and child pornography be addressed by a comprehensive approach in which the constituent elements of criminal law common to all Member States, including effective, proportionate and dissuasive sanctions, form an integral part together with the widest possible judicial cooperation.

The Decision obliges member states to legislate against, and lay down an appropriate range of penalties for, the production, distribution, dissemination, transmission, supply, acquisition and possession of child pornography. While the UNCRC identifies a minor as anyone under the age of 18, it also recognises that different countries' laws concerning the age of majority often consider individuals to be 'adults' before they reach 18. However, the Decision recognises a 'child' as any person below the age of 18 years and calls on member states to amend their legislation accordingly. (In response the UK Sexual Offences Act, 2003 pushed the outer boundary of childhood from 16 to 18, but as Gillespie (2003) noted this differs from the age of consent (16) and as a result may cause problems.) The Decision also calls on states to outlaw morphed or computer-generated images (see further Chapter 3).

Law enforcement trumped by new technologies

Just when suppression of the child pornography trade seemed within sight as national legislatures finally began to take seriously the harms caused by magazines and videos, the Internet arrived on the scene. The digital age has created the potential for abuse on a hitherto unimaginable scale. Within a generation the oft photocopied and much sought after *Lolita* magazine has been replaced by a bewilderingly large and varied catalogue of abuse, which can be accessed via a few commands on a computer keyboard. The paedophile subculture has become amorphous and dislocated in a physical sense but virtually united. Before examining what sustains this subculture it is important to consider the extent to which deviant opportunities have been transformed by the Internet, and it is to the revolution in information technology that we turn our attention in the next chapter.

Chapter 2

The role of the Internet

According to Adler (2001a: 233), the 1990s witnessed a 'return of the repressed' whereby despite intensive efforts to eradicate the trade in child pornography it grew exponentially. Many attribute this to the rapid development and subsequent widespread availability of the Internet. As Krone (2005a: 1) observed: 'It appears that a once limited trade has seen remarkable growth, with the potential to intrude into the homes and workplaces of all those connected to the Internet'.

Although there is evidence to suggest that paedophiles have been using computers to communicate since 1982 in the USA (Jenkins 2001: 44) and 1985 in the UK (Akdeniz 2002: 6), it was only in the 1990s that social concern with Internet-related child sexual exploitation became widespread. In his novel *Strega*, Andrew Vachss (1987) tells the story of the pursuit and destruction of a paedophile ring involved in exchanging child pornography images over the telephone system. In an interview with *The Spectator* (9 April 1998), Vachss is quoted as saying: 'When I wrote about predatory paedophiles trading kiddie porn over modems in 1987, book reviewers were unanimous in telling me what a sick, fevered, crazy imagination I had'. A few years later what had seemed far-fetched was commonplace.

Paedophiles adapted very quickly to the new technology. Jenkins (2001: 41) noted that: 'Perhaps ten years before the Internet became known to the general public, computer databases and bulletin boards were becoming the favoured tools of child pornographers, a strikingly precocious use of computer technologies'. As early as 1983, investigations of NAMBLA found its members were using computers to distribute details of potential victims as well as pornographic images and stories. By the time the general public became familiar with the Internet, some paedophiles had become so computer-savvy as to perpetrate real-time online sexual abuse.

The Internet-using population

The Internet has transformed the way millions of people lead their lives. So successful has been its integration into so many areas of daily life that it can be easy to forget how truly profound its impact has been. Businesses, educational institutions and the organs of the state, not to mention individuals, have embraced this multimedia technology with gusto and many have come to rely on it to structure their approach to communication, work and leisure. Life before the Internet and all its timesaving services can be hard to imagine. European and North American teenagers have not known a time when 'google' did not exist as a verb, 'surfing' was a purely acquatic pursuit and 'Spam' was a type of tinned luncheon meat. This transformation has taken place at high speed. In the space of a generation, the Internet moved from being an expensive and unwieldy communications resource used primarily within the US academic and defence communities to becoming a cheap and user-friendly mass consumer product. (For an entertaining and informative account of the context in which the Internet developed see Naughton 2000.)

Put simply, a computer network is two or more computers connected together so that they share information, and the Internet is the largest computer network in the world. More accurately, it is a network of networks. It allows communication between millions of smaller domestic, academic, business and government networks regardless of their geographical location on the planet. Although the Internet is a global system with no fixed physical location or central control point, access is localised making it cheaper than conventional methods of communication, such as telephone or mail, where prices rise with distance (Akdeniz 1999). There is no central point of control, no way of imposing order on content, no admission criteria for participating. It is free flowing and anarchic but works brilliantly. At times referred to as the 'Information Superhighway', the Internet comprises a multitude of services, all of which facilitate the exchange and retrieval of information. Any computer connected to the Internet can transmit and receive electrical impulses that can be converted into text or graphics. Newer technologies, such as wireless broadband and satellite, are replacing the traditional reliance on fixed-line public telephone networks to allow faster connections between computers. With the right technology this information transfer is almost instantaneous. Writing in *Wired* magazine, Kelly (2005) seemed awestruck at how quickly we have come to take so much for granted:

> The accretion of tiny marvels can numb us to the arrival of the stupendous. Today, at any Net terminal, you can get: an amazing variety of music and video, an evolving encyclopedia, weather forecasts, help wanted ads, satellite images of any place on Earth, up-to-the-minute news from around the globe, tax forms, TV guides, road maps with driving directions, real-time stock quotes, telephone numbers, real estate listings with virtual walk-throughs, pictures of just about anything, sports scores, places to buy almost anything, records of political contributions, library catalogs, appliance manuals, live traffic reports, archives to major newspapers – all wrapped up in an interactive index that really works.

Alexander (2002: 980) highlighted the growth of the Internet by selecting a few key statistics: 'In 1981, fewer than 300 computers were linked to the Internet, but by 1993 that number had risen to over 1,000,000. In 1996, only three short years later, that number had grown to 9,400,000; the number had skyrocketed to sixty million in December 1999.' Today, estimates of the number of computers connected to the Internet vary wildly, but the general consensus is that it has entered the hundreds of millions.

Estimating the number of Internet users is even more problematic considering its integration into academic and business life, not to mention the increasing popularity of home computers and Internet cafés. One computer may be accessed by any number of people while the number of users online changes every second. Relying on numerous sources of information (for example, the Central Intelligence Agency's *World Factbook*; *Computer Industry Almanac*; *Nielsen/NetRatings*), ClickZ Stats (2006) estimated that by the end of 2005 the worldwide Internet-using population stood at 1.08 billion people. It is projected that this will increase to 1.8 billion by 2010. In 2005, the USA had the highest number of Internet users at almost 204 million while China had 111 million, Japan had 86 million, Germany had almost 49 million and the UK had just under 38 million. In the Netherlands, 78 per cent of all households had access to the Internet in 2005, the highest rate in Europe. Lithuania had the lowest level at 16 per cent (see Table 2.1).

Table 2.1 European households with Internet access (per cent) and households with broadband connection as a percentage of those with Internet access, 2005

	Internet	Broadband		Internet	Broadband
Netherlands	78	69	Estonia	39	77
Luxembourg	77	51	Italy	39	34
Denmark	75	68	Spain	36	58
Sweden	73	55	Cyprus	32	14
Germany	62	38	Portugal	31	63
United Kingdom	60	52	Poland	30	51
Finland	54	67	Slovakia	23	31
Belgium	50	81	Greece	22	3
EU average	**48**	**48**	Hungary	22	49
Slovenia	48	40	Czech Republic	19	27
Austria	47	50	Lithuania	16	73
Ireland	45	16	France	Not available	
Latvia	42	30	Malta	Not available	

(*Source*: Central Statistics Office 2006: 56, 58)

Internet connection speed is determined by whether the connection is dial-up or broadband. Because broadband enables a greater quantity of information to be transferred at a faster speed, increasing numbers of customers are switching over. According to Point Topic (2005), a UK-based independent organisation providing information on broadband communication, the total number of broadband lines worldwide grew to 190 million during the third quarter of 2005, an increase of 25 per cent from 31 December 2004.

The variety of resources and services offered online has revolutionised the way in which we send and retrieve information. Although often thought of interchangeably, the World Wide Web is only one of many services offered on the Internet. The Web is a collection of interconnected documents; a vast online encyclopaedia providing information on almost any subject imaginable. Retrieval of information from the Web is facilitated by search engines (for example, Google, Yahoo), which drill through masses of data and locate information on the topic of interest, often in a matter of milliseconds. The resources available on the Web are viewed using a browser (for example, Netscape Navigator, Internet Explorer). Other popular applications that run on the Internet are Electronic Mail (email), Internet Relay Chat (IRC), and Newsgroups (which make up Usenet, a precursor of the Internet). This cluster of Internet activities is sometimes referred to as 'cyberspace', which Akdeniz (1999: 8) defined as, 'a nowhere location without any known borders but available to any with an Internet access'. To take advantage of the range of services provided by the Internet requires users to register with an Internet Service Provider (ISP) and obtain an account.

Illegal content and Internet misuse

When Bill Clinton took office as the forty-second president of the United States in early 1993, there were fifty known Web sites in the world. By 1998, as his second term in the White House got underway, the number had grown to 1.3 million, and was doubling every few months (Jenkins 2001: 47). In 1996, when announcing the Next Generation Internet initiative, Clinton himself commented: 'When I took office, only high energy physicists had ever heard of what is called the World Wide Web ... Now even my cat has its own page'. Indeed, 'Socks' the White House cat had, for a time, its own fan club and online newsletter.

The immensity of the Web today is hard to grasp. According to Kelly (2005), the total number of Web pages, including those that are dynamically created upon request and document files available through links, exceeds 600 billion. Unsurprisingly, the pornography industry has taken full advantage of the opportunities afforded by cyberspace, and indeed has been credited with laying some of the foundations for e-commerce more generally. Yar (2006: 106–7) makes the interesting point that Internet pornographers played a role in pioneering some of the technological and commercial developments, such as secure credit card payment systems, that demonstrated the potential of e-commerce. They were the first Web entrepreneurs.

The (estimated) number of pornographic Web sites jumped from 28,000 to 60,000 between 1998 and 2000. Internet pornography was an instant success, the booming trade accounting for 11 per cent of the entire US$9 billion e-commerce pie in 1998 (Alexander 2002). Explicitly sexual material continues to grow in popularity. Recent statistics compiled by Ropelato (2006), the accuracy of which – like so much in cyberspace – cannot be verified, suggest that there are currently 4.2 million pornographic Web sites and that every day there are 68 million search engine requests for pornography (constituting 25 per cent of the total number of searches). Darlington (2004) noted that in January 2000 the world's first Internet sex convention was held in Las Vegas. Despite tickets costing US$275, more than 5,000 delegates attended to find out about, and place orders for, the latest technology.

Revenues from traditional sex-related magazines and videos are in decline as more and more consumers shift their attention to the Internet. Sales of *Penthouse* magazine fell from a peak of 5.3 million copies in September 1984 to 327,000 in 2005. Similarly, *Playboy* sold 7.1 million copies of its November 1972 issue, the largest sales figures for any magazine in history, but circulation had fallen to 268,000 by the end of 2005. Due to declining sales, the last edition of *Australian Playboy* was published in January 2000.

In *Sex on the Net*, Yaman Akdeniz (1999: 5) explained that the Web offers 'photographs, erotic text and audio stories, video clips including live feeds, live sex chat, with almost anything imaginable in content from straight sex to gay and lesbian to fetish and ultra hard-core sexual encounters together with specialised themes such as Asian babes and celebrity porn'. In the years since these words were written the variety and quantity of content has increased and the boundaries of acceptability have been further tested. Every conceivable sex-related topic, including a dizzying array of sexual fetishes, has its own Web pages and discussion groups. A significant amount of activity centres on the bizarre and it is difficult to imagine that there is any taste that is not now catered for. There are even devotees of sites that feature urinating grannies or grown men wearing nappies, dog collars and embarrassed grins. The Internet is also a sinister place, where individuals have committed suicide before an online audience, cannibals have found willing victims, alienated young men have learned bomb-making skills, and young people have shared secrets about how to be successfully anorexic.

But there is something for everyone in cyberspace – not everyone is seeking out the grotesque – and there are numerous sites catering for the most benign interests. A Google search carried out on 22 August 2006 revealed that the keyword 'pornography' yielded 41.8 million results. However, 'sociology' yielded 165 million, 'criminal justice' 158 million, 'knitting' 35.8 million and 'running' 1.4 billion. For every person hunting down extreme pornography there are many others searching for the ideal training shoe for over-pronation, the most up-to-date scholarly literature on crime and punishment and how best to deal with a dropped stitch without unravelling an entire garment-in-progress.

Still, it is sex that concerns us here. The pace of development is such that men and women are even beginning to use their machines as glorified sex toys. Lane (2001: 278) described the emerging technology of 'teledildonics'. Essentially what this entails is an individual connecting a piece of apparatus to their computer so that other people can control it remotely. In this way a gentleman in Los Angeles can manoeuvre himself into his preferred piece of equipment, go online and invite a stranger in Hong Kong to engage with him. The latter uses his, or her, computer to control the speed and intensity at which the gadget moves and stimulates. If both have the same device there is scope for mutual satisfaction. One popular product carries the brand name 'Robo-suck'. In this cyberworld, Freud's characterisation of human sexual interest as polymorphously perverse seems somewhat understated.

While some of the material on offer may be considered offensive, most of it is legal and viewing, along with self-censorship, are left to the individual's discretion. Material is sought out and downloaded according to personal preferences and often what is accidentally stumbled upon can redirect an individual to new areas of interest. Like browsing in a library, the most interesting discoveries are sometimes serendipitous.

Diverse cultural norms, along with widely different legal systems, mean that a single definition of pornography will never be universally recognised. What's more, changing standards of obscenity and acceptability, fluctuating tolerance for censorship, along with increasing ease of travel and communication would ensure the failure of most attempts to regulate adult content. For example, despite fierce resistance *Playboy* magazine finally went on sale in Indonesia, a predominantly Muslim country, in April 2006. Just as it was declining in its traditional heartlands it was finding new markets. (It hit the top shelves in Ireland, a predominantly Catholic country, in 1995.)

Illegal material and criminal activity are other matters entirely. New techniques for corrupting the innocent use of computers will evolve as the cyber-environment expands. The potential for the Internet's services to be misused by individuals in their pursuit of sexually deviant interests is a longstanding cause of concern. More specifically, the use of the Internet to exploit children sexually presents parents with a growing number of fears. Because the Internet has become mainstreamed within schools and colleges and commonplace within homes, and because children readily adapt to new technologies, the attraction to those with sexually deviant appetites is obvious. This has become a cause of burgeoning anxiety, reinforced by emerging evidence that the Internet is pivotal to the distribution of child pornography and the provision of resources and contacts for paedophiles.

How does the Internet facilitate child sexual exploitation?

Until recently the child pornography producer, like any amateur photographer, required a darkroom, chemicals, film, paper, camera equipment, skill, time and privacy. More importantly, he required access to real children. When the trade was legal, the distributor required a retail outlet and the collector had to travel to it. When the trade became illegal, both parties took their chances with the postal system.

Contrast that with the situation today. For a modest investment, a home PC package contains a computer, scanner, photocopier and printer, often a Webcam and always an internal modem. Software packages for editing photographs and videos come as standard. Add the Internet and access to a child, and the average desktop computer becomes a pornography studio. If a child is not available in person, there are many potential victims online, only too willing to send their photograph to their new best friend.

It has been estimated that the fastest modem connection available in the mid-1980s would have taken 28 hours to download a picture file that was 2.5 megabytes in size. Twenty years later the same operation took a little over three minutes (Ferraro and Casey 2005: 13) and the time lag continues to fall. This quantum leap in transmission speed was one of the primary drivers of the efficient distribution of child pornography images.

The Internet brings with it accessibility, affordability and anonymity. For the price of a local telephone call, or a modest monthly subscription, individuals can access a global network of more than one billion Internet users from the privacy of their own home, 24 hours a day, 365 days a year. Durkin (1997) identified four ways in which the Internet is misused to exploit children: to traffic child pornography; to locate children to molest; to engage in inappropriate sexual communication with children; and to communicate with other paedophiles.

For general purposes, **Web sites** are the most popular means of distributing information. They can be set up to ensure access only by selected individuals via passwords, and many sites, including those catering for adult pornography, generate revenue through selling services by subscription and hosting advertisements. This is also how some child pornographers have managed to make a lot of money. For example, Operation Blue Orchid began in May 2000 when Russian authorities asked the US Customs Service for assistance in identifying the owners and customers of a Russian-based Internet site that was selling child pornography (*US Customs Today*, April 2001). The Blue Orchid Web site, which operated between March and October 2000, promoted for sale collections of videotapes and CD-ROMs of adults sexually abusing 8- to 15-year-old children. The *Thief's Punishment* series, which was made in December 1999, contained two videos that depicted the forcible rape and physical abuse of a 15-year-old boy. Other collections available for purchase were entitled *Russian Flowers*, *Girls*, and *Man and Boy*. The films sold for US$300 each or two for US$580 and attracted customers from 15 different countries.

The US Customs CyberSmuggling Center made an undercover purchase of a video from the site and subjected it to forensic investigation. They sent their findings to the US Customs Attaché's office in Moscow. Moscow City police used this vital information to identify the creator and business manager of Blue Orchid. He was arrested in December 2000 when he returned to his home with a 13-year-old boy, later identified as a frequent victim in the *Russian Flowers* series. Had the boy been a year older no crime would have been committed, as the age of sexual consent in Russia was lowered to 14 in 1996 (Ferraro and Casey 2005: 53). (In 2002 it was raised to 16.) This arrest led to the identification of the Blue Orchid Webmaster, a search of whose residence found a computer revealing every client's name and address. US Customs forwarded all the information to the appropriate field offices in the USA. Investigations also took place in Sweden, Denmark, and the Netherlands.

Newsgroups are basically discussion forums. They offer a means for people with common interests to communicate. Participants do not interact in real time but contribute to discussions by posting messages to the group and returning later to see what, if any, response their observations have elicited. Participants can join and leave discussions at their discretion. The groups are organised according to subject area such as Recreation, Science, Society and Alternative. The latter category carries the prefix alt., and is where the more counter-cultural and outright weird discussions are to be found. One hesitates to imagine the kind of exchanges underway on alt.sex.snuff.cannibalism, alt.torture or alt.eunuchs.questions (group description: did it hurt?).

Anyone can set up a newsgroup and a small number are devoted to paedophilia. Newsgroups provide a degree of anonymity and a place for like-minded people to correspond. They allow for the attachment of a picture file to a posting. It is more likely, however, that as trust develops individuals may reveal their email addresses to each other so that the sharing of pictures can be carried out privately. Estimates put the total number of newsgroups at tens of thousands but many are believed to be inactive. Akdeniz (2001: 1) believes there are approximately 200 sex-related groups, some pertaining to legitimate discussions of sex-related topics. Newsgroups are complemented by Web-based bulletin board systems (BBS) that allow individuals to place comments and queries and follow 'threads' of discussion.

Internet Relay Chat (IRC), unlike newsgroups, allows for real-time communication. Chat rooms are organised according to shared themes and allow for a significant degree of anonymity. Exchange of files is achieved by 'going DCC', that is, leaving the IRC server system and setting up a direct computer-to-computer link. IRC was used by the notorious Wønderland Club (see Box 2.1) but it was modified to ensure that the participants were not available or readily visible to non-club members (Sommer 2002: 179). The breaking up of the Wønderland Club in September 1998 brought to public notice how the Internet could be used by paedophiles to network and exchange contraband material. Although there had been earlier police operations, Cathedral was the first large-scale international exercise in this area. While not representative of the majority of investigations of this type, it nonetheless demonstrates the nature and complexity of this criminal activity.

Box 2.1: Operation Cathedral and the Wønderland Club

Operation Cathedral started in California in April 1996. It quickly developed into the largest operation of its kind in the history of international policing. This is what it involved.

A ten-year-old girl went to stay for the weekend at her friend's house. While she was there her friend's father, R, sexually abused her live on camera. He took instructions over the Internet about what to do next from other members of the so-called Orchid Club who had logged on and were watching. These images were stored on R's computer and he later traded them in an Internet chat room. Some weeks later, R was arrested on suspicion of molesting another child, leading police to the first child who disclosed her abuse. Police went back to R's home and seized his computer. R was sentenced to one hundred years for his crime, and twelve other men in other parts of the USA also received custodial sentences for their roles in the Orchid Club.

R's computer provided a link to three men in the UK, one of whom was a computer consultant living in Sussex. The police raided his house, seized his computer and found evidence of the existence of another and more extensive club which had 180 members in 49 different countries. This was the Wønderland Club. It was highly

---

organized, with a chairman, a secretary, a management committee, a procedure for vetting new members and five different levels of security calculated to keep unwanted eyes away from their activities. The ø was employed as an extra security measure by making the group's name alphanumeric.

The club made extensive use of complex passwords and encryption technology. To gain entry, a candidate member was required to produce 10,000 child pornographic images and, within the club, one gained status by finding new children to abuse, thereafter providing fresh pictures as evidence. Some of the computers later seized by police had encrypted material on them which was never viewed or produced in court because the codes proved impossible to break.

It was agreed through Interpol that the National Crime Squad (NCS) of England and Wales should coordinate the worldwide police action that would be necessary to arrest the Wønderland members and close down the club. From information in the possession of the NCS, Interpol had links or leads to suspects in 49 identifiable countries. However, only 15 police forces were invited to an initial conference called by Interpol. It was agreed that the swoops on suspects' addresses would be coordinated in order to deny them the opportunity to warn fellow club members who could then destroy or hide evidence. A time was fixed: 04:00 GMT on 2 September 1998. Just before the operation was due to begin, two countries, the Netherlands and Canada, pulled out, leaving 13 participants. The Dutch police acted later and arrested the suspects identified in their country. This brought the total number of participating countries to 14. Canada did not act against its identified suspects, either at the time or afterwards.

The police were able to identify photographs or videos of 1,263 different children, only a handful of whom have since been located. Over 750,000 child pornographic images were seized along with over 1,800 hours of digitised videos of child sex abuse. One individual had over 180,000 individual pictures on his computer. The 107 men who were caught were, in the main, well educated, employed and in a wide range of professions, but with a preponderance who worked with computers. Eight individuals committed suicide before they could be dealt with by the courts.

(*Source*: Carr 2001: 28–30)

Peer-to-peer file sharing technologies, such as Napster and Gnutella, have recently been popularised as a means of enabling people to exchange music. They allow anyone with an Internet connection to become both a server and a client, thus permitting people across the world to connect directly to each other's machines without having to use a third party, such as an Internet Service Provider. There is some suggestion that child pornographers are already using these technologies to communicate directly with each other in ways which further reduce the possibility of detection. Ropelato (2006) estimated that one in three peer-to-peer downloads involves pornographic content and, more disturbingly, that there are 116,000 daily Gnutella requests for 'child pornography' (see also Ferraro and Casey 2005: 38–9).

It is accepted procedure for users of Internet services to adopt nicknames. While most are innocuous, or even humorous, some individuals choose a name that is a declaration of intent. Rather than making them less visible, the name is a statement of preferences and priorities. In his observation of messages posted to newsgroups and bulletin boards, Jenkins (2001) came across the following monikers: DaughterLover, PussyPig, Loligagger, Baldpubes, Dad.

In addition to facilitating the trade in illegal images, the Internet enables sexually deviant adults to make contact with children for sinister purposes. Paedophiles are well aware that the remarkable pace at which the online community is expanding is in large part driven by the devotion shown by young people to the potential of the new technologies. Newsgroups, and especially chat rooms, offer a level of anonymity that would hinder interaction in the real world. Online, however, it enables an offender to develop a trusting relationship with a young person without revealing their true identity. A number of contacts can be nurtured in parallel and, over time, the basis of the relationship can change – what were risqué exchanges between 'friends' can become tools for exploitation. A 21-year-old Canadian man, who operated under the names Marco1812000 and Supalover666, befriended over 40 British girls aged nine to 15 and urged them to remove their clothes. They obliged and sent him the photographic evidence. He then allegedly threatened to send the photographs to their relatives and to rape or kill them if they did not perform sex acts over a Webcam. Many of the girls came from the same area and it was thought that the offender had hacked into his victims' email address books to identify their friends and contacts (*Sunday Times*, 30 July 2006).

Such activity is not uncommon. A US survey of 1,500 regular Internet users aged between 10 and 17 found that almost one in five had received an unwanted sexual solicitation in the previous year. Five per cent of those surveyed reported that contact of this kind made them feel very or extremely upset or afraid. There were occasionally aggressive demands for offline meetings. None of the solicitations led to an actual sexual contact or assault. These uninvited communications usually took place in chat rooms. One in four reported unwanted exposure to sexual material. In most cases this happened when they were searching the Web, but sometimes the material was transmitted to them via email or instant messaging. Few of these incidents were reported (Finkelhor *et al*. 2001).

Webwise is an Internet safety programme of the National Centre for Technology in Education in Ireland. In a survey of 848 students aged between 9 and 16, which formed part of a wider EU initiative, it was found that all of the children used personal computers and 91 per cent had one at home. Ninety per cent of those with a computer at home reported having an Internet connection. One in 15 of those surveyed had met in real life someone they had first encountered on the Internet. Most reported very positive experiences but 11 per cent said the other person tried to physically hurt them. In every case where the child was harmed they had been expecting to meet another child, but it was actually an adult who showed up (http://www.webwise.ie).

In her book *Katie.com*, Katherine Tarbox (2000) tells the story of her online seduction. A top student and nationally ranked swimmer, Katie grew up in an affluent area of Connecticut. At 13 she was lonely and self-conscious and like so many young adolescents craved the company of someone who would understand her:

> I thought I wanted someone who would share my interests – music, reading, movies – someone who was intelligent and kind and funny. Someone I could learn from. The problem was, middle-school boys had none of these qualities, and they were only interested in girls for their bodies ... New Canaan was a town filled with beautiful people and I was pretty much the opposite ... That was when Abby [sister] came home for the summer and brought along her computer fully equipped with America Online. Suddenly there was an entire new world opening up to me in on-line chat rooms and the World Wide Web, and it was limitless. (p. 24)

Katie spent hours on the computer every day, even logging on at night if she could not sleep. Her parents issued the basic warnings about not giving out personal contact details but with their hectic work schedules there was seldom anyone around to monitor her activities. Also this was a time when the Internet was in its infancy and its potential was poorly understood. In September 1995, Katie met '23-year-old Mark', and by the end of their first chat she had disclosed her personal phone number: 'I really didn't expect that he was going to use my phone number. But part of me hoped he would. And I was excited that I had met someone just like me, but of the opposite sex. He even liked Mozart! At last I had connected with another kind, intelligent soul. Best of all, he recognised me as someone different from the typical thirteen-year-old ... I thought he *must* be all right' (pp. 30–1; emphasis in original).

Mark's first phone call followed a few hours later in the early hours of the morning. The grooming began: 'Well, I have been thinking about you all day and I just thought why think about you when I can talk to you? So I figured I would call' (p. 34). Mark maintained regular contact through emails and telephone calls. He became Katie's confidant and sweetheart. He was there with a kind word and caring voice whenever she turned to him. At last she had a soul mate. In one exchange he wrote:

> I'm really having strong feelings for you Katherine. I finally know that now. I know it BIG TIME! I can't get you out of my mind. You just pop up in whatever I think about. And you know what? It feels good! It really makes me happy inside just to know that I'm thinking about you, and that the most wonderful girl has entered my life. (p. 75)

Mark emphasised the need to keep their relationship secret and six months after the initial contact he persuaded Katie to meet face-to-face. He flew from California to Dallas where Katie was taking part in a swimming competition. Mark booked a room in the team hotel and Katie visited him there. Within a few minutes of entering the room he assaulted her. As she recalled it: 'He tried to reach into my pyjama bottoms through the fly opening. I pulled his hand away. He did it again, and I pulled his hand away again. Then he pushed down on me hard, letting me know he would not be resisted again. Instead of being angry and shouting at him to stop it, I was confused and speechless. Mark was supposed to be better than this' (p. 95). At that point Katie's mother arrived at the door with hotel security and the police (her room mate had been aware of her whereabouts and informed her mother). Before opening the door, Mark tried to persuade Katie that she should not tell anyone what had happened or else he would go to jail.

Mark, or Frank Kufrovich as he really was, turned out to be a 41-year-old financial consultant with a history of seducing and assaulting young girls and at least one young boy. He was found to have an interest in child pornography. Kufrovich was one of the first people to be dealt with under the US Communications Decency Act, 1996 and he was jailed for 18 months. Throughout the prosecution and for several years afterwards Katie had mixed feelings about him. The excitement and friendship she had experienced conflicted with feelings of shame and guilt that she had been responsible for causing so many problems for her former 'boyfriend'. This case illustrates the lengths to which some men will go to molest a child and how emotionally confused the target of their attention can become. This emotional turmoil exacerbates the problems associated with reporting such activity.

Katie's story shows how individual children can be targeted and groomed. Another tactic used to attract potential abuse victims is the genre of Web site that is designed to pique the interest of children as well as adults. They make subtle use of colour, text and imagery and are as disconcerting as they are child-friendly. Some offer logos (such as fluttering butterfly wings) to be used by those who share a sexual interest in children. It is difficult to imagine that this kind of logo could be used anywhere other than in a world of virtual reality. But the fact that such symbols are available tends to add a veneer of collegiality to members of this 'club'. Box 2.2 illustrates how the Web can be used to attract children and prepare them for more intimate contact.

Box 2.2: A Welcome to Sugar and Spice!

Hi! I am SO glad you are here!
Welcome to the site for all young girls who want to learn more about love and about people called girl lovers. Some of the things that I am going to tell you are much different from what other people have told you. You might even disagree with some of the things that I say. That's OK. You have the right to your own opinion about things. But you also have the right to know all the sides of a story so that you can decide for yourself what you want to think, feel and believe.

What Is a Girl Lover?
The love that you have with most adults that you know is probably either family love or friendly love. You love your parents and your aunts and uncles, and there are probably some adults who are friends of your family with whom you are also friends. Most adults do not ever develop deeper feelings than this for young girls. But there are some adults who see them as much more than young girls. Rather than just seeing a child, these adults have a heightened appreciation for the

---

physical and spiritual beauty of young girls. These people are called girl lovers. Girl lovers care very much about girls and are committed to making them happy and protecting them. A true girl lover would never do anything to hurt a young girl. Girl lovers love to spend time with girls, because they appreciate the thoughts and emotions of girls and are eager to experience the world the way that you do. They enjoy seeing the world through your eyes!

Good People and Bad People

A long time ago, girl lovers were called pedophiles. Back in those days, people understood that pedophiles were simply people who loved children in the same way that girl lovers love girls today. Unfortunately, when people hear the word pedophile now, they think it means child molester. A child molester is a very evil person who hurts children. Girl lovers do not like child molesters at all, and think that child molesters should go to jail. While a girl lover wants to make girls happy and do only things the girl wants to do, child molesters are selfish people and want to force girls to do things that they don't want to do. Unfortunately, even some good people can become bad. Some girl lovers lose the ability to exercise self-control and become selfish, and these things sometimes result in them doing bad things. The main difference between girl lovers and child molesters is very simple: girl lovers want to love and to give, while child molesters only want to take and are not interested in love.

(*Source*: *The Human Face of Paedophilia* Web site (now defunct))

The attraction of the online world to young people is shown by the huge popularity of social networking sites such as Bebo and MySpace, which allow users to develop their own Web page, diary and photo gallery and to communicate in a variety of ways, such as writing blogs (regularly updated journals of personal commentary) and exchanging messages. According to *Nielsen NetRatings*, these are the fifth and sixth biggest online sites in the world, when rankings are by audience size. Almost one third of British visitors to MySpace, and half of those to Bebo, are under 18 (*PCPro*, news, 4 July 2006). Bebo and MySpace were to be banned in Irish schools in September 2006 because they were considered too time-consuming (*Irish Independent*, 30 June 2006). There were also concerns that they were being used by mischievous students to post abusive, and possibly defamatory, comments about teachers and other pupils. Of course, blocking access to these sites will have a limited impact as young people will still be able to access the networks from home, libraries, Internet cafés and other places.

In the USA, under the Deleting Online Predators Act of 2006, any federal institution that receives funding for computers and Internet access will have to put filters in place to prevent access to social networking sites and what it describes as 'trendy chat rooms' unless it is for an educational purpose and under adult supervision. This was not because of a belief that schoolchildren were spending so much time on these sites that it might begin to affect their studies but out of concern for child protection. Under Section 2 of the legislation (which passed the House of Representatives on 26 July 2006), Congress found that:

1 sexual predators approach minors on the Internet using chat rooms and social networking websites, and, according to the United States Attorney General, one in five children has been approached sexually on the internet;

2 sexual predators can use these chat rooms and websites to locate, learn about, befriend, and eventually prey on children by engaging them in sexually explicit conversations, asking for photographs, and attempting to lure children into a face-to-face meeting; and

3 with the explosive growth of trendy chat rooms and social networking websites, it is becoming more and more difficult to monitor and protect minors from those with devious intentions, particularly when children are away from parental supervision.

It must be acknowledged that a sense of hysteria tends to accompany this debate and, as White (2006: 75–6) has argued, there is a case for resisting the calls for ever-tighter regulation on the basis that the Internet is not the only place where potential molesters proposition children. This threat exists, and is more immediate, in public swimming pools, malls and recreational areas where offenders and victims are physically proximate. These environments are not viewed with equal alarm and subjected to such close legislative attention. The fact remains that children are most at risk from someone they know; stranger molestation is mercifully rare.

The Internet also allows adults with a sexual interest in children instant access to others who share their proclivity, even if they are thousands of miles apart. It provides a level of inscrutability that is unattainable in the real world. It reduces the possibility of apprehension and encourages a culture of impunity. This facilitates open discussion of the kinds of sexual desires which must be kept hidden in wider society. It also allows for the exchange of ideas about how best to identify and find potential victims. Importantly, it provides a measure of social support and the development of a seemingly more noble perspective; child molestation becomes 'intergenerational intimacy' or the free choice of individuals separated by age but united in affection. Paedophiles become members of the 'minor-attracted community' or principled men struggling for the 'emancipation of mutual relationships between children and adults'. These are but a few examples of the kind of self-serving language to be found on Web sites frequented by paedophiles.

Crimes against children become reinterpreted as tragic love stories when offenders share accounts of the price they have paid for following their feelings; as they see it, they are the real victims of society's prejudice and stupidity. This is illustrated by the following extract from a letter published in the *NAMBLA Bulletin* in May 1982. It was written by a prisoner in Nassau County Jail who was serving time for sex crimes involving children. (Other publications by the same organisation describe those imprisoned for sex with children as 'unacknowledged political prisoners'.)

> And for what reason is all this punishment? (For, mark my words, being here is punishment, even though I am guilty of no crime, just as in all totalitarian countries.) Just because I looked after, loved and cared for several boys over a number of years, boys who were my good friends as I was theirs; and allegedly allowed that love to develop naturally into physical affection (for, remember, here in Amerika [sic] hugging is against the law). They're supposedly being 'protected'. From what? And from whom?
>
> They neither want to be, nor did they ask to be 'protected' from their grown-up friends. They only want to be protected from the efflorescent evil of over-ambitious detectives and DA's [district attorneys] who seek promotion, publicity, and political advancement with utter disregard for the kids' feelings or the ruination of their lives. For boys and men alike, police intervention into their friendships is a total disaster, even if, later, charges are dismissed. The damage to both is irreparable.

It is common for adults with a sexual interest in children to use language that attempts to neutralise the exploitation inherent in adult-child sexual relationships. Consider the following two cases. A police officer paid a prostitute to find him a girl aged between seven and ten to have sex with. He told her he did not see it as sexual abuse because he was willing to pay for the 'service'. After his arrest child pornography was found on his home computer (*The Irish Times*, 19 November 2002). A 30-year-old man whose partner was expecting their first child received a suspended sentence for possession of 138 photographs and eight videos depicting children aged between eight and 16 years engaged in sexual activity with each other and adults. In his own words: 'It's not a turn on. I did not get off on it. It was just curiosity. I felt sorry for the kids in the pictures and films' (*Irish Independent*, 10 May 2005).

A study by Rind *et al.* (1998) published in the *Psychological Bulletin*, a prestigious journal of the American Psychological Association, concluded that the widespread belief that child sexual abuse caused profound harm was not supported by the evidence. In a review of 59 studies based on samples of college students, they found that any negative effects were neither pervasive nor particularly intense and that men fared much better than women. These findings quickly found their way onto Web sites hosted by those with a sexual interest in children who felt they had found objective support for their views. The study attracted a level of interest and controversy that is highly unusual for academic work. (For a unique exploration of the – largely positive – views of young boys involved in sexual relationships with older men, see Sandfort 1982.)

Forde and Patterson (1998: 1) observed that the Internet provides paedophiles with the opportunity to build informal networks and peer-to-peer contacts on a previously unimaginable scale: 'For the relatively small cost of reorganising their activities around personal computer technology, paedophiles are able to operate internationally'. From the frequently asked questions list of the Usenet newsgroup alt. support.boy-lovers, Durkin (1997: 15) cited the following to illustrate this point:

> Alt.support.boy-lovers is a forum for males to discuss their feelings towards boys. It is intended to provide a sense of peer support for those having difficulties with their feelings, for boy-lovers who feel isolated with their orientation, and for those who have no other avenue of discussion than via a group such as this.

Durkin examined a sample of newsgroup postings and determined that they served two major functions: validation and information. Newsgroups provide a supportive environment that facilitates the discussion of adult fantasies and sexual contacts with children. This allows offenders to neutralise the harms they are causing and to normalise and legitimise aberrant interests. Guilt is replaced by relief as the reality dawns that even the most apparently idiosyncratic perversions are not unique. Conduct that should cause alarm is sanitised through repetition and the elicitation of positive feedback. Brenner *et al.* (2004: 30) elaborated on this theme:

> While not widespread, 'child love' websites have been growing in popularity. These sites use terms such as child lovers, boy lovers and girl lovers to describe the activity they promote. While these sites make it clear they do not host child pornography, they offer message boards, chat rooms and other methods for communicating that can be used to establish a community for those interested in child love and related topics. It is not clear how many of those who frequent these sites are interested in child pornography, but the sites give those who are interested an opportunity to share knowledge and ideas, including ideas about how to avoid law enforcement. The North American Man/Boy Love Association, for example, includes an entrapment warning on its website. Other similar sites provide information about anonymity, encryption and evidence elimination.

Durkin (1997: 16) fears that the supportive social context afforded by the Internet may encourage some individuals to victimise children by putting them in touch with other potential offenders. As well as hardening their resolve in this way they will share techniques and find partners in crime. Durkin and Bryant (1999) suggest that 'cybersex' and the immediate reinforcement provided by online communication allow individuals to breathe life into deviant sexual fantasies that would otherwise have self-extinguished. They conducted a study of 41 admitted paedophiles who participated in discussions on alt. support.boy-lovers. Findings indicated that more than one half offered accounts in the form of justifications for their orientation and behaviour. The most frequent was the claim that children were not harmed as a result of sexual contact with adults.

One case study, described by Quayle and Taylor (2001: 606), illustrates the ways by which one individual misused a range of the services offered by the Internet to further his sexual interest in children. In their words his progress involved distinct stages:

This was achieved through initially accessing child pornography, which intensified his levels of sexual arousal and behaviour and fuelled his desire to engage in a relationship with a child. His move to chat rooms allowed him to engage initially as a child persona in 'cybersex' with people presenting as both adults and boys, and then as an adult in order to access boys offline. We can see a progression in offending that moved him closer to behaviour that was clearly sanctioned online: that of the sexual predator. This is paralleled in changes in his sexual behaviour and language. Pornography was an important feature in that through it he accessed a like-minded community, secured a role in that community and was provided with a vehicle that allowed both solitary and mutual sexual expression. Pornography cemented both adult and child relationships, giving him status through the size and quality of his collection.

Scale of the problem

In the vast majority of countries today, the production, distribution, and possession of child pornography are illegal. What's more, it is against the law simply to view child pornography in some countries while in others viewing the material online can lead to charges of possession due to the inevitability of downloading images while browsing child pornography sites. This makes serious research very problematic. While some jurisdictions (for example, Ireland) offer exemption from prosecution for *bona fide* researchers, others fail to acknowledge a need for any such legal protection. In the USA, for example, simply viewing child pornography is a criminal offence, leaving researchers reluctant to risk legal consequences by studying this phenomenon. Kincaid (1998: 171) noted: 'If we look for studies of the actual material, the kiddie porn itself, we find nothing, since it is against the law to look at what may exist, much less own it'. In the UK a tiny number of academics and doctoral students have concerned themselves with the various manifestations of paedophilia. They have attracted police attention and been vulnerable to false allegations regarding their motivation (Thompson and Williams 2004).

On top of this, the public condemnation and outrage reserved for child pornography offenders mean that few individuals are willing to risk leaving themselves open to even the mere suggestion that they were involved with child pornography. As Jenkins (2001: 19) noted: 'Viewing child porn material is a criminal offence, in a legal environment in which it is all but impossible for even the most inept of prosecutors to lose a case. Nor given the horror attached to the offence, is there likely to be much public outcry about judicial railroading: in this area of law, only the most egregious cases of police entrapment have inspired any media complaints whatsoever'. Thus, the few studies published will show a bias towards those countries, generally wealthier ones, where police action has been more widely publicised and where researchers have been able to access reliable criminal justice sources (Carr 2001: 7).

In the days before the Internet, arrests for possession of child pornography involved a modest number of pictures either printed on paper or stored on tape. Sometimes the original negatives were seized too. It is likely that the majority of collectors only managed to obtain a small quantity of what they wanted due to prohibitive costs, difficulties identifying reliable sources and the risk of detection; to receive the material by mail meant revealing an address. Carr (2003: 11) noted: 'In 1995, arguably the last year before the Internet started to take off in the UK, the Greater Manchester Police Abusive Images Unit seized the grand total of 12 indecent images of children, all of them on paper or on video. In 1999 the same squad seized 41,000, all bar three of them were on computers and had come from the Internet'. Similar findings emerge from Australia where Burke *et al.* (2002: 80) reported that between 1989 and 1994 around 12,000 items of child pornography were seized across the country. By contrast, in 2001 a single offender was apprehended with more than 21,000 images and 1,300 stories depicting the sexual abuse of children. Media reports detailing recent police investigations and court cases indicate that the Internet has swollen the market for child pornography.

According to estimates published in the April 2001 issue of *US Customs Today*, approximately 100,000 Web sites were involved with child pornography. In addition, the Internet Watch Foundation, an industry supported 'hotline' in the United Kingdom, estimated that there were around one million images of child abuse in circulation on the Internet and this number was reckoned to be expanding at the rate of about 200 a day (Robbins and Darlington 2003). Clearly though, given the covert nature of this activity, there is no way of determining with any degree of accuracy how many child pornographic images or videos are in existence. It is probably safe to say that most of the material currently produced originates in private homes, away from the eyes of authority, and is bartered rather than sold for profit. It is available only to the initiated and is circulated narrowly and privately. What enters the public domain gives no more than a hint of the scale of the problem.

The last four decades have seen patterns of production and distribution alter dramatically on a number of occasions due to a changing legal environment (for example, the legalisation and then criminalisation of child pornography in some countries) and the introduction of new technologies (for example, the camcorder and then the Internet). The lifespan provided by the Internet means that material from the 1960s and 1970s remains in circulation, making it difficult to chart modern trends in consumption.

Taylor and Quayle (2003) suggest that one approach to exploring the parameters and changing shape of the problem is to interrogate the COPINE archive created from images downloaded from publicly available newsgroups on the Internet. The archive has two main components: first, pictures which are known to be over fifteen years old, and second, a searchable pool of new (less than ten years old) and recent (ten to fifteen years old) pictures. Among the images held in the COPINE database, more than half are of girls but there has been an increase in boys in the newer pictures. In these new pictures, some 40 per cent of the girls and over 50 per cent of the boys are between the ages of 9 and 12, the rest being younger. Children over the age of 12 or 13, when the onset of puberty makes age determination difficult, are underrepresented.

Among the newer pictures of children involved in explicit sexual activity, the overwhelming majority are white, with Asian children more likely to appear in posed images. There is a marked absence of black children in any of the age groups (but see Kelly 1992: 116–17). Anecdotal information from interviews with offenders suggests that many collectors show a preference for thin, fair children, where genitalia are clearly visible and where there are no secondary sexual characteristics, such as pubic hair (Taylor *et al.* 2001). The COPINE researchers have noted that the age of children in the photographs, particularly the girls, has been dropping (Taylor and Quayle 2003).

In a study of 9,800 pornographic images randomly selected from 32 Usenet newsgroups in the mid-1990s, Mehta (2001) found that around one in five involved children or adolescents (5.1 per cent were 'simple nudes', 10.6 per cent appeared to be adolescents and 4.4 per cent were clearly paedophilic; the latter two categories were distinguished by an emphasis on the genital or anal region). Groups included in this study covered a wide range of sexual interests including bondage, coprophilia and bestiality, but a number were clearly targeted at child lovers (for example, alt.sex.pedophilia, alt. sex.intergen and alt.sex.fetish.waifs).

However, Taylor (1999: 7) believes that attempts to quantify the number of images available are not worthwhile because:

> There is an arbitrary relationship between pornographic video films and the number of video captures; for example, a single video of 30 minutes might yield 3 or 300 video captures, depending on the energy and particular interests of the person scanning. All of this distorts the meaningfulness of any numerical answer.

In order to gain some understanding of the scale of this problem, Taylor suggests that it is more sensible to look at the numbers of children involved in child pornography than to attempt to quantify the amount of material available. He acknowledges that very few children who appear in child pornographic photographs and videos are ever identified. For example, the Interpol database contains more than 400,000 images. Yet it has helped in the identification of only 360 victims (Interpol media releases, 6 May 2005; 15 September 2005).

Children of all ages, including infants, are used to produce pornography. At greatest risk are those who are vulnerable, perhaps through poverty, substance misuse, sex work or neglectful parenting. Child sex tourism is a major source of child pornography. This has been given a boost by the low-cost travel opportunities afforded by budget airlines and the opening up as mass tourist destinations of places that were formerly the preserve of the most intrepid travellers (for example, Thailand, Vietnam, the Philippines).

In addition, research suggests that there is an increase in images with 'domestic qualities', indicating that much of the material currently being produced originates in private homes (Taylor 1999). This is not surprising given that the family home is the setting for so much predation and abuse. To give just one example, James Taylor (43), a married father of three, came to the attention of authorities in Scotland after police involved in an international investigation were tipped-off that he had been posting child pornography on the Internet. When his home was raided they found disks containing 2,280 indecent images of children. Most had been downloaded from the Internet but computer specialists were able to recover some horrific images of Taylor's own making which he had tried to delete. These included graphic images of him raping a 13-month-old baby girl and other indecent images of a naked 6-year-old girl asleep in bed. Both had stayed over at his home on occasion. Taylor was sentenced to five years imprisonment, later raised to eight on appeal (*BBC News*, 3 September 2003, 27 January 2004; *The Scotsman*, 19 September 2006). Where the abuse is family-based, love and loyalty may inhibit the child from disclosing. As Operation Hamlet shows (Box 2.3) victims can be rendered so powerless that grotesque abuse can extend over time and across networks of families.

Box 2.3: Operation Hamlet

In 2002 a member of the public made a report to the Swedish Hotline, Rädda Barnen, about an image of a young girl being abused by an unidentified man. When the report was processed, the hotline staff recognised a logo on a T-shirt worn by the perpetrator and identified the likely country as Denmark. The report was forwarded to the Danish Hotline and Danish Police for further investigation. As a result of a swift investigation, the victim (a 9-year-old girl) was taken into care and her mother and stepfather, Eggert Yensen, were arrested. The couple were later found guilty of raping their daughter and selling pornography. Yensen was sentenced to three and a half years in prison and his wife was ordered to receive psychiatric care.

A joint investigation by the US Customs Service and the Danish National Police targeted a ring of paedophiles, of which Yensen was a member, who molested their own children (aged 2 to 14 years) and distributed the images on the Internet. In at least one case they exchanged children to be sexually abused and photographed. The abuse involved sado-masochism and other forms of torture which in some cases was broadcast live over the Internet. As a result, by March 2003 there were 16 US search warrants issued, 19 US arrests, 12 international arrests, and more than 100 children taken into care. The ringleader was a father of four based in Clovis, California.

In a press conference announcing the success of the operation, US Customs Commissioner Robert Bonner declared that: 'I have seen some horrendous crimes in my time, but these crimes are beyond the pale. These crimes are despicable and repulsive. People who engage in these kinds of despicable acts – sexually exploiting children – especially their own children – should be removed from their children forever and incarcerated for as long as the law allows'.

(*Source*: based on Bonner 2002; Huda 2005: 5; INHOPE 2004: 10; Jones and Skogrand 2005: 31–2)

How has the Internet changed the nature and use of child pornography?

Because there is no way of estimating the amount of child pornography that was in circulation prior to the advent of the Internet, it is possible that the quantity has not increased but has simply become more available and more copied. The evidence suggests otherwise. There is a consensus that the Internet has massively expanded both the supply of, and demand for, this material. A vicious cycle has been initiated whereby the new technologies allow more people to view this material, which in turn stimulates a greater appetite for new images and places more children at risk of exploitation.

The Internet creates a vast number of new criminal opportunities. A false sense of security is created by the anonymity which it affords. The perceived lack of risk lowers inhibitions, tempting people to become involved who under different circumstances may never have encountered the objects of their desire. Alternatively their desires might have been different in the pre-computer age. As well as being an outlet for those whose sexual preference is settled, the Internet allows an unprecedented degree of inquisitiveness, and the danger is of curiosity hardening into deviance. In a Swiss study, Frei *et al.* (2005) found that two-thirds of men investigated for purchasing child pornography from Landslide productions (see Box 4.2) gave as their motivation 'curiosity', 'fascination' or 'investigation'.

In other words, the Internet *per se* may be a trigger for a significant number of individuals to access child pornography. In an interesting study published in the *British Journal of Criminology*, Demetriou and Silke (2003) explored the extent to which deviant opportunities online were availed of by those who came across them, but had not sought them out. They set up a Web site to offer free games and software. When visitors entered the site they were presented with links to the legitimate content but also to illegally obtained software and hard-core pornography. Links to the latter two categories were not genuine and when people clicked on them they were sent a message to the effect that the relevant page was under construction or that it was unavailable because too many people were trying to access the site at the same time.

The most popular section of the site, by some margin, was the hard-core pornography, which most visitors attempted to access. Indeed more people were interested in hard-core pornography than in free games even though they must have been surprised to find such material there at the outset. Overall, a minority of the more than 800 visitors to the site restricted themselves to legal and non-pornographic material. This is a powerful example of how the anonymity afforded by the technology, in conjunction with the availability of deviant content, can generate a high level of illicit activity. (The potentially disinhibiting nature of the Internet is discussed by Suler 2004.) This willingness to yield to temptation suggests that some of those who stumble upon an opportunity to access child pornography will seize it, and of these, some will then begin to seek it out.

Jan Wong of Canadian newspaper *The Globe and Mail* demonstrated how easy it is for the average computer user to find their way to disturbing material. Box 2.4 shows how entering a few keywords in an Internet search engine can have dramatic consequences. The investigation that formed the basis of Wong's article was inspired by comments from a convicted child murderer. In a statement to police, Michael Briere said that he could not understand why the kind of revolting material that he felt had led to his killing a 10-year-old girl was not more difficult to access on the Internet. In the killer's own words: 'The simplicity of getting material … it's close to mind-boggling. For me, I have never understood how come the whole thing wasn't shut down. You search for the word "baby" and it will find stuff there'.

Wong's report is sickeningly graphic and readers may be upset by it. Some of it is reproduced as a reminder that images of child pornography have real victims whose dignity is destroyed. The subject matter of this book touches on lives that have been broken by a form of criminality that seems to be growing and that is extremely difficult to combat. The conventions of academic writing, with their emphasis on value-neutrality and tolerance for difference, should not be allowed to blind us to the importance of these key facts.

Box 2.4: Depravity made easy

[A colleague] suggested googling 'underage'. In a nanosecond, we were in cyber-hell. Something called Pedo World flashed across the screen. And then a series of colour photos of children popped up. They were mostly girls. One child stood innocently in a bathtub; others wore black garter belts or thongs that somehow fit their narrow hips. One girl looked as young as four. Others were probably five or six years old. Some appeared to be about 10, the age when they lose their baby fat.

The photos were amateurish and badly lit. They appeared to be taken in ordinary homes, a rumpled living room, a cheaply tiled

---

bathroom, a sunny back yard. One terrible photo showed a little girl, maybe six years old, lying on a couch, naked from the waist down. A man, completely naked, was touching her vagina with his hand. He could have been her father.

I clicked on that photo. It took me to a message board where anonymous visitors exchange passwords and links to other so-called child-porn sites. Above, a message screamed: Shocking Lolitas Portal. Suddenly, new photos, worse than before, tumbled onto the screen. At the same time, a dozen new websites appeared unbidden, awaiting my perusal at the bottom of the screen. The porn appeared to be taking control of the computer. The tiny X in the top-right corner, the icon you click to exit a site, had vanished. Clicking backward led me to a new, equally bad, site. I was trapped in cyber-porn.

Then a series of photos flashed on the screen that made us sick. It showed men raping little kids, including a little girl who couldn't be older than four. I hadn't touched the keyboard or the mouse when another set of photos replaced them. They showed a pot-bellied white man, his face hidden, having sex with two scrawny Asian girls, perhaps five or six years old.

The *Globe* has passed the URLs of these websites to Toronto police.

(*Source*: From 'A Journey into Depraved Cyberspace' by Jan Wong, 19 June 2004, *The Globe and Mail*)

Forde and Patterson (1998) found that the tremendous flexibility of the Internet enabled paedophiles to congregate at virtual locations that changed according to circumstances. At the beginning of their study, most Web pages proclaiming an interest in boys were located in Western Europe. When Internet Service Providers started withdrawing services this resulted in a period of upheaval with many pages relocating to Canada. However within a short space of time pages had returned, but now to Eastern Europe, with new servers under development in Russia. Owners of these pages were internationally connected and technologically astute. They constructed their sites so that transferring physical locations was a trivial consideration. Jenkins (2001: 68-69) effectively illustrates this issue:

Unknown to the [Internet service] provider, the Californian now loads ten or twenty or five hundred photographs or videos featuring illegal child porn material ... The hypothetical individual now announces the posting of the series on the Maestro [Bulletin] board or one of its counterparts, where the message is read and acknowledged gratefully by other 'loli fans', who might be located in the next town to him or in Budapest or in Singapore – there is no way of knowing ... Duly alerted, consumers then flock to the site advertised, which may be based in any of twenty countries, and they download the pictures. The images will exist at that site only for a few hours before they are removed and the site ceases to exist.

There is something of a cat-and-mouse pursuit about this. Jenkins elaborates:

There is a continuing battle of wits between posters and the administrators of the server ... The subculture has had some success in evading this surveillance by giving Web sites codeword titles relating to sport, such as soccer, volleyball, and so on ... The best indication that a home page is offering improper material is when a new site suddenly attracts thousands of hits within a few hours, and this is usually sufficient for server administrators to examine its contents and suppress it.

Similarly, Taylor and Quayle (2003) suggest that another effect of the Internet may be that it shortens the chain of production, private distribution and eventual public dissemination. New photographs can appear much more quickly in the public domain than previously. As already noted, modern technologies facilitate the distribution of digital footage capturing real-time abuse, effectively reducing the chain of production, distribution and consumption to instant make, send and receive, as exemplified by the depraved activities of the Orchid Club (see Box 2.1, pp. 38–9). The same authors argue that as more people come in contact with child pornography, the demand for more extreme material will escalate. In addition, once uploaded to the Internet, there is practically no control over what happens to an image. The potential distribution knows no limits. According to Bowker and Gray (2004), this has created a longer duration of harm for the victims.

The Internet challenges what we may have thought about child pornographers. Distinctions between producers and consumers become blurred. Modern technology allows anyone with a digital camera, computer and modem to make and trade their own child pornography. In addition, the massive storage capacity of the average personal computer presents challenges in terms of assessing risk. Prior to the Internet, a large child pornography collection would have been indicative of an enthusiast of long-standing, somebody who had devoted much time, effort and money to amassing his collection. But the Internet allows an individual to download a huge amount of material in a very short space of time. In other words, a collection of 5,000 images possibly reflects the quality of an individual's Internet connection rather than the effort they expended to painstakingly build a collection.

Perhaps the most extreme example is the 34-year-old accounts clerk from Lincolnshire, England, who was convicted in March 2004 of the possession of over 495,000 images of children in a collection of up to 20 million pornographic images. The man's lawyer argued that his collecting behaviour was akin to that of a trainspotter and stressed in mitigation that he was not a paedophile as the images of children constituted only a small fraction of his archive and he had 'no interest in sex with children'. He was jailed for five years (*The Guardian*, 3 March 2004). Clearly, it would have been impossible for this individual to have viewed every one of these images. Devoting just one minute to each of his images of children equates to almost a year of continuous viewing without any breaks for work, sleep, food or recreation. To view his entire collection, at one minute per picture, would require thirty eight years of unbroken attention. It would seem that the compulsion to collect can become an end in itself (see further Box 3.3, p. 88).

Although not yet recognised by any of the official diagnostic manuals, a condition known variously as Computer Addiction, Internet Addictive Disorder or Cyberaddiction has been described by Orzack and Ross (2000). It refers to individuals who become restless and irritable when not using their computer, who lie about the amount of time they spend engaged in computer-related activities, and whose family, work and educational commitments are neglected in favour of virtual reality. Davis (2001) believes that use of the term 'addiction' is inappropriate as customarily it requires evidence of a physiological dependence. Instead, to describe a similar cluster of behaviours and consequences he has suggested the label 'Pathological Internet Use'. In 2000, a special issue of the journal *Sexual Addiction and Compulsivity* (Vol. 7, No. 2) was dedicated to problematic aspects of cybersex and emerging treatment options.

Historically, most child sexual abuse has taken place within established family or institutional structures. To some extent this reflects the availability of suitable targets. The Internet changes this context dramatically. It allows adults with a sexual interest in children to make contacts in any part of the world. The Internet has thereby introduced a new class of sex offender: one who gets to know a child remotely and is then willing to travel in order to pursue the relationship. The Internet has also introduced a new intermediate stage in the development of certain relationships, namely the grooming process. As such, it may accelerate the individual along the route to contact offending. Carr (2003: 2) elaborated:

> It has created the possibility of a kind of intimacy at arms' length that, in former times, could only have been attempted through correspondence and therefore was very different indeed. A paedophile can work with this intimacy, through the grooming process, to sexualise a child and bring them to a point where they have won their trust, and perhaps also their affection. At that stage the child may well have become open to the possibility of a meeting in real life and to complying with or submitting to the paedophile's sexual advances. By then the person's age may have become, as they see it, an irrelevant detail. They will continue to see them as being 'still the same person I have come to know and love'.

Box 2.5 shows that the grooming process can take place across thousands of miles and over an extended period of time before it is consummated. Considerable effort must be required to persuade a 12-year-old girl to obtain her passport from her parents under false pretences, travel to a major international airport to meet her 'lover' who has flown in from another continent, and then flee the country with him. It is obvious why this case caused alarm among parents who realised the importance of the Internet in their children's lives but were frightened of its implications.

Box 2.5: The US Marine and the English Pre-Teen

A former US marine who admitted abducting a 12-year-old British girl he met in an Internet chatroom was jailed for four-and-a-half years. Toby Studabaker, 32, from Michigan, pleaded guilty at Manchester Crown Court to child abduction and to inciting a child to commit gross indecency. Studabaker could not be charged with unlawful sex or rape because he is not a British citizen and the intercourse took place abroad.

Following the development of a relationship on-line over the course of a year, the girl disappeared from her parents' home on 13 July 2003. After tricking her mother into handing over her passport by saying she needed it for a bus pass, she met up at Manchester airport with Studabaker who had flown in from Detroit. The pair flew to Heathrow and onwards to Paris.

Greater Manchester Police launched one of the biggest investigations in its history, contacting the FBI, which began delving into Studabaker's background, as well as Interpol and the French police. FBI profilers discovered that Studabaker, who claimed he was a devout evangelical Christian, had joined the armed forces after two sex allegations involving minors were leveled against him.

Three days following her disappearance, the victim contacted her mother having seen a CNN news bulletin about her case. Studabaker took her to an airport and she flew home. He was arrested in Frankfurt on 16 July and extradited to the UK the following month.

Sentencing him, Mr Justice Leveson said: 'The nature and tone of some of your communications, including the so-called cybersex, demonstrates that you, then 32 years old, were intent on sexual intimacy with a girl you knew to be 12.' He added that adults who use the Internet to prey on and 'groom' children for sex should expect harsh sentences. He said: 'Although the Internet can be a force for very great good, it is not always so and its abuse can slip under the guard of parents who are not aware what their children can get involved in while on the Web.'

(*Source: The Scotsman*, 13 February 2004; 3 April 2004)

Bowker and Gray (2004) made the point that the Internet enables a single offender to groom multiple victims in parallel. Compared to the real-world situation, the Internet allows an offender to maximise the returns on his investment of time and effort; he reduces the odds of being caught and increases his chances of snaring a victim. Finally, the Internet presents young people with increased opportunities to access illegal content. This has the potential to facilitate the grooming process in the sense that young teenagers who have already had access to sexually explicit images, and for whom a tryst with an older individual might be an enticing prospect, could be more receptive to just such an approach. In this way the wide availability of this material may prime them for abuse as well as desensitising them to its effects.

Evolution of the Internet

The rapid development of the Internet and its related services shows no sign of faltering. Like so many other technologies, while the Internet will continue to enhance the quality of life for millions, human nature will ensure that it also contributes to the exploitation and harm of some. Ray Wyre (2003), an experienced clinician, has warned: 'We need a recognition that the addictive qualities of sex, the freedoms of the Internet and widespread access to computers have come together with explosive consequences'.

There are plenty of signs that individuals are becoming more creative in their use of the Internet and related technologies in order to engage in criminal activity. The Internet has facilitated new ways of committing old crimes (for example, fraud) as well as creating entirely new criminal activities (for example, hacking). Child pornographers rapidly identified the potential of the Internet to enable covert and profitable activity. The law is always one step behind, as illustrated by attempts to define, prevent and punish online grooming (McAlinden 2006).

There is evidence that the Internet is facilitating a return to commercialisation. Recent police investigations, such as Operations Falcon and Avalanche in the USA (see Boxes 2.6 and 4.2, p. 62 and p. 119–20), indicate that there is big money to be made from the pornographic exploitation of children. Despite the well-known risks associated with using a personal credit card to purchase illegal material online, it appears that a number of sites providing such an opportunity still exist. Accordingly, the UK government announced plans to establish a Child Exploitation and Online Protection Centre in 2006. The Centre will target the assets (for example, homes, cars, bank accounts) of those who profit from selling child pornography on Internet pay-per-view sites and the money seized will be used to further tackle the problem (*The Sunday Times*, 13 November 2005). Some of these sites will no doubt have been designed to entrap the unwary but the nature of the material displayed on others suggests that they are the work of hardened criminals.

Similarly, a coalition of financial organisations, including all of the major credit card companies, banks and ISPs, was formed in 2006 with a view to sharing information about Web sites that are advertising and selling images of child pornography and then stopping any further payment to their accounts. The group aims to eradicate commercial child pornography by 2008 (Malone 2006); an admirable mission, albeit one that is unlikely to succeed.

Box 2.6: Operation Falcon

On 15 January 2004, a child pornography enterprise based in Belarus and a Florida credit card billing service were charged in a global Internet pornography and money-laundering scheme involving thousands of paid memberships to some 50 pornography Web sites. According to the indictment, Regpay Co. Ltd. was a credit card processing company providing billing services to dozens of child pornography Web sites and also operated at least four of its own Web sites, which accounted for nearly a quarter of the US$3 million in credit card membership fees it generated in the six months ending in August 2003. Another credit card processing company, trading as IServe, pleaded guilty in federal court in Newark to a conspiracy to launder money for Regpay and its principals.

In addition, 15 people were arrested or surrendered in New Jersey as part of the wider investigation targeting individual subscribers of child pornography Internet sites connected to the Belarussian enterprise. They and another nine suspects already charged were found to have possessed child pornography on their home computers. Arrests included a family physician, at least three previously convicted sex offenders, a campus minister, part-time teacher and church youth coordinator, and an 85-year-old retired engineer. At least 20 other individuals were also arrested nationwide during the investigation of Regpay.

(*Source*: retrieved 3 June 2006, from
http://www.criminaldefenseassociates.com)

Some recent reports suggest that rather than using a credit card to pay for their purchases a trend is developing to pay in 'digital gold'. This can be bought at dozens of Web sites using a credit card, bank account or wire transfer. It can then be stored in an account on the Caribbean island tax haven of Nevis and exchanged for goods or services with someone who accepts it as a form of payment. The company that created this new currency is called E-Gold and it settles 60,000 transactions each day, worth about US$10m. A number of paedophiles are known to have used these offshore gold-trading accounts in the belief that their transactions would take place anonymously and far from the prying eyes of police or prosecutors. This seems to be a mistaken belief as this same company has cooperated with the FBI and child protection organisations in the UK (*The Times*, 11 March 2006).

It seems that going to such lengths to cover one's traces would hardly be worthwhile unless significant sums were being transacted.

On occasion they may be. For example, it is reported that a German amateur video depicting the mass rape of young girls was produced during the Bosnian war and can be bought for US$8,000 (Stewart 1997: 211). For an individual wishing to transfer such a large amount of money the attractions of a parallel, and discreet, banking system are obvious.

The technology continues to evolve and downsize. The number, and power, of handheld computing devices are increasing rapidly. Mobile telephones can record, store and transmit video footage and photographs, with newer models allowing high-speed Internet access. Using infrared or radio signals they can transmit data to a personal computer without the need for a physical connection. Until recently the material may have been easy to obtain but it was still necessary to find the time to spend in privacy at a computer equipped with all of the relevant cables and plugs. Even this slight inconvenience has disappeared: the tools of the trade are now pocket-sized and the search for child pornography can be carried out anywhere, any time. The opportunities are almost limitless with the biggest constraint being the imagination of the individual user.

Of great concern is not how the technology will evolve, but rather how we can attempt to respond to a pattern of adaptation the shape of which cannot be predicted with any confidence. The quantum leaps in computing power, miniaturisation, connectivity and affordability over the past decade make it difficult to read even the immediate future. Who could have foreseen thirty years ago that wireless telephones would be in the grasp of every teenager, let alone that they would have allowed access to a virtual cornupcopia of pornography.

The real-life consequences of these technological changes are addressed in the next chapter.

Chapter 3

Why does it matter?

In recent years, few issues have inflamed public passions like child pornography. Krone (2005a) conducted a search of a global English-language newspaper archive and found that the amount of media attention given to the issue of child pornography had risen dramatically; between 1990 and 1994 there were 4,573 articles that referred to this topic compared with 51,270 between 2000 and September 2004. This is nothing short of an explosion of interest.

Despite this growing obsession, there is little understanding of what this kind of crime actually entails and why people (almost exclusively men) are attracted to it. Tate (1990: 13) believes that 'the greatest single obstacle to the fight against child pornography is that too few people ever get to see it … consequently they never see its effects nor understand what went into its production'. This is particularly problematic in the USA where Jenkins (2001) has highlighted the fact that there is no protection in law if academics come into contact with this material as part of their work. To get around this legal impediment Jenkins had to resort to a number of elaborate stratagems when he was researching his book, such as deactivating the 'autoload images' feature on his computer and thereby preventing images automatically downloading while he was monitoring bulletin boards. He also used an old computer so that his financial loss would be limited in the event that the police initiated an investigation against him and seized his equipment.

Notwithstanding these impediments to understanding, it is possible to articulate the harmful effects of child pornography and to say something about the characteristics of those who are attracted to it. The kind of material that is of interest can be categorised by content and the resulting classification provides a basis for making more nuanced, and consistent, legal decisions. Before examining these issues is it is necessary to address the question of what is meant by 'child pornography' and to explore how this concept has varied over time and across countries.

The problem of definition

At the First World Congress Against the Commercial Sexual Exploitation of Children, Healy (1996: 2) highlighted the difficulties in defining child pornography:

> The question of what constitutes child pornography is extra-ordinarily complex. Standards that are applied in each society or country are highly subjective and are contingent upon differing moral, cultural, sexual, social and religious beliefs that do not readily translate into law. Even if we confine ourselves to a legal definition of child pornography, the concept is elusive. Legal definitions of both 'child' and 'child pornography' differ globally and may differ even among legal jurisdictions within the same country.

While child pornography is almost universally condemned, the legislative response varies considerably. Renold and Creighton (2003) noted that although the majority of countries in the world (over 120) had legislation on child prostitution and general obscenity that could encompass child pornography, few had legislation specifically designed to combat child pornography. Despite several international instruments expressly calling for states to enact bespoke legislation a number have still not responded, relying instead on laws dealing with pornography in general or laws that outlaw the corruption of minors (Carr 2001: 10).

Accordingly, jurisdictions differ with regard to the nature of prohibited material. While some seek to cover every type of visual and audio representation, others exclude paintings and drawings, and some exclude texts. For example, in Ireland, England and Wales no distinction is made in law between computer-generated images and actual child pornography pictures. There is ambiguity about the former in other jurisdictions, and in the USA they enjoy the protection of the First Amendment as no harm was involved in their production.

Pseudo-photographs were initially prohibited in the USA under the Child Pornography Protection Act, 1996, but this provision was overthrown by the Supreme Court in 2002 in *Ashcroft v. Free Speech Coalition* (see Ryder 2003: 122–3). Ferraro and Casey (2005: 236–41) argued that the decision in *Ashcroft* clearly referred to 'virtual' images (namely those that are completely rendered by the computer and which involve the depiction of no real children) but that whether 'morphed' images (namely where parts of children's bodies are affixed to adults' or vice versa) constitute child pornography remains a somewhat open question. Either way the onus is now on the prosecution to demonstrate that the images are of actual children. As information technology becomes more sophisticated it will become increasingly difficult to differentiate between true images of abuse and computer-generated child pornographic images. The need for such discrimination adds a further layer of complexity to the criminal process and adds to the burden on law enforcers.

Variations across jurisdictions regarding the legal status of children further blur the picture. While the UNCRC recognises a 'child' to be anyone under the age of 18, this is not a universally accepted standard. In addition, the age of consent for sexual activity varies from 7 for boys in Namibia (12 for girls) to 18 in India (for boys and girls) while some states have no specific stipulation at all (for example, Austria, Turkey) (see http://www.interpol.org for different countries' laws). Namibian law absolves from prosecution any male who has unlawful carnal knowledge of a girl under the age of 16 if 'the girl at the time of the commission of the offence was a prostitute' (Combating of Immoral Practices Act 1980: Section 14). Prostitution, *per se*, is not an offence in Namibia. It is clear that such a legal context is a recipe for sexual exploitation.

The definition of child pornography is influenced by cultural factors, particularly local attitudes towards childhood sexuality. Ideas of what is acceptable vary considerably from country to country. For example, the comic books (*manga*) that are so popular in Japan often involve depictions of graphic sex and violence. Material that is unblushingly read in public by Japanese adults would be viewed with disquiet elsewhere. According to a report in the *Index on Censorship*, when a tough package of laws was introduced to combat child pornography in 1999, *manga* were excluded (Glosserman 2000). The variety of *manga* that includes the most graphic content is known as *hentai*. These cartoon strips can contain fantasy material of the most disturbing kind, including the violation and mutilation of children.

Furthermore, even after the law changed in 1999, 'the individual's right to possess child pornography and distribute it, recreationally, online' was preserved in Japan (Graham 2000: 472; see also Khan 1999). This suggests a continuing level of toleration that is unusual by international standards. Similarly, Article 240B of the Dutch Penal Code protects from prosecution those in possession of child pornography for 'scientific, educational or therapeutic purposes'.

Standards of obscenity change over time depending on evolving social and political values. These shifts can be sudden. Consider Edwards's article, 'Pretty Babies: Art, Erotica or Kiddie Porn?', which appeared in the journal *History of Photography* in 1994 accompanied by a number of photographs. These included images of naked children in explicit poses taken by Lewis Carroll, Robert Mapplethorpe and Sally Mann. It is debatable whether academics writing in this area today would support their argument with such illustrations. This might be because sensibilities have changed or because the risk of adverse comment, perhaps even legal action, has led to a degree of self-censorship. Whatever the reason the change in perceived acceptability seems undeniable.

The response to the sex education book *Show Me!* is a case in point. This was a subject of controversy when it appeared in the mid-1970s (initially in German, but soon translated into English) because it included graphic photographs of children's erotic play, teenagers' sexual exploration and sexual intercourse. The captions for the photographs were suggested by the children involved and information for parents was provided by a psychologist. When the publisher (Macmillan) attempted to import the book for distribution in Canada it was banned by Customs. The ban was lifted a month later and the book went on sale but proceedings were soon taken on the grounds of obscenity. When the case came to court the judge ruled that the book was not obscene and did not offend community standards of tolerance because children were 'sexual beings' and the book would assist parents in dealing with this reality in a positive and healthy way (Ryder 2003: 133). As a result, the book circulated freely around the country. Around twenty-five years later a copy surfaced in the belongings of a man prosecuted for possession of child pornography. The judge had no hesitation in declaring it as pornographic in the strongest terms: 'when viewed objectively the book is thinly disguised child pornography. It blatantly sexualizes children. It also sends the message young children are capable of engaging in sexual activity and that such activity should be encouraged and promoted' (Ryder 2003: 134). What had initially been seen as a fact of life was now a temptation to corruption.

A final illustration of how attitudes have shifted is provided by the hugely influential work into human sexuality carried out by Alfred Kinsey and his colleagues at Indiana University and supported by the National Research Council in the USA with funding from the Rockefeller Foundation. The first volume of findings, *Sexual Behavior in the Human Male*, appeared in 1948, and sold 200,000 copies within months. It reported multiple orgasms in children aged between five months and 14 years and chronicled attempts to bring two-month-old babies to orgasm (Kinsey *et al.* 1948: 175–81). These observations had been timed with stopwatches. According to Reisman (2003: 134–42), over 300 children were involved and the Kinsey team collected these data from imprisoned sex offenders and cooperative members of paedophile organisations. This kind of sexual contact with children was criminal at the time but this did not prevent it being recorded for posterity in the interests of 'science'. Indeed for many years this aspect of Kinsey's work attracted no comment, despite the enormous impact his findings had on attitudes to sexuality. It is difficult to imagine that such research would receive ethical approval at a university today, let alone that it would receive the backing of prestigious funding bodies.

Even the term 'child pornography' itself is considered unsatisfactory by some commentators who believe it trivialises the images of rape and torture that it can entail. Edwards (2000: 1) advises us to 'begin by resisting the term "child pornography" just as we should resist the term "ethnic cleansing". Both expressions lend credence to the definition and meaning attributed to these actions by the perpetrator'. This criticism carries some force and would have been especially pertinent in the period when hard-core images of children were legal or seen as (barely) acceptable trappings of a particular form of sexual expression. They were 'just' another form of adult entertainment. But things have moved on. In most societies today the term 'child pornography' has powerful negative connotations and any association with it is highly damaging to an individual's character and life chances. As a descriptor it is unambiguously negative and loaded with horror and for these reasons it was felt appropriate to use it throughout this book. There is a stark discontinuity between explicit pornography involving consenting adults, which is legal unless deemed to be obscene, and that involving children, where meaningful consent cannot be given and where there are no legal protections.

Harmful effects

Despite difficulties in reaching a uniform definition, there is a reasonable degree of consensus around the justification for outlawing child pornography, namely the harm it causes to those it depicts. There are seven elements to this.

1   The link to child sexual abuse

First and foremost, child sexual abuse and child pornography are inextricably linked; in the majority of cases, child pornography cannot be produced without a child being sexually abused. The exceptions are where images are computer-generated or the material in question is a written record of a fantasy (and perhaps when children are photographed surreptitiously in compromising situations). It is impossible to describe these images without risking upset on the part of the reader. As noted by Tate (1992: 15–16):

> The pictures, films and tapes range from revealing stills of naked children, through more explicit shots of their genitalia thumbed apart, to the recording of oral, anal and vaginal abuse and intercourse. Commonly the children are required to have sex with other youngsters as well as with adults (both male and female). Frequently they are made to urinate on each other or their abusers. Almost invariably their faces, chests or genitalia are coated in semen when adult men ejaculate over them. Occasionally they are photographed having sex with an animal.

Edwards (2000: 17) reminds us of the fall from grace of ageing rock star Gary Glitter (aka Paul Gadd) who received a four month prison sentence in 1999 for downloading thousands of images of children in scenes of bondage and degradation. One girl, who appeared to be 7 or 8 years old, was pictured with legs strapped together, mouth gagged and hands tied behind her back. She bore the marks of a cruel beating and her humiliation was entitled 'Lovers guide to better child sexual abuse'. Other pictures showed children being urinated upon.

Thus, child pornography is regarded as the evidence – stored on film, videotape or computer disk – of sexual assaults on children. It is a record of a crime scene. What's more, the level of interaction with the material is seen to be irrelevant. In Carr's opinion (2003:

9): 'Possessors are simply active abusers by proxy. They could not possess or look at the images if someone else did not do the abusing for them. If they did not do what they do, fewer children would be abused'. According to Adler (2001a) this conception of child pornography, that it is sexual abuse, persists as the foundation of the approach taken by courts, legislators, politicians and the media.

Graphically illustrating this point, Jenkins (2001: 2-3) details one set of images to appear online:

> [W]e might consider the more recent KG and KX series, the 'kindergarten' photos, which together represent perhaps the most prized collections currently available on the Net. KG is a series of hundreds (maybe thousands) of nude images of several very young girls, mainly between the ages of three and six years old, with each item including the girl's name – Helga, Inga, and so on. The photographs date from the mid-1990s, and they likely derive from either Germany or Scandinavia. In the words of one fan of the series, 'Once upon a time. There was a chemist that had earned his Ph.D. Well, he got married and along with his wife opened up a day care centre. Well, as the story goes, he managed to take pictures of lots and lots of things. Eventually he got busted'. The KG collection exists alongside a still more sought-after version, KX, which depicts the same children in hard-core sexual situations with one or more men. Put simply, most are pictures of four- and five-year-old girls performing oral sex and masturbation on adult men. The immense popularity of the KG images ensured an enthusiastic market for KX, which entered general circulation in early 2000.

The extent to which there is a causal relationship between viewing child pornography, fantasising about sex with a child and perpetrating child abuse is less clear (see point 6 below). In some cases what is desired is the image and the idea of actually molesting a child would be considered abhorrent.

2 Aggravation of original abuse

The process of recording emphasises the powerlessness and degradation of the victim. It also tends to exaggerate the abuse, as the child is required to perform for the camera. Child pornography becomes a virtually indelible record of an act of violation and the victim continues to be exploited as long as the image is in circulation. According to Taylor and Quayle (2003: 31), 'each time a picture is accessed for sexual purposes it victimises (if only by proxy) the individual concerned through fantasy'. These authors argued that victims must live with the consequence of their image being swapped, traded and sold, perhaps perpetually. Victims lived in fear of someone they knew seeing a pornographic image of them and this aggravated the original trauma.

This dimension of harm is highlighted in the accounts of adult survivors of child pornographic exploitation. The following extract is based on a statement made in January 2002 by 'Sandra' to the Washington-based organisation Concerned Women for America:

> When I was four years old until I was fifteen I was taken to people's houses as a child prostitute. Inside those homes I was shown newspaper type magazines filled with haunting pictures of children like me that looked drugged, dazed and lifeless ... Pictures were also taken of me. I clearly remember standing cold and naked, exposed to all while someone would tell me how to pose. It was harder than the physical and sexual abuse because there wasn't any fighting or struggling to keep me distracted. I would try to go numb or disappear but no matter how hard I tried I couldn't. The pain that I felt and shame was too strong for me to go numb. After it was over and I would go home I was always worried and scared where those pictures would wind up, and who would see me. I still have those same concerns at age thirty. Those pictures could be anywhere. (Retrieved 7 August 2006, from http://www.cwfa.org.)

The extent to which images remain in circulation is demonstrated by the fact that the *Lolita* magazine series, which ceased publication in the mid-1980s, is still found in raids of the homes of those involved in child pornography. If further proof were needed of the extent to which this material endures it is to be found in Issue 48 of the aforementioned magazine which featured a Victorian picture-spread carrying the headline 'Exciting photos taken of Lolitas in action when photography was just starting' (Tate 1992: 208–9).

3 Rarely identified victims

The children exploited through child pornography have no voice. Although the objects of others' perverse viewing pleasure, in this important way they remain invisible. The victims of child pornography are rarely identified, located and given the help they need. In the Wønderland case (see Box 2.1, pp. 38–9), of 1,263 different children whose pictures were found, only 18 were identified (*BBC News*, 16 January 2002). Returning to Sandra's story:

> I have tried to look for more survivors of this abuse, and, to tell you the truth, they are hard to find. It isn't that they don't exist. It is just that some have died, or are not mentally able to speak about their trauma, or sadly have turned to prostitution or drugs to hide from the pain. Just because they aren't able to talk about it doesn't mean that it doesn't exist. The problem is that it is such a horrible abuse that it destroys a person's life so strongly that it makes it almost impossible to talk about.

Box 3.1 illustrates the amount of time, effort (and luck) required to identify a single child victim. Even still, the details presented below involve the most basic synopsis of a lengthy cross-jurisdictional investigation. A full account of the amount of work this operation involved would require a book of its own.

Box 3.1: The Björn tape

The first time that the Amsterdam Vice Police came across the Björn tape was in July 1991 when it was intercepted by a customs officer. The tape had been sent from Denmark and the sender refused to speak about its origin. Three months later a Frenchman was arrested in Amsterdam while he was trying to get child pornography pictures developed. A copy of the Björn tape was found in his hotel room and he stated that he had borrowed it from an Englishman called John.

In January 1993 the Amsterdam Vice Police arrested a Swiss national who was suspected of the kidnapping and possible murder of several children. He turned out to be in possession of the Björn tape, as were a number of other child abusers who came to police attention during the 1990s. At the end of 1996 Dutch police searched an apartment on an Amsterdam canal. It was occupied by a local man who, together with his Belgian girlfriend, had sexually abused two 8- and 11-year-old boys from Thailand and made a videotape of this. During the search a suitcase full of videotapes of child pornography was recovered. It included what were probably the original Björn tapes.

The images show Björn, aged nine or ten, being carried into a room by a man with a blanket over his head. He is tied to a chair and ordered to carry out sexual acts on the man standing next to him. There follows a long sequence when Björn is seriously sexually abused by two men. Sometimes the boy's pain is clearly audible, his voice is

---

scared and he tells the men to stop. He appears drugged. During the filming the men go to some lengths to avoid recognition. The room in which the filming takes place never fully appears in the picture. The film was made to be sold. One of the men says clearly: 'This film is gonna make a lot of money.'

In 1997 continuing detective work revealed that a boy called Björn had reported a crime of sexual abuse against his stepbrother Richard and his friend John. The crimes had occurred in or around 1990 in an apartment in the east of the Netherlands. The apartment was located and searched: it was the place where the tape had been made. Eventually, Richard was sentenced to two years imprisonment. John had gone to Thailand many years earlier but was arrested at Heathrow airport in London when he made a trip home in August 1998. He received a prison sentence of six years.

(*Source*: Marshall *et al.* (1999))

Given that it took seven years of dedicated police work across several European countries to identify Björn and bring his abusers to justice, it is not surprising that victim identification is the exception rather than the rule.

Holland (2004) also highlights the fact that the focus in child pornography investigations is on the offender rather than the child. She gives the example of Joseph Millbank who was sentenced to six years imprisonment in January 2002 (later increased to ten years) for a string of offences committed across Scotland. It was not until March 2003, 14 months after he was convicted, that 13 families were notified that their daughters had been abused by Millbank.

4   A tool of seduction and blackmail

There is a body of opinion that child pornography is not merely the product but also the cause of abuse. It can be used during the grooming process as a tool of seduction. In this way the shockwaves of the initial abuse extend to new victims. Those who have been exploited through pornography are used to perpetuate sexual exploitation. They become unwilling (and unwitting) participants in further victimisation. In a Canadian study, Langevin and Curnoe (2002) found that when pornography was used by sex offenders during the commission of an offence it was usually to groom the potential victim. In a small number of cases the offender showed pictures of themselves engaged in sex with other children.

In his review of the safeguards for children living away from home in England and Wales, Sir William Utting (1997: 100–1) pointed to a number of harmful consequences of child pornography. He concluded that exposure to pornography could desensitise children and lower their inhibitions. Images showing children smiling could be used to 'prove' to younger children that what they were looking at was 'fun': the camera does not lie. With older children it could serve the purpose of sexual excitation, instruction and normalisation.

Utting also suggested that child pornography can be used to entrap children gradually so that they become vulnerable to even greater harms. The embarrassment and fear that others will see what they have done, or a mistaken belief that their involvement in the original sexual act means they have done something criminal, can be used as blackmail to force the child to remain silent, and compliant. This might be especially true if the child is shown abusing other children. Kelly *et al.* (1995: 34) highlight the cycle of abuse:

> What emerges from examining the production and use of child pornography is a pattern of mutually reinforcing connections: child pornography is itself a document of the abuse of one child; it is then used by abusers to reinforce their will to abuse; they may in turn show it to children they wish to abuse to secure their co-operation; some of these children may, in turn, be photographed or filmed whilst being abused and/or trained to pose for pictures. The process then begins anew.

It becomes increasingly difficult for those caught up in such a scenario to extricate themselves, intact.

5   The normalising of adult sexual interest in children

Over time regular consumption of child pornography numbs an individual to the harm caused to a child and encourages a view of children as legitimate sexual objects. Often, paedophiles use such material to legitimise their behaviour. As one participant in a sex offender treatment programme put it: 'Why is it a crime? It's in my head so what is the harm?' (Hudson 2005: 64). Keeping their own and others' records goes some way to normalising and (possibly) reinforcing their behaviour. Jenkins's (2001) study of the postings to child pornography bulletin boards revealed that participants used language that neutralised the harm inherent in child pornography and supported the illusion that children were consenting participants in sexual behaviour. The extent to which this self-deception can become ingrained is shown by one participant's request: 'Does anyone know where I can get movies of 8 to 12yr old girls being raped? Not hurt, just being forcefully deflowered' (cited in Jenkins 2001: 86).

DeYoung (1989) studied the language used in newsletters, booklets and brochures published by NAMBLA. She found that a number of justifications were common, namely denial of injury, condemnation of the condemners, appeal to higher loyalties and denial of the victim. These serve the purpose of convincing the individuals in question that their behaviour or obsession is not abnormal, but is shared by thousands of other sensitive, intelligent and caring people.

In his controversial book, *Paedophilia: The Radical Case* (1980: Chapter 10), self-confessed advocate of 'child love' and former chairperson of PIE, Tom O'Carroll clearly highlights why child pornography causes concern:

> I would say that erotica has had a powerful influence on my own attitudes ... I could never quite bring myself to believe, having been brought up in a severely anti-sexual family, that some children might be interested in sex. I learnt about their sexuality intellectually, through the writings of the sex researchers, but only through erotica did I come to see the possibility that it was real, not just an intellectual exaggeration: until I actually saw a picture of a five-year-old boy with an erection, I did not believe it could happen to such a young child. Nor could I believe that children of that age could have intercourse with each other, until I saw photographic evidence with my own eyes. And of course, having seen photographs of adults engaged in sexual acts with children, in which the latter definitely appeared to have been enjoying the experience, I was sustained by a hope that one day I might do such things myself.

O'Carroll admits to having been in love with many children.

6 The inciting of viewers to abuse children

There is much debate, predominantly regarding work with sex offenders, as to whether the use of child pornography stimulates sexual fantasies of children, relieves impulses to commit offences, or leads to a desire to act out those fantasies. COPINE researchers interviewed convicted child pornography users and found that while some had convictions for sexual offences against children, others did not (Quayle and Taylor 2002). Howitt (1995) found that child abuse (both as victim and perpetrator) predated exposure to child pornography. Carr (2003) believes that child pornography fuels sexual fantasy about adult-child sexual relationships, and that even if this is true of only a minority of cases, eliminating such material reduces the overall risk of child sexual abuse.

Seto and Eke (2005) carried out an interesting longitudinal study. By following a sample of known child pornography offenders through police records for an average of two and a half years after their conviction (or release from custody) they established that 6 per cent incurred a new child pornography charge. A further 4 per cent came to attention for new contact sexual offences. Those with a prior criminal record, particularly if it included a contact sex crime, were most at risk of reoffending. This is a modest, but significant, level of recidivism especially given the relatively brief follow-up period. It cannot tell us about the direction of causality (for example, whether exposure to pornography preceded contact abuse) but supports the notion that, at least for the more serious offenders, perpetrating abuse and viewing pornography are intertwined.

The case of *Curley v. NAMBLA* demonstrates why many believe that child pornography incites its users to sexually abuse children, and worse. In 2000 Barbara and Robert Curley took a lawsuit against NAMBLA. Their son Jeffrey was 10 years old when he was murdered by two men in 1997, one of whom was Charlie Jaynes. The men took Jeffrey to the Boston Public Library and accessed NAMBLA's Web site, before attempting to sexually assault him. The young boy fought back and Jaynes gagged him with a gasoline soaked rag, eventually killing him. The two men then sodomised his dead body before dumping it in a river. According to police, Jaynes had eight issues of a NAMBLA publication in his home at the time of his arrest. The parents alleged that: 'NAMBLA serves as a conduit for an underground network of pedophiles in the United States who use their NAMBLA association and contacts therein and the Internet to obtain child pornography and promote pedophile activity'. When the case was dismissed against NAMBLA, the Curleys continued the suit as a wrongful death action against individual NAMBLA members. In relation to Charles Jaynes (who had been sentenced to life imprisonment and becomes eligible for parole in 2021), the claim was that:

i. In the Fall of 1996 Charles Jaynes also known as Elizah Woods, Anthony Scaccia and Scott Eastman of 42 Peterson Avenue, Brockton, Massachusetts joined NAMBLA.
ii. Prior to joining NAMBLA Charles Jaynes was heterosexual.

iii. After joining NAMBLA Charles Jaynes received and read the NAMBLA Bulletin, accessed and read the NAMBLA Web site which is provided by John Doe Inc. and by said means of communication began to collect child pornography and various pedophile material.

iv. As a direct and proximate result of the urging, advocacy, conspiring and promoting of pedophile activity by John Doe Inc., NAMBLA, [and other named persons], Charles Jaynes became obsessed with having sex with and raping young male children.

v. As a direct and proximate result of the urging, advocacy and promoting of pedophile activity by John Doe Inc., NAMBLA, [and other named persons], Charles Jaynes stalked Jeffrey Curley of Cambridge, Massachusetts who was ten years old and tortured, murdered and mutilated Jeffrey Curley's body on or about October 1, 1997. (*Source*: United States of America District Court of Massachusetts, 16 May 2000. Docket No. 00cv10956 GAO. Transcript of lawsuit paragraphs 27–31. http://www.thecpac.com/Curleys-v-NAMBLA.html)

At the time of writing this case had not been finalised.

7 Affects on health and well-being

Child abuse victims are at risk of a range of physical, emotional, behavioural and sexual harms (World Health Organization 1999). Health consequences range from the bruises, welts and fractures that appear immediately to longer-term challenges such as sexually transmitted infections, substance misuse and self-destructive impulses. Sometimes the outcome can be fatal. Because child pornography is a record of abuse its victims are vulnerable to all of these adverse health consequences. Their distress is amplified by the permanent trace of their abuse that may exist in cyberspace and, tragically, outlive them.

Silbert (1989: 226) described the impact of coerced participation in child pornography production on 100 boys and girls, whose average age was 14 years, but one of whom was 6 when violated in this way. She found that:

... they talked about a great deal of soreness and irritation in genital, vaginal, and anal areas. They remembered feeling generally flu-like during the period. They described symptoms such as vomiting, a lot of headaches, a loss of appetite, and sleeplessness. Emotionally, most described themselves as extremely moody and unable to continue on with the friendships they had had before because they felt they were now so different. Those used by adults to make pornography over a longer time described more intense emotional isolation as time passed. They also talked of growing feelings of anxiety, and many experienced direct fear.

Clearly, children who are used as fodder for pornographic magazines and films bear the marks physically as well as emotionally. No matter how resilient the young person, this is a trauma that is likely to endure. Even when the scars heal their ability to trust others remains seriously impaired, and in Silbert's view the long-term impact is more debilitating than the immediate effects, akin to a form of 'psychological paralysis' (ibid: 229). They come to believe that they are worthless and this is a state of mind that proves resistant to change. Nightmares and flashbacks act as painful reminders of the traumatic events.

Who are the child pornographers?

Producers (including photographers, creators of home videos and publishers), distributors (including advertisers, hosts and administrators of Web sites, and individual traders), and collectors of child pornography all sexually exploit children. Some do not have a sexual preference for children but have exhausted what adult pornography has to offer and are on the look out for more bizarre images. Others have no sexual interest either in children or child pornography and their involvement is motivated purely by profit. Recent indications that organised criminal gangs have become involved in the child pornography trade (Carr 2003) suggest that this type of entrepreneur will grow in number. There are also pranksters or misguided individuals conducting private investigations or exposés who have been found in possession of child pornography. None of these individuals would be considered paedophiles in the psychiatric sense of the word.

According to the latest version of the *Diagnostic and Statistical Manual of Mental Disorders* published by the American Psychiatric Association (DSM-IV-TR 2000) the criteria required for a diagnosis of paedophilia are:

a) Over a period of at least six months, recurrent, intense, sexually arousing fantasies, sexual urges, or behaviours involving sexual activity with a prepubescent child or children (generally age 13 years or younger).
b) The person has acted on these urges, or the sexual urges or fantasies cause marked distress or interpersonal difficulty.
c) The person is at least age 16 years and at least five years older than the child or children. (This diagnosis does not include an individual in late adolescence involved in an ongoing sexual relationship with a 12- or 13-year-old.)

This was a change to the previous definition which stated that a person who molested children was considered to have a psychiatric disorder only if his actions caused significant distress. In other words, a remorseless child molester whose actions did not impair his social or work relationships would not be diagnosed as a paedophile. The current criteria would seem to suggest that if an individual's sexual fantasies of children cause no distress and have no behavioural sequelae, then the individual is not a paedophile.

Because 'paedophilia' is a psychiatric classification, and because it is impossible to fix pubescence at an exact age, law enforcement agencies often employ a broader definition (Healy 1996: 3). This incorporates adults with a sexual preference for individuals legally considered children, including ephebophiles (persons with a sexual preference for pubescents) and hebephiles (where the sexual preference is for adolescents). Throughout this text a looser definition than the psychiatric one is used, following the general practice in the relevant social science literature. We are not primarily concerned with the duration of the 'condition' or the precise level of sexual maturity of the parties involved. Our interest resides in the extent to which the illicit desire for children gives rise to criminality, and how society responds.

Attempts to tally the number of child pornography enthusiasts are as pointless as the guesstimates of the numbers of victims and images in circulation. The illegal nature of every aspect of this trade leaves few individuals willing to admit their involvement. Such is the revulsion which child pornography usually invokes it is a rare individual who would admit to even viewing this material. As Jenkins (2001: 19) expressed it: 'It is inconceivable that an active child pornographer will allow himself to be interviewed or to permit an academic any kind of access to his traffic'. This is quite a change from the 1970s when such material was openly available and freely traded. Studies involving child pornography offenders are limited to those who have been caught, are in custody or receiving treatment, and are willing to participate. The data collected are at best representative of a very small minority of this group of offenders.

Where a degree of consensus exists is around the fact that those who come to the attention of the authorities represent only the tip of the iceberg. Jenkins (2001: 1) monitored child pornography newsgroups and bulletin boards over a two-year period and was astounded by the thriving community of enthusiasts he encountered online. He quotes one of the gurus of this electronic world, 'Godfather Corleone':

> In fact, extremely few persons actually get arrested and sent to jail, that is a myth really. There are thousands of vhs's [videos] out there ... thousands of people present at this bbs [bulletin board] and millions of loli-lovers in various countries, yet you only see a couple of persons getting arrested, and the media writes about it like they have been busting Al Capone.

If 'Godfather Corleone' is to be believed, and what sketchy evidence is available would tend to support his view, then the vast majority of child pornography offenders remain outside the awareness of the authorities and beyond the reach of the law. Many of those who are caught exhibit a certain naivety. Consider the case of George Sherman, whose activities came to the attention of the FBI and the Customs Services in Canada and the USA. As outlined by Anglin (2002: 1110–11) Sherman was sent a letter, purportedly from the owners of 'Foreign Films Etcetera ... a business specializing in visual materials "very much outside the norm"', but really from an agent of the US Postal Inspection Service. Sherman began a correspondence with the agent and ordered a video entitled *Boys-3* and a set of photographs called *Chicken for Hire*. He had been sent promotional material describing the video as containing 'sexual activity between two boys aged 12 and 13' and the photographs as portraying 'uninhibited boys aged 8 to 15 engaged in various sexual acts'.

As if this was not a sufficiently extraordinary display of trust with a previously unknown organisation trading in what were clearly prohibited items, Sherman was kind enough to complete and return a survey questionnaire where he indicated his interest in pornographic genres such as 'chickenhawk', 'incest' and 'young, underage'. Despite being warned that some of the materials were 'very illegal', Sherman indicated an interest in buying and trading them; hardly the acts of a clever criminal. To cap it all, Sherman took receipt of his order personally and signed for it. When his apartment was searched a short time later he had already made a copy of the video and hidden it in his oven with the original. The photographs were found under a cushion in the living room. Reading the facts of this case one cannot help but be struck by the feeling that a more sophisticated offender would have seen the warning signs early on and steered well clear of such an obviously hazardous enterprise.

In fact Jenkins (2001) believes that the majority of Internet pornographers are alive to the police presence on the Internet and the more sophisticated among them treat every communication with a 'newbie' as if they were dealing with an undercover cop. It has become something of a standing joke that the most active online traders are law-enforcement personnel, as are the most enthusiastic customers, each trying to sting the other. Even genuine participants are not as they seem. In a study of online chat rooms supposedly for young gay males, Lamb (1998) estimated that around nine out of ten visitors were adults masquerading as children, usually seeking to exchange sexual fantasies or pornography.

So what do we know about this community of 'loli-lovers'? Krone (2004) has devised a typology which describes an escalation in both the seriousness of offending and the degree of commitment to the activity. He divided offenders into nine groups and these are summarised in Box 3.2.

Box 3.2: A typology of child pornography offenders

1   A *browser* may come across child pornography unintentionally (for example, via spam) but then decide to keep it.

2   If a person has a *private fantasy* involving sex with a child, no offence is committed. If that fantasy is preserved as something more than a thought, then it may be an offence. The representation of that fantasy in text or digital format on a computer may be sufficient to constitute the possession of child pornography even if the offender has no intention of sharing it with any other person.

3   Among *trawlers* there is little or no security employed and minimal networking. Some are oriented to a range of sexually explicit material of which child pornography is a part but not the focus; their tastes are extreme but wide. Others are sexually curious and experiment with, but do not pursue, child pornography.

---

4   The *non-secure collector* purchases, downloads or exchanges child pornography from openly available sources on the Internet or in chat rooms that do not impose security barriers such as passwords, encryption or the requirement to trade a minimum number of images. There is a higher degree of networking among non-secure collectors than among trawlers.

5   The *secure collector* makes use of security barriers. In addition to encryption, some groups have an entry requirement that locks members into protecting each other, such as requiring interested parties to submit child pornography images to join (for example, the Wønderland Club demanded an entrance fee of 10,000 original pictures; see Box 2.1, pp. 38–9).

6   The *online groomer* is a person who has initiated online contact with a child with the intention of establishing a relationship involving cybersex or physical sex. Child pornography is used to 'groom' the child; it is displayed to lower the child's inhibitions concerning illegal sexual activity.

7   *Physical abusers* are actively involved in the abuse of children and use child pornography to supplement their sexual craving. The physical abuse may be recorded for the future personal use of the adult but there is no intention to distribute it further.

8   The *producer* of child pornography is involved in the physical abuse of children. He provides the images of that abuse to other users of child pornography.

9   The *distributor* of child pornography may or may not have a sexual interest in child pornography. His sole motive may be financial gain.

(*Source*: Krone 2004: 4–5)

O'Connell (1998) analysed Usenet newsgroups that were dedicated to child sex on the basis that these were a concrete expression of paedophile networking. From this she came up with a classification of the roles played by posters to newsgroups and formed some interesting insights into how this activity was socially structured. There were a number of distinct spheres of activity. Some took it upon themselves to carry out a range of administrative functions, including drafting responses to FAQs (frequently asked questions) and providing technical information about how to use the Internet securely. These are the first points of contact for novices and are responsible for explaining key elements of 'Netiquette'. Others advise on how to procure relevant literature and join support groups such as NAMBLA. Another group contributes by posting child sex stories, whether based on imaginary or real events, for the titillation of visitors. Some play a part by building a supportive and non-threatening context where illicit desires can be discussed openly. The backbone of the social group is provided by those who post and trade child erotica and pornographic images without whose efforts there would be little to explain, support and validate. It should be noted that not all of the visitors to these newsgroups are promoters of child pornography. A number become involved with the explicit intention of posting derogatory comments or naming and shaming convicted paedophiles.

While there is very little empirical information available about the characteristics of Internet child pornography offenders, some interesting findings have emerged. In May 2004, Patrick Walsh, Director of the Granada Institute in Dublin, a leading centre for the treatment of sexual abuse, addressed the fifth Annual Prosecutors' Conference in Ireland. He outlined the results of a study which he had carried out with 35 Internet child pornography offenders. These men ranged in age from early twenties to sixty and were of above average intelligence, often educated to third level. They tended to have histories of well-paid employment, commonly in sales, engineering, accountancy and computing. None of them were involved in the so-called caring professions. Almost 80 per cent showed patterns of obsessive collecting behaviour. They went to great lengths to catalogue their archives of images.

All of the offenders described how they frequently masturbated when they viewed their images. This reinforced the behaviour and it became a habit. In practically every case they became satiated and bored and felt compelled to continually seek out new, and sometimes more extreme, images. Their use of the Internet was a continuation of pornographic magazine collecting that often went back to adolescence. There was an addictive quality to their computer use and the offenders expressed a unanimous view that this part of their lives was out of control.

Almost two-thirds of them were or had been married, but their marriages often lacked emotional depth. Walsh described them as 'intellectually articulate' but 'emotionally illiterate'. He found them to have a 'somewhat childlike quality' and to have difficulty forming deep relationships. (Similarly, in a US study Stack *et al.* (2004) found that the lack of a happy marriage was a predictor of

Internet pornography use, along with weak ties to religion and the use of prostitutes.) They also tended to be thrill-seekers and reported deriving satisfaction from successfully bending or breaking rules in other domains of their lives. This ranged from submitting false claims for expenses to shoplifting.

Walsh compared the characteristics of this group with contact child sexual abusers. He found a difference in psychosexual adjustment. The Internet offenders believed that their maternal relationships had been seriously disrupted in early life. They tended to describe their mothers as distant, controlling and emotionally unavailable. To adapt to this situation they withdrew and sought solace from their private thoughts. In the contact abuse group the maternal relationship was described as intact and strong but there was often an absent or inadequate father figure. (For a review of the issues around the classification, diagnosis and assessment of child molesters, especially the variability among individuals in terms of personal characteristics, life experiences, criminal histories and reasons for offending, see Prentky *et al.* 1997.)

While our knowledge about the characteristics of child pornographers is limited, it appears that they do not conform to a particular stereotype. Unlike other offenders they are not typically young, male, working-class, urban-dwelling recidivists. This is a kind of crime unusually blind to socio-economic differences and those apprehended for it make a stark contrast with the persistent property and drug offenders who clog up criminal justice systems around the world. Few of them were previously known to the authorities. The British edition of Avalanche, codenamed Operation Ore, first came to public attention with the arrest of two police officers who had worked in a high profile case involving child abduction and murder. Also brought into the net were two Members of Parliament, doctors, judges, legendary rock star Pete Townshend of The Who, and more than 50 other police officers (*The Guardian*, 13 January 2003). Carr (2003: 15) estimated that between 70 and 95 per cent of those arrested under Operation Ore had no previous convictions and were not known to law enforcement authorities or social services.

Operation Auxin in Australia in 2004 revealed offenders to be police officers, military personnel, lawyers, ministers of religion, doctors and nurses. In France in 1997 a major child pornography investigation revealed that many of the 235 men charged had jobs that brought them into contact with children, including 31 teachers, two holiday centre directors, two priests and six doctors, one of whom was a paediatrician (*The Independent* (London), 23 June 1997).

A similar pattern was found in the canton of Lucerne under the Swiss edition of Operation Avalanche where those arrested tended to be middle aged, middle class and without previous convictions (Frei *et al.* 2005).

The Canadian study by Seto and Eke (2005), referred to earlier in this chapter, identified 201 adult male child pornography offenders from police records. This was clearly a male pursuit. Just a single female was identified and she had been charged with a man. The average age was 38 years and the range was wide, extending from teenagers to senior citizens. More than half (56 per cent) had a prior criminal record. One in four (24 per cent) had a history of contact sexual offences and 15 per cent had prior child pornography offences on their records. This level of established criminal conduct goes against the international trend.

Alexy *et al.* (2005) compiled data on 225 cases of Internet child sexual exploitation from a variety of media outlets including newspapers, magazines and watchdog organisations (such as Pedowatch.org). Once again the higher socio-economic groups dominated, with almost two-thirds classified as professionals and fewer than one in ten unemployed. The overwhelming majority were male (95 per cent) and the average age was 37 years (range: 15–66). The individuals concerned fell into three groups. Traders were involved in the collection, production and distribution of child pornography. They were the greatest in number, making up 59 per cent of the sample. Travelers engaged in discussion with children online and through manipulation and coercion attempted to arrange meetings for sexual purposes. They accounted for 22 per cent of cases. Combination trader-travelers participated in trading child pornography as well as travelling, sometimes significant distances, with a view to engaging in sexual interaction with a child. The remaining 19 per cent fell into this category.

McLaughlin (2000) catalogued the characteristics of persons arrested during a three-year Internet law enforcement project conducted by the Keene Police Department in the US state of New Hampshire. Suspects were encountered in chat rooms, newsgroups and other sites. Over 200 offenders were arrested (all but two of them male) and over two million child pornographic images were seized. The average age was 36 years (range: 13–65) and there was a wide spread of occupations including students (22 per cent), labourers (22 per cent) and computer specialists (13 per cent). Those with known access to children represented 41 per cent and those with a prior arrest for a sex crime represented 12 per cent.

erman and Wilson (2002: 96) reported that during one British e investigation of Internet child abusers (Operation Appal) a ber of the 48 suspects targeted were themselves children; six were under 17 years of age and one was only 13. The youngest child had over 300 images hidden in his bedroom including some that showed the abuse of babies. He was placed on the Sex Offender Register. This raises complex questions about how to disentangle curiosity and naïvety from hardened criminality, and what is likely to be achieved by punishing a child for possession of pornographic images of other children, especially in a scenario where the subjects of the images are age appropriate.

Why the attraction?

Healy (1996: 7) identified eight reasons why individuals use child pornography. These can be stated briefly:

1 *Arousal and gratification*: To stimulate their sexual drive. Some may only fantasise but for others reading and viewing are a prelude to actual sexual activity with minors. (On occasion the pornography can be used as an alternative to contact offending.)

2 *Validation and justification*: To convince themselves that their behaviour or obsession is not abnormal, but is shared by thousands of other sensitive, intelligent and caring people.

3 *To lower children's inhibitions*: Pictures of other children having sex are used to assist in seduction and encourage reluctant children to participate. Images are often used to show a child what the offender wants them to do. Pornography may be used under the guise of 'sex education' to create sexual arousal in the child.

4 *To preserve a child's youth*: This ensures that there will always be an image of the child at the age of sexual preference.

5 *Blackmail*: Sexually explicit images help ensure the silence of the victimised child. Threats to show the pictures to parents, peers or others are powerful. Child victims will not always report pictorial records – even if they report sexual abuse – because they may be ashamed of what happened to them as well as fearing that they might have been considered willing participants.

6 *A medium of exchange*: Used as a means of establishing trust and camaraderie with other like-minded people and as proof of good intentions when establishing contacts. It is a medium of communication with fellow exploiters in public and private sex markets. It is the currency of the subculture.

7 *Access*: Pornography can be exchanged to gain access to new markets and children.

8 *Profit*: Although most do not sell child pornography, sometimes homemade videos and photographs are offered for sale on a one-to-one basis. It is not unheard of for self-produced materials to be sold to finance trips overseas to popular sex tourist destinations. Occasionally, the sale of child pornography over the Internet can be big business (for example, see Box 4.2, pp. 119–20).

One behavioural characteristic shared by many of those with an interest in child pornography is a tendency to collect, swap and sort images. On occasion, as we noted in the previous chapter, this activity takes place on a pathological scale and gives rise to archives containing hundreds of thousands of photographs. The importance of the phenomenology of collecting cannot be overestimated (see Box 3.3 below). This can be an integral part of the behaviour, and the reluctance to part with their prized images is one reason why paedophiles are often found in possession of huge numbers of photographs, meticulously filed and cross-referenced. The Internet affected the size of collections but not their essence.

Tremblay (2006: 154) gives the example of a series of 300 pictures of a boy called Nathan. The pictures are spread over a period of several years, beginning when Nathan was around 9 years old. The first 60 or so pictures show him fully clothed and only a couple of dozen depict any sexual contact. The explicit pictures are extremely difficult to obtain, and as such are valuable currency. Tremblay argues that the Nathan collection is popular partly because it shows the evolution of an apparently consensual relationship between photographer and subject but also because the pictures have to be sorted into chronological order, the gaps are hard to fill, and the challenge to the collector is satisfyingly substantial. The need to collect the full series becomes an important goal, independent of the pleasure gained from viewing the images. This is a solitary pursuit that can become hugely time-consuming and fill a void in an otherwise empty life.

Box 3.3: Collecting passions

Collections are *important*. They are central to the collector's life and he is willing to spend considerable time and money on the acquisition of new material.

Collections are *constant*. No matter how much he has it will never be enough. The impulse to gather material is deep-rooted and enduring.

Collections are *organised*. They are usually maintained in a detailed, neat and orderly fashion, aided by computers and related storage devices. Given the large numbers of images involved – tens of thousands are not uncommon – a well-defined filing system is essential.

Collections are *permanent*. Although a collection might be moved, hidden or given away (perhaps to another enthusiast when an investigation is underway), it is unlikely ever to be destroyed. It is his life's work and helps to define who he is.

Collections will be *concealed*. The obvious need to keep a collection securely hidden must be balanced against the desire to have easy access to it. Computers have greatly facilitated collectors in this respect.

Collections may be *shared*. Paedophiles frequently have a need or a desire to show and tell others of a like mind about their collections. The paedophile is constantly seeking validation for his efforts.

(*Source*: Reynolds (1998). These characteristics of collections first appeared in a document produced in 1988 by the Obscene Publications Branch (see Tate 1992: 212).)

Features of contemporary child pornography

Modern technology means that child pornography is produced and stored in a number of different formats, including photographs, movies, audio files and text-based accounts. Prior to the widespread availability of affordable communication devices and recording technologies, child pornography generally took the form of printed magazines and relied on postal services to reach a limited audience. However, rapid technological advances and falling prices for electronic goods facilitate non-commercial production and storage of images and allow for their large-scale distribution.

Child pornographic and erotic images can be quickly, easily and cheaply produced using digital cameras. These bypass traditional requirements to send film to a laboratory for processing and allow images to be directly transferred onto a personal computer and printed off in the privacy of one's own home. Computers facilitate the storage of large amounts of material (on hard drives, floppy disks, tapes, CDs or DVDs) and allow for cheap and quick distribution via the Internet. The time lag between production and consumption has been reduced to such an extent that the ultimate in instant gratification is now possible: using a cheap and simple Webcam, abuse can be viewed, and recorded, as it is perpetrated (see Box 5.1, pp. 158–9).

Even the most basic home computer purchased in 2006 would have at least 80 gigabytes of storage space. This is enough to hold well in excess of 100,000 colour photographs even if no efforts have been made to compress them. Sophisticated users could take advantage of readily available software to squeeze these files into a smaller amount of disk space. This makes them easier to copy and share. A massive amount of material can very quickly be accumulated by collecting a number of these compressed files.

Taylor and Quayle (2003) believe that the production and distribution of child pornography films are poorly understood, but there are grounds for thinking that moving images are the major contemporary source of child pornography. This trend is likely to intensify as digital photography becomes more widely available. The recent rollout of camera phones also presents new challenges. Consider the case of the teenage schoolgirl in the south of Ireland whose sexually explicit image was rapidly circulated among secondary school students around the country via camera phones. Within days she had become a national talking point. The incident received coverage in the print and broadcast media, was raised as a matter of concern in parliament and there were calls for new regulations (Terry Leyden, *Seanad Debates*, 22 January 2004, Vol. 175, Col. 72). The police began an investigation under the Child Trafficking and Pornography Act, 1998, warning that anyone found in possession of the image, or distributing it, could be prosecuted and jailed (*RTÉ News*, 22 January 2004; *The Irish Times*, 23 January 2004).

As we have seen, it is not uncommon for contemporary collections of child pornography to contain material dating back to the 1970s when it was legal in a number of countries. With respect to the newer material becoming available, Taylor and Quayle (2003) found that the age of children seems to be dropping and children are being photographed in more degrading settings. Furthermore, according to the same authors, there is growing involvement of children from developing countries: 'Thailand, the Philippines, India and more recently South America, are locations from which child pornography production has increasingly been evident. Most notable of all, however, are the increasing number of children from Eastern European countries. The amateur producers of this material ... tend to be Westerners, who deliberately set out to establish contacts with disadvantaged children' (p. 45).

Lanning (2001: 52) distinguished between child pornography ('the sexually explicit visual depiction of a minor including ... photographs, negatives, slides, magazines, movies, videotapes, or computer disks') and child erotica ('any material, relating to children, that serves a sexual purpose for a given individual'). Child erotica can consist of anything, provided that the verbal or visual representation involves children. Generally speaking possession and distribution of such items remain within the law. Carr (2003) suggested that the presence of such material in a collection might be indicative of an active abuser on the grounds that these images were likely to be much closer to potential fulfilment in real-world situations than hard-core pornography. In other words, images depicting hand holding or cuddling, even innocent parent-child images, represent more achievable goals than extreme sexual violations.

Taylor (1998) noted that text-based material and erotica were much more likely to be recent and many Internet paedophiles expressed a preference for this material over sexually explicit photographic images. (A content analysis of postings to the newsgroup alt.sex. stories by Harmon and Boeringer (1997) found explicit references to paedophilic sex in 19.4 per cent of the narratives examined.) Taylor argued that the existence of child erotica emphasises the significance of understanding the way in which the paedophile sexualises what otherwise may be quite innocent material. An examination of the viewing preferences of NAMBLA members reinforces this point.

The Seattle journalist, Mathew Stadler, reporting on a weekend spent at NAMBLA meetings, revealed that they derived erotic stimulation through watching children on network television, the Disney channel, and mainstream films. He concluded that he had 'found NAMBLA's "porn" and it was Hollywood' (cited in Kincaid 1998: 115). Similarly Adler (2001b: fn 99) found that in June 1998 the Web site of *Paidika*, a self-described journal of paedophilia, provided a link to *Vogue Bambini*, an Italian fashion magazine for children's clothes, and featured a cover from the magazine depicting children wearing heavy winter coats. In her words, 'the mundane innocence of pictures is often their draw' (p. 944).

Tremblay (2006: 155) describes a North American television sitcom, *Malcolm in the Middle*, that was originally based on a family with four sons. The first episode showed two of the boys wrestling on the floor in their underwear for about five minutes. This caused a high level of activity on *Free Spirits*, a major computer network for paedophiles, and subsequent episodes were viewed by groups of similarly inclined men who got together specifically for this purpose. Between episodes there was endless speculation about who would be next to disrobe on screen. This is a good example of how family entertainment can serve unintended purposes and how the most unremarkable household scenes can have a libidinal appeal.

Before the Internet became widely available, Howitt (1995) conducted a study of paedophiles with extensive offending histories who were undergoing assessment or treatment at a private clinic in Britain. He found that exposure to explicit child pornography was uncommon, and that some expressed a strong distaste for such material despite not having encountered it. Instead offenders generated their own 'erotic' materials from relatively innocuous sources such as television advertisements and clothing catalogues featuring children modelling underwear. Sometimes they added sexual details to the images by drawing. One individual, Charlie, found erotic arousal in pictures cut from Scout magazines. Another, Graham, said that he had no interest at all in pictures of naked children. His fantasies were fuelled by newspaper cuttings of boys shown in uniforms, with a strong preference for short trousers. Just like child pornography, such seemingly innocent material is more widely available and easier to manipulate today. The scrapbook and glue of twenty years ago have been replaced by the perfect 'cut and paste' of the digital age. But the point remains that even if the supply of pornography were reduced to zero (an impossibility of course) the resources for sexual gratification would remain abundant.

Contemporary collections are increasingly seen to contain computer-generated images. Sometimes these involve the manipulation of a real image (for example, a child's hand is superimposed onto an adult's penis, or pubic or facial hair is erased to make an adult look like a child) but they can also involve the creation of a virtual image of a child. Computer technology has made image manipulation extremely easy with advanced graphics software making it difficult to differentiate simulations from the real thing. This is presenting greater challenges for both law enforcement and international campaigns against child pornography. For example, a 36-year-old former priest, prosecuted in the north of Ireland, had in his collection a picture that he had created by superimposing a photograph of a girl's face onto the body of a naked 14-year-old. The offender knew the girl personally as she was involved in a youth council he had helped set up (*The Irish Times*, 15 October 2003).

The extent to which computer-generated graphics can carry an erotic charge is illustrated by the appearance of Web sites containing nude images of Lara Croft, digital heroine of the Tomb Raider computer games. Some programmers have written code that allows users to play Tomb Raider with Croft naked throughout the game. Another product of animation, UltraVixen, appeared as a centrefold in the January 1998 issue of adult magazine *Rage* (Lane 2001: 59-61). The line between the real and virtual worlds is becoming increasingly blurred.

COPINE researchers found that the creators of computer-generated images often demonstrated great technical skill and competence and it was apparent that they devoted a considerable amount of time to their work (Taylor and Quayle 2003). While computer-generated images do not usually involve harm to 'real' children, awareness is growing that such creations are not entirely benign. In the theme paper for the Second World Congress on the Commercial Sexual Exploitation of Children, Carr (2001: 21) argued:

> Civilised society has declared that the depiction of children as sexual objects is unacceptable. It has done this not just because of the harm it generally does to the children who are its immediate victims. It is also because viewing child pornography can desensitise adults and lead them towards further harmful or abusive behaviour, and therefore also puts other children at risk ... Child pornography is often used by sexual predators quite deliberately to lure children into abusive relationships. In that context, therefore, whether or not the image is real or artificial is of no significance.

Quayle and Taylor (2002: 8–22), in interviews with convicted downloaders, have attempted to expand our understanding of why individuals use child pornography. Highlighting the role of modern technology, these authors identified the following half-a-dozen ways in which child pornography is used in today's society. There are clear points of overlap with Healy's scheme outlined above (pp. 86–7).

1 The most dominant function of child pornography is as a means of achieving *sexual arousal*, with most images accessed for masturbatory purposes.

2 Child pornography enthusiasts obtain pleasure from *colleu.* pictures as part of a series, even when the material is not attractive or sexually arousing.

3 Those who traded images and who used Internet Relay Chat to communicate cited the importance of *social contact* with others with shared interests. Collections also provide status for individuals and facilitate networking.

4 Linking up with others on the Internet provides important social support that often *replaces unsatisfactory relationships* in the real world; life and its problems are avoided when the computer powers up. Sexual satisfaction can be sought and gained, over which the individual has perfect control.

5 Some individuals claimed that seeking child pornography helped them to control their interests and explore the nature of their problem; in their view it can be seen as a form of *therapy.*

6 The *Internet* facilitates rapid, easy and anonymous access to child pornography. The Internet itself was held responsible by some individuals for their interest in child pornography, with many citing the compulsive elements of searching, downloading and storing.

A psychological perspective

Taylor and Quayle (2003) argued that understanding and responding to child pornography require us to think psychologically rather than legally. Evidence that child pornography collections are supplemented by child erotica indicates the need to account for material which is not strictly pornographic in nature. Child erotica can serve identical functions to child pornography. For example, photographs of JonBenet Ramsey singing and dancing were popular among those with an interest in Internet child pornography (Singular 1999: 48). The 6-year-old North American Beauty Pageant Queen was murdered in 1996 (see further Chapter 7).

Clearly then the materials used in child pornography vary greatly, making it difficult to conduct comparative research. In this regard the classification of images produced by the COPINE project marked a significant step forward. Founded upon images downloaded from publicly available newsgroups, the archive quickly grew to in excess of 150,000 still pictures and 400 video clips. In May 2004, it was transferred from University College Cork to Interpol's offices in France where the resources were in place to build on what COPINE had achieved. Through Interpol this valuable collection will continue to be available to police forces around the world.

The taxonomy was developed principally from a psychological perspective and is therefore more extensive than any criminal law classification, particularly with its inclusion of 'indicative material' at Level 1. This way of grading material (see Table 3.1) has become extremely influential in legal and clinical circles. An abbreviated version of the COPINE scheme was adopted by the Sentencing Advisory Panel (2002) in London when they published their guidelines on sentencing in child pornography cases. These were drawn up after an extensive consultation exercise which included consideration of a lengthy written submission from the aforementioned paedophile apologist Tom O'Carroll.

The Sentencing Advisory Panel offered a structured legal approach to assessing the seriousness of an individual offence and selecting the appropriate penalty. It related the choice and length of sentence to the nature of the material and the degree of engagement with it and recommended that sentencers should always view for themselves the images involved in a particular case. It prepared a five-level descriptive typology of images based on a collapsing of several of the COPINE categories. The first COPINE category was omitted and the next five were collapsed into Level 1. COPINE categories 7 to 10 can be mapped directly onto levels 2 to 5. The levels of the SAP scheme can be summarised as follows:

1 Images depicting nudity or erotic posing, with no sexual activity.
2 Sexual activity between children, or solo masturbation by a child.
3 Non-penetrative sexual activity between adult and child.
4 Penetrative sexual activity between adult and child.
5 Sadism or bestiality.

While conceptual clarity around the issues at stake is required, particularly with regard to offence seriousness, it is essential not to lose sight of more fundamental concerns.

Our next task is to examine, in the second part of the book, the way a single country has grappled with the problem. Before doing so, it is salutary to return to the question raised in the title of this chapter, and shift the focus of the analysis from a somewhat academic discussion about how best to classify images, to a flesh and blood example of 'why it matters'. In essence this is about how children's

Table 3.1 COPINE categories of material used by persons with a sexual interest in children

Level	Name	Description of picture qualities
1	Indicative	Non-erotic and non-sexualised pictures showing children in their underwear, swimming costumes, etc. from either commercial sources or family albums; pictures of children playing in normal settings, in which the context or organisation of pictures by the collector indicates inappropriateness.
2	Nudist	Pictures of naked or semi-naked children in appropriate nudist settings, and from legitimate sources.
3	Erotica	Surreptitiously taken photographs of children in play areas or other safe environments showing either underwear or varying degrees of nakedness.
4	Posing	Deliberately posed pictures of children fully, or partially clothed or naked (where the amount, context and organisation suggest sexual interest).
5	Erotic Posing	Deliberately posed pictures of fully or partially clothed or naked children in sexualised or provocative poses.
6	Explicit Erotic Posing	Emphasising genital areas where the child is either naked, partially or fully clothed.
7	Explicit Sexual Activity	Involves touching, mutual and self-masturbation, oral sex and intercourse by child, not involving an adult.
8	Assault	Pictures of children being subject to a sexual assault, involving digital touching, involving an adult.
9	Gross Assault	Grossly obscene pictures of sexual assault, involving penetrative sex, masturbation or oral sex involving an adult.
10	Sadistic/Bestiality	Pictures showing a child being tied, bound, beaten, whipped or otherwise subject to something that implies pain. Pictures where an animal is involved in some form of sexual behaviour with a child.

(*Source*: Taylor *et al.* 2001: 95–6)

lives are destroyed for the pleasure of adults, predominantly men. The following vignette – based on an account in Tim Tate's (1990: 180) important book *Child Pornography: An Investigation* – shows the price paid to satisfy corrupt desires.

 On 27 August 1984, in a hotel room in Amsterdam, Thea Pumbroek died. She had taken a cocaine overdose.

For much of her life Thea had been involved in the production of pornographic videos and her death occurred while she was yet again under the camera.

Nobody remembers her. The records of her death appear to have vanished. Even on the Internet she has left no trace. Her humanity has been effaced.

Thea Pumbroek was 6-years-old.

Part II
A National Case Study

Chapter 4

Ireland in focus

At the end of the twentieth century the pornographic exploitation of children did not appear to be a problem in Ireland. In 1998 the Irish Society for the Prevention of Cruelty to Children (ISPCC) found that there was very little evidence of forced participation in, or exposure to, child pornography among callers to its Childline service. Consultations with health board care workers by the Working Group on Illegal and Harmful Use of the Internet also failed to elicit evidence of such activity (Department of Justice, Equality and Law Reform, 1998a: 36).

Nor were any hints to be found in official statistics, policy documents or academic treatises. Prior to 2000 no information relating to child pornography was presented in the annual crime statistics produced by *An Garda Síochána* (the national police force). The Department of Justice, Equality and Law Reform published *The Law on Sexual Offences: A Discussion Paper* in 1998. This was silent on the question of child pornography. Tom O'Malley, a leading authority on sex crime and sentencing, completed two influential books around this time: *Sexual Offences: Law, Policy and Punishment* (1996) and *Sentencing Law and Practice* (2000). Neither referred to a child pornography problem.

As far as is known, there was never a representative paedophile organisation in Ireland and there is little evidence that child pornography was circulating in the country in significant quantities. Official records detailing publications prohibited by the Censorship of Publications Board as indecent or obscene suggest a tiny number of complaints about material that may have involved the sexual exploitation of children (see the *Register of Prohibited Publications*, 1930 to the present, and Table 4.1 below).

Nevertheless, in June 1998 the Child Trafficking and Pornography Act completed its passage through the Houses of the *Oireachtas* (parliament). It came into operation a month later. For the first time, the term 'child pornography' was included on the Irish statute book and sanctions of increasing severity differentiated between possession, distribution, production and the pornographic exploitation of minors. In 2000, only seven offences were recorded under the Act in the crime statistics (*An Garda Síochána* 2002: 79). By any measure this was a low level of activity. It could be argued that the legislation was a solution in search of a problem.

However, within months of these *Garda* figures being released, public anxiety about child pornography began to grow. On foot of information received from the American authorities, police searched more than 100 homes and business premises in a series of dawn raids on 27 May 2002. Codenamed Operation Amethyst, the investigation exposed Irish involvement in the international child pornography trade and gave the problem a local dimension for the first time.

Sensationalist reporting captured the public's attention by presenting a crime wave of greater magnitude than anyone had imagined. One report claimed that *Gardaí* had 'confiscated evidence that shows paedophilia is indulged on a frightening scale here' (*Irish Examiner*, 31 May 2002). Overnight, parents began to view child pornography as an immediate threat to their children. What was presented as most shocking was the background of those who were investigated. Among others, the homes of a solicitor, a judge, a bank manager, a schoolteacher, a business executive, a health board official and a choirmaster were raided. Ireland is a parochial and close-knit society and people felt it easy to relate to the offenders, whether based on personal knowledge of their circumstances, place of abode or position in society. This fuelled media interest. As the account in the *Irish Examiner* newspaper continued:

> Pillars of society all of them and all suspected of an evil secret
> that should instead make them the outcasts of society ... Nor is
> it something which, like drug dealing, happens on street corners
> or dark clubs, practiced by shady looking characters. Under
> the veneer of ultra respectability, some of the most respected
> in the community can be the greatest threat to children and it
> could be right next door to you or working next to you. None
> of the almost 100 men who will be questioned have a previous

criminal record. They were practically all from better class areas and many of them are married. They are the kind of people from whom you wouldn't mind getting a reference for a job.

In particular, the Internet was presented as a sinister place where sexual predators lurked, waiting to entice unsuspecting children into the rapidly expanding child pornography industry. Child pornographers, it was stressed, were active abusers who presented an ongoing threat to children. Media reports fuelled a growing panic by portraying a previously undetected culture of child abuse. Irish society was still reeling from a decade of disclosures and allegations, which during the 1990s saw child sexual abuse emerge as its 'best kept secret'. High-profile cases revealed the extent to which the sexual violation of children had been allowed to take place for decades. Surveys confirmed what many already suspected, namely that child sexual abuse had reached epidemic proportions. A national study by a team of researchers from the Royal College of Surgeons in Ireland found that more than four in ten of the women surveyed reported some form of sexual abuse or assault in their lifetime (McGee et al. 2002). The figures for men were lower but no less alarming with over one quarter reporting that they had been victims of sexual abuse or assault. It is unsurprising then that the mere suggestion of a further dimension of abuse elicited such a strong reaction.

As the Amethyst and other child pornography cases proceeded through the courts, the public became vocal in its disapproval of what was perceived as lenient treatment of sex offenders. The sentence handed down in the case of a well-known celebrity chef provoked national outrage, with many people believing that his wealth, and in particular his ability to pay a 'fine' of €40,000, helped him to avoid prison. Lurid media coverage fuelled the conspiracy theorists. The Star newspaper was one of many to carry provocative front-page headlines, blaring: 'You're rich, you're free but you're still a sick pervert' (17 January 2003). It continued: 'Money talks, and yesterday it kept a child porn pervert free of even a soft suspended jail term'. However, the individual in question was not 'fined', a fact lost on most commentators. He received 240 hours community service in lieu of a nine-month prison sentence and had his name placed on the Register of Sex Offenders for the mandatory term of five years. He also made a voluntary contribution of €40,000 to the court poor box in aid of a local charity, the Edith Wilkins Foundation, which helps street children in Calcutta.

Politicians joined in the condemnation. Enda Kenny, leader of *Fine Gael*, the main opposition party, called for mandatory jail sentences for people convicted of using child pornography, warning that 'the public may see the sentence ... as too lenient ... and there was now a danger that people will believe there is "one law for the rich and one for the poor". He said this "vile" crime should be dealt with in the circuit court which can impose higher sentences than the district court which tried the ... case' (*The Irish Times*, 20 January 2003). Child protection groups also expressed their disapproval. The chief executive of the ISPCC said the sentence did not reflect the seriousness of the offence and sent out the wrong message (*RTÉ News*, 16 January 2003).

The saturation media coverage which the chef's treatment attracted focused public attention on sentencing in child pornography cases, and contributed to the growing belief that there was an unacceptable level of disparity in the decisions made by judges. *The Irish Times* (18 January 2003) opined: 'The manner in which the courts have dealt with persons charged with possessing child pornography has been inconsistent'. Other cases which were perceived to have attracted lenient sentences also generated intense concern.

In a very short period of time, Ireland was forced to come to terms with a problem that had been identified in other countries more than a quarter of a century before. The child pornography issue became a lightning rod for public fear and discontent. The recent arrival of the Internet and a level of uncertainty about its potential to facilitate, or even encourage, this kind of crime put the criminal justice system under pressure to respond. But understanding of the issues fell well behind the level of public, political and media concern. To begin a process of understanding, the research which gave rise to this chapter was commissioned by the Department of Justice, Equality and Law Reform in September 2004 when the glut of Operation Amethyst cases had completed their journey through the courts. Before presenting the key findings it is important to sketch the background against which a legislative response to child pornography was formulated.

A legacy of ill treatment

Mirroring international developments, health professionals in Ireland began to 'discover' child sexual abuse during the 1980s. Lalor (2001) outlined a brief history (for a more detailed critique see Ferguson, 1996). In 1983 the Irish Association of Social Workers hosted a workshop on incest. The first official reference to the phenomenon was made in the same year, in the Department of Health document, *Guidelines on Procedures for the Identification and Management of Non-accidental Injury to Children*. However, this concentrated mainly on physical abuse and it was only in a 1987 publication, *Guidelines on Procedures for the Identification, Investigation and Management of Child Abuse*, that the sexual abuse of children was identified as a separate issue to physical abuse or 'non-accidental' injury. It is perhaps no coincidence that this was the first year that the Roman Catholic Church in Ireland insured itself against child sexual abuse by its priests (*The Irish Times*, 6 February 2003).

O'Sullivan (2002) has argued that while the period from the 1980s may have been when the vulnerability of children to sexual abuse was publicly defined, and the parameters of this problem began to be articulated, the issue had been identified half a century earlier. In 1930, the government established a committee to inquire into juvenile prostitution. In his submission to this body the *Garda* Commissioner [police chief] described cases of incest, sodomy and unlawful carnal knowledge and bemoaned the lightness of sentences imposed by the courts. Some of the victims were as young as 4 or 5 years and the number of cases appeared to be rising. The Commissioner felt that when girls aged under 13-years-old were involved, whipping should be part of the punishment, 'not just a few strokes, but the most severe application the medical advisor will permit'. It is noteworthy that while the committee reported in August 1931, its report was suppressed on the basis that public discussion of such issues would be undesirable (Kennedy 2000).

The women's movement is frequently singled out as having played a central role in the growing awareness of child sexual abuse, as it brought to the fore issues that had previously been considered out of bounds, such as domestic violence and rape. More specifically, Rape Crisis Centres identified survivors of child sexual abuse as a major client group in the mid-1980s. Statistics from the Department of Health (1996: 49) revealed that the number of notifications for alleged sexual abuse rose from 88 in 1984 to 1,242 in 1989. This no doubt reflected a rise in reporting rather than actual incidences of abuse, resulting from increased professional awareness, media scrutiny and public concern.

Of particular significance in terms of raising awareness about the harms associated with childhood sexuality was the death, in 1984, of 15-year-old Ann Lovett. Ann died in childbirth at the grotto of the Catholic church in Granard, County Longford. Her infant son perished with her. Her parents, the subsequent inquest was told, had been unaware of her pregnancy. This was the catalyst for an outpouring of public grief as people shared experiences of concealed and painful pasts in letters read out on national radio by the country's most popular broadcaster, Gay Byrne. The tragic event began a process whereby there was virtually nothing that could not be discussed in an intimate way on the airwaves, facilitating the exposure of further 'hidden Irelands'. O'Toole (1990: 174–5) elaborated in the following way: 'A sort of secret history of modern Ireland emerged that day with stories from every decade since the 1940s, stories that had been told to no one, stories that had been bottled up and swallowed down'.

The report of the Irish Council for Civil Liberties Working Party on Child Sexual Abuse (1988: 12–13) identified a number of factors which prevented an adequate response to child sexual abuse, despite a growing awareness of the problem. It noted:

Problems in identifying and dealing with sexual abuse, such as late disclosure, inadequate legal and social responses, lack of resources and professional discomfort, seem to reflect unresolved moral questions in Irish society, which appear too threatening or divisive to debate freely and rationally.

The report continued:

Anxiety about moral and sexual norms in Ireland has limited open debate about the sexual rights of individuals and the parameters of sexual abuse. It has made disclosure difficult and has influenced the values, attitudes and practices of those to whom sexual abuse is disclosed. Debate and dissemination of information are essential to free victims of sexual abuse to seek help and to be assured of sensitive, effective assistance.

This report highlighted what many subsequently came to recognise as the very root of the widespread problem of child sexual abuse in Ireland; namely a deeply ingrained culture of submissive acceptance of church and state control over individual behaviour and morals. What was socially acceptable was rigidly defined, and those in authority worked in close cooperation to ensure that any transgressions were dealt with harshly. The Magdalene laundries represent a striking example of this culture of intolerance. Run by female religious orders and generally supported by the state and society at large, the laundries held young women who had been sent there for what was seen as sexual misconduct or to protect their virtue. The conditions were austere, the labour was demanding and the forced adoption of babies was standard practice. It has been estimated that up to 30,000 young women and girls were sent to such laundries (*The Irish Times*, 1 September 2003). The last one closed in 1996.

Those that suffered most from this culture of non-disclosure and intolerance were the most vulnerable in society: children. When Minister for Education Brian Lenihan visited Artane Industrial School in Dublin in 1968, he was approached by a 15-year-old boy who begged him to intervene and 'stop them [the Christian Brothers] beating us'. The Minister is reported to have responded by saying to his driver, 'Get me out of this fucking place' (cited in Raftery and O'Sullivan 1999: 380). If a government minister felt that it was acceptable to voice such an unsympathetic attitude to children in care, it is little wonder that society more generally was prepared to ignore the problem. This attitude prevailed for many years before the reality and pervasiveness of child abuse – physical, sexual and emotional – began to trouble the nation's conscience.

Just as television exposés had proved critical in prioritising these issues in the USA (see Chapter 1), Irish society was galvanised into action by two documentaries shown on *RTÉ* (the national broadcaster). These were the three-part series *States of Fear*, which was broadcast in May 1999, and *Cardinal Secrets*, which aired in October 2002. These programmes exposed the harsh treatment experienced by children in institutional care, the extent to which the authorities colluded to cover up known abuse, and the apparent impunity that characterised the actions of a number of sadistic priests and religious brothers. They led to a lengthy period of national self-examination, outpourings of anti-clericalism and attempts by church and state to make redress to those who had been brutalised as children.

Acknowledging child sexual abuse

The 1990s heralded a new climate of openness and accountability, unearthing aspects of Irish life that had previously been pushed behind the scenes. This openness was ushered in, to some extent at least, by a new brand of investigative journalism that was not afraid to challenge powerful institutions. As argued by Ferriter (2004: 664):

> There was a growing awareness of the many failures of independent Ireland, particularly with regard to ... vulnerable children, and the appalling treatment many of them endured. Giving a voice to victims became a major cultural concern in the 1990s, aided by a vastly expanded media. Irish people were listening to and seeing things that would have found no outlet in the 1970s.

The volume of personal accounts of child abuse was staggering and highlighted the extent to which Irish citizens had accepted without question the unreasonable and unyielding demands of those in authority (see, for example, O'Connor's (2000) account of how the predatory and bullying behaviour of Wexford priest, Fr Sean Fortune, intimidated an entire community).

Not surprisingly, the Roman Catholic Church took a big fall. Charged with the moral and spiritual leadership of the overwhelming majority of Ireland's population, the hypocrisy of the church was met with ferocious anger. Not only had a number of clergymen, all of whom had taken a vow of celibacy and promoted sexual propriety, sexually abused children but their religious superiors knew of this behaviour and often failed to handle it effectively. With dismaying regularity a complaint was responded to by relocating the alleged offender to a new parish. Such a tactic facilitated the continued abuse of children. In addition, victims of clerical abuse often found the Church leaders' responses lacking in compassion and justice (Goode et al. 2003).

Public awareness of child sexual abuse by members of the clergy began with media coverage of the Fr Brendan Smyth case. Known as the 'paedophile priest', Smyth's catalogue of predation came to light in 1994. For more than four decades he had abused children in Ireland (both north and south), as well as Scotland, Wales and the USA. During this time, senior clergy within the Catholic Church in Ireland preferred to deny and hide his actions by moving him from parish to parish rather than recognising the criminal nature of his behaviour (Moore 1995). They confused vicious crime with moral weakness and overestimated the redemptive power of self-awareness. A request for his extradition from the Royal Ulster Constabulary remained for seven months in the office of Harry Whelehan, the Irish Attorney General, and some ministers were alleged to have had knowledge of the case. Taoiseach (prime minister) Albert Reynolds's determination nevertheless to appoint Whelehan President of the High Court led to both their resignations in November 1994 and brought down the government.

As Moore (1995: 16) observed: 'There were few people in Ireland who did not believe that the Fr Smyth extradition affair once again raised questions about the special relationship between the Catholic church and the state'. Smyth pleaded guilty to 74 charges of indecent and sexual assault of 20 young people over a period of thirty-six years. He was sentenced to twelve years imprisonment. In August 1997, one month after his incarceration, Smyth collapsed and died in the exercise yard of the Curragh prison. Such was his notoriety that he was buried in a secret pre-dawn ceremony, attended by seven of his fellow Norbertine priests and a handful of local people. The high emotion surrounding the case kept his family away and ensured a *Garda* presence. At the request of one of his victims the word 'Rev' was later removed from the headstone on his grave.

Other high-profile cases of clerical abuse, including those of Fr Ivan Payne and Fr Thomas Naughton in Dublin, and Fr Donal Collins in Wexford, found a similar response by the church's hierarchy. Allegations were ignored and the abuser was repeatedly placed in positions of trust with access to children, whom they duly abused. As Murphy *et al.* (2005) made clear in their study of the diocese of Ferns, the police and public were part of a wider conspiracy of silence and inaction. Deborah's story shows that sometimes even parents could not believe that men of God would stray so far from the path of righteousness:

The abuse is alleged to have started when she was five years of age in the mid 1970s. She alleged that the abuse continued for a number of years and that when she was seven years of age Fr. Grennan tried to penetrate her. Deborah's mother ... stated that although Fr. Grennan was a regular visitor to their home and on occasion stayed overnight, nothing improper occurred between Fr. Grennan and her daughter. She said that Fr. Grennan would sometimes sleep in Deborah's bed; if she was already asleep she would not move her, but she was quite certain that if anything had happened, Deborah would have told her ... Deborah committed suicide in 2002, aged 31. (Murphy *et al.* 2005: 84–5)

During a visit to the Vatican by Irish Catholic bishops, Pope Benedict expressed his 'personal anguish and horror' at what had happened in Ferns (*The Irish Times*, 27 October 2006). This was the strongest language he had ever used in relation to clerical child sexual abuse. It shows how the profane behaviour of some of those in religious life in Ireland shook not only the confidence of a once unquestioningly subordinate population but ultimately caused tremors all the way to the apex of the institutional church.

In the interests of balance it is important to point out that as few as 31 Catholic priests and religious brothers in Ireland were convicted, between 1991 and 1998, of child sexual abuse (Ferriter 2004: 737). It is difficult to say what proportion of those in religious life this represents as the offences in question went back several decades in some instances and the number of men who pursued, and then dropped, a vocation during this period cannot be counted. There is little doubt, however, that convicted sex offenders accounted for no more than a fraction of one per cent of the clerical population. The 1991 census, for example, shows just over 9,000 priests, nuns and religious brothers. This is half of the number for 1951 and more than twice the number in 2002. (More detailed information is available for the Archdiocese of Dublin. A press statement issued in March 2006 revealed that between 1940 and 2006, around 2,800 priests were appointed to the Archdiocese. Their behaviour resulted in criminal convictions for eight of them and civil actions being brought against 32. Allegations of child sexual abuse were made against a cumulative total of 91 individuals over the 66-year period.)

Breen (2007) has shown that the level of media coverage generated by members of religious orders is out of all proportion to their contribution to the problem of sexual abuse. In a study of reportage in *The Irish Times* he found that where the profession of the perpetrator of child sexual abuse was identified, more than two-thirds of stories (68.3 per cent) related to clergy and others in religious life. This compared with the finding of a major national survey (McGee *et al.* 2002: 89) that such perpetrators were responsible for the victimisation of 5.8 per cent of all boys and 1.4 per cent of all girls who had been sexually abused.

Only one nun, Nora Wall, a former Mercy sister, was ever convicted. In 1999 she was the first woman to be found guilty of rape, the victim being a 10-year-old girl who had been a resident in a childcare centre of which Ms. Wall was administrator. She was given the maximum sentence of life imprisonment. Her co-accused, Pablo McCabe, was sentenced to 12 years. He was a homeless, alcoholic, mentally ill, petty criminal who suffered from Parkinson's Disease. In announcing the sentence Mr. Justice Paul Carney referred to the incident as 'gang rape'. The trial and conviction took place at a time of heightened sensitivity to the problem of the sexual abuse of children in institutions, especially those run by religious orders.

The *RTÉ* series *States of Fear* had ended a month earlier, generating widespread debate and indignation.

The conviction was overturned within weeks when it came to light that one of the witnesses should not have been called (by order of the Director of Public Prosecutions). The DPP issued an unprecedented statement to the effect that Ms. Wall and her co-accused were entitled to be presumed innocent of all charges. In December 2005 the Court of Criminal Appeal certified that she had been the victim of a miscarriage of justice (see O'Brien 2006, for the background to this unprecedented series of events).

The demonisation of the clergy could easily have disguised the extent of family-based child abuse, which was far more prevalent, were it not for a number of exceptionally brave young Irish women who disclosed their personal experiences of incest and the appalling failure of the state to protect them.

The Criminal Law (Incest Proceedings) Act, 1995, was a direct consequence of a high profile child sexual abuse case which became public knowledge in 1993. The so-called Kilkenny Incest Case involved the physical and sexual abuse perpetrated by a man against his daughter between 1976 and 1991. She was first sexually abused at age 11 and became pregnant when she was 16. Over the course of fifteen years the victim had repeated contact with hospital and Health Board personnel due to the injuries she sustained at the hands of her father. The investigation focused on why these contacts did not register concern and lead to an investigation of her family. It became a defining case and, as the following quotation illustrates, was the focus of intense interest throughout the country and in parliament.

> The revulsion and horror which has swept the country at the details of the Kilkenny Incest Case and the brutality and torment suffered by this young woman at the hands of her father must not be allowed to take from the necessary lessons we must learn from this case. The tears I and many others shed as we read the horrific details of this case were tears of sympathy for this young woman and for her mother who must have suffered greatly as she watched her daughter suffering and who was herself oppressed. They were also tears of frustration and anger that these horrors can still be perpetrated against an innocent young woman in our society in the nineties. (Nora Owen, *Dáil Debates*, 3 March 1993, Vol. 427, Col. 688)

The publication of the McGuinness report (1993) into this case resulted in an immediate commitment from the government to release IR£35m (€44m) over three years to implement in full the Child Care Act, 1991. More significantly, two judgments made in the Central Criminal Court in February 1995 in relation to the Kilkenny Incest Case, highlighted shortcomings of Section 5 of the Punishment of Incest Act, 1908. The first was that proceedings must be held *in camera*, in an environment of total secrecy where only the parties immediately involved were permitted to be present. The second related to the fact that the Act precluded information relating to sentencing in incest cases from being disclosed. This meant that a health board social worker, for example, concerned for the welfare of an incest victim, could not be told if the offending parent had previously received a sentence for incest. Indeed the social worker could not even be told that a prosecution had taken place. This greatly hampered adequate child protection.

The situation was remedied by the Criminal Law (Incest Proceedings) Act, 1995, which provided that access and reporting arrangements in incest cases were to be subject to the same provisions as applied to cases of rape and sexual assault. This allows for the exclusion of the public from legal proceedings but enables representatives of the press and others, with the court's permission, to attend. It also stipulated that the verdict and sentence must be announced in public.

The extent to which intra-familial abuse existed in Ireland was further revealed after a Sligo man was convicted of raping and abusing his children over a twenty-year period ending in 1993. Joseph McColgan inflicted a reign of terror on his wife and children, during which time the North Western Health Board had 392 contacts with the family. His daughter, Sophia, who gave up her anonymity to highlight the inexplicable lack of action by the authorities, was sexually and physically abused by her father between the ages of 6 and 21. The sustained level of cruelty to Sophia, her mother and her siblings, caused universal horror (see Box 4.1).

Box 4.1: Getting away with murder (almost)

Joseph McColgan, a farmer from Ballymote, Co Sligo, pummelled his children with fists and feet and beat them with anything he could lay his hands on, including shovels, hammers, carpet beaters, brooms and thin sticks that would whip around their little bodies. He tried to drown them, strangle them and he even dropped a concrete block on his son Gerard's fingers when the child, about six or seven, could not move rocks fast enough as he made him labour in the fields.

One of the most harrowing aspects of their abuse was that the children constantly tried to alert the authorities to their torturous existence, but they were ignored. Gerard ran away more than 50 times, telling anyone who would listen about the beatings his father gave him. But each time he was brought back home. Each time he would receive an even worse beating from his father. Even Mrs McColgan begged the authorities in 1979 to take her children into care when a savage beating landed 9-year-old Sophia in hospital. At that stage, Sophia had been raped by her father on a near daily basis for three years. A doctor's notes at that time refer to both Sophia and Gerard as 'battered children'.

In 1984 a social worker wrote: 'It is my opinion that I am dealing with a very pathological family. The degree of abuse both physical and sexual is at an extraordinary [sic] high level. I have formed a professional opinion that he [McColgan] is an extremely sick man ... and seriously sexually perverted. He ... keeps control by terrorising. His sexual activities regarding the children can only be called criminal.'

At this stage, every orifice of Sophia's body had been invaded by her father's penis, fingers and tongue. When that was not enough, he used implements. He made her have sexual encounters with Gerard, while he watched and masturbated. When her father did not have a condom, he would use a cattle syringe to inject spermicide.

In 1993, after he battered and raped his 21-year-old daughter Michelle, he tried to run her down with a motorbike, a move that proved to be his downfall. She told a doctor that her father had raped, beaten and attempted to kill her repeatedly for 15 years. The doctor contacted the Gardaí and social workers and McColgan was charged with physical and sexual abuse and brought to trial.

Throughout it all, Sophia insisted she was not a victim or a survivor, just an ordinary person. After the court case she said: 'The silence is gone, there is no more silence now. We did it for all the victims.'

(*Source*: From 'Diary of Abuse: How a Father Beat and Raped his Children Daily for Almost 20 Years' by Collette Keane, *Irish Examiner*, 16 February 2004)

In 1995, McColgan was sentenced to a cumulative total of 238 years in prison, having been convicted of 12 sample charges of rape, assault and grievous bodily harm (the sentences were to run concurrently, giving a total time to be served of twelve years). Three years later, the McColgans reached an IR£1m (€1.27m) settlement in their High Court negligence action against the North Western Health Board and their family doctor. Neither the board nor the doctor admitted liability. Summing up her experiences, Sophia McColgan commented that: 'There is still far too much of the "leave it behind" attitude.

y has to wake up' (cited in Lalor 2001: ix). Her father was
n prison in 2004, after serving his full sentence less 25 per
ᵒn. He had taken part in no treatment programmes. (For
ᵗount of what life was like in the McColgan household
_998.)

Further allegations reinforced the growing perception of an
endemic culture of child abuse. The shock when a number of high-
profile members of the professional swimming community were
accused of sexual misconduct was aggravated by evidence that the
Irish Amateur Swimming Association, the sport's controlling body,
had failed to act on reports that some of its members were a direct
threat to children. In 1998, Derry O'Rourke, the Olympic swimming
coach of 1980 and 1992, was sentenced to twelve years imprisonment
for the sexual abuse of swimmers, some as young as 10 years old.
In January 2005, he received a further ten years for the rape and
indecent assault of another girl he had trained. George Gibney, the
Olympic coach for the 1988 games, fled the country after successfully
preventing a case against him from proceeding. He was facing 17
charges of rape (*The Irish Times*, 24 September 2005).

By the time the 1990s drew to a close the sordid and painful
reality of child sexual abuse had moved centre stage, sweeping away
a culture of secrecy, denial and disbelief that had prevailed for too
long.

Concern about commercial sexual exploitation

While it is often the media who are first to give public expression
to societal concerns, transcripts of political debates offer valuable
insights into the issues defined as priorities by the legislature of the
day. A detailed search of all *Dáil* (lower house of parliament) and
Seanad (upper house) debates (the complete text of which, dating back
to the foundation of the state in 1922, is available online at http://
historical-debates.oireachtas.ie) revealed that while the problem of
child sexual abuse received increasing political attention during the
1980s and early 1990s, the commercial sexual exploitation of children
was not identified as a cause of concern.

The expression 'child pornography' was used for the first time in
a parliamentary debate in 1984. Reflecting the climate of the day and
the growing professional awareness that children required specific
legal protections, child pornography was presented as a health issue
and was briefly referred to in the wider context of the government's

childcare agenda. Child pornography was not mentioned again in a parliamentary debate for seven years. On this occasion – July 1991 – it was described as a pressing threat to vulnerable children, but no evidence was presented in support of this claim. There was no further mention of this supposedly 'alarming' problem for another four years. This lack of sustained interest is striking given that over this period child pornography had been legalised and then prohibited in a number of European countries and had attracted a high level of political action across Europe and North America.

While clearly not an urgent concern, the production of child pornography was not completely unknown. John Charles McQuaid, Catholic Archbishop of Dublin, was contacted in 1960 by *Gardaí* who had been informed by their British counterparts that the chaplain to Our Lady's Hospital for Sick Children in Crumlin, Dublin, had sent pornographic photographs of children to be developed in England. McQuaid interviewed the priest in question, Fr Paul McGennis, and 'arranged for him to have treatment which was considered successful at the time' (Raftery and O'Sullivan 1999: 256). In 1997 McGennis was convicted of sexual offences carried out in the 1960s involving two young girls, one of whom was a patient in Crumlin. (In an historical footnote that sheds light on the priorities of the day, the same archbishop sent a letter to the home address of the Secretary of the Department of Justice in 1965, enclosing a brochure that had been given to him by a chemist. It promoted adult home movies such as *Stripped for Action* starring Jane Blonde, special agent 008. His Grace was concerned to block the entry of this kind of merchandise into the country and the Department reassured him that while brochures might have slipped through the post undetected it was unlikely that any films would get through; *The Irish Times*, 30 December 2006).

While Irish society was beginning to absorb a litany of child abuse allegations and disclosures during the 1990s, the Celtic Tiger roared into existence, bringing with it previously unimagined wealth. In the space of a decade, unemployment virtually disappeared, migration patterns reversed, incomes soared and property prices became a national obsession (for reviews of Ireland's changing socio-economic context see Nolan *et al.* 2000 and Fahey *et al.* 2007). But the rising tide did not lift all boats and society's most vulnerable children experienced the downside of economic prosperity with some reports indicating that child prostitution and homelessness were on the increase (see for example, *The Irish Times*, 24 September 1996). Figures compiled by Mayock and O'Sullivan (2007) show that between 1998 and 2004 the number of homeless young people declined somewhat, but that the problem proved stubbornly resistant to eradication in a country that was rapidly becoming one of the wealthiest in the world. A booming economy and cut-price airfares meant that more people could find the time and money to travel and evidence emerged of Irish involvement in the child sex tourism industry. As highlighted in the *Dáil* by the Minister for Justice:

> Deputies will be aware that information has come to light that implicates Irish people in child sex tourism ... Up to recently we had no reason to believe that Irish people were involved in this repulsive trade either as promoters or as sex tourists. Even if only a handful of Irish people are so involved, it is incumbent on us as legislators to take action. (Nora Owen, *Dáil Debates*, 14 November 1995, Vol. 458, Cols. 366, 370)

Clearly the potential existed for the commercial sexual exploitation of children both on Irish soil and by Irish tourists.

Closing legal loopholes

As Irish society began to come to terms with the inescapable conclusion that child sexual abuse was an ingrained problem rather than an occasional aberration, the government came under increasing pressure to prove both to the electorate and also to the international community that it was actively addressing the issue. Child protection was seen to be prioritised.

In response to the judgments made in the Central Criminal Court in February 1995 in relation to the Kilkenny Incest Case, the Criminal Law (Incest Proceedings) Act became law in July 1995. Shortly afterwards, faced with the formal examination of the country's first national report to the UN Committee on the Rights of the Child, the government accepted the Sexual Offences (Jurisdiction) Bill, which became law in 1996. This instrument extended the criminal law of the state to try sexual offences against children committed by Irish citizens or residents outside Ireland's territorial boundaries. The returning 'sex tourist' now faced a prison sentence of up to five years. The legislation was largely of symbolic value: there is no evidence that during the first decade of its existence anyone was charged under it.

Child pornography also began to receive political attention at this time and was now identified as a criminal justice, as opposed to a health, issue. A member of the opposition asked the Minister for Justice 'the plans, if any, she has to prepare legislation to criminalise the sale of magazines portraying child pornography and bestiality; and if she accepts that this type of publication, which is not banned under the Censorship of Publications Act, is frequently to be found in cases of child sex abuse' (John O'Donoghue, *Dáil Debates*, 26 October 1995, Vol. 457, Col. 1706).

Interestingly, the minister's response indicated that a *Garda* investigation into the sale of child pornography was underway, although no details were disclosed. Her response highlighted a glaring loophole in the law, which in effect confirmed the argument that child pornography was not illegal in Ireland at the time.

> Section 9 of the Censorship of Publications Act, 1946 makes provision for the Censorship of Publications Board, on receipt of a complaint from any person, to prohibit the sale of a magazine which they consider to be indecent or obscene ... A complaint must be accompanied by a copy of the book in question or, in the case of a magazine, by three recent issues of the magazine. (Nora Owen, *Dáil Debates*, 26 October 1995, Vol. 457, Col. 1706)

According to the law, a magazine containing child pornography could only be banned if it resulted in a complaint that was upheld by the Censorship of Publications Board. Thus, if a magazine did not come to the board's attention it was not illegal. It is probably fair to assume that very few individuals would have unwittingly come in contact with this material. Prior to the arrival of the Internet, obtaining child pornography was time-consuming and costly, and enthusiasts risked public vitriol by declaring an interest in such publications. Anyone who had access to child pornography was unlikely to flaunt it. In other words, an apparently lax legal environment, in a country where sexual morality was tightly controlled, would have had little practical effect.

The *Register of Prohibited Publications* which is available for consultation on the Web site of the Department of Justice, Equality and Law Reform (http://www.justice.ie), does not provide details of the content of books or periodicals banned by the Censorship of Publications Board, which first sat in 1930. While it is not always advisable to judge a book by its cover, a number of titles listed in the *Register* would certainly suggest that some child pornography was finding its way into the country. One publisher in particular, Bens

imited in London, stands out as specialising in dubiously
 publications, a number of which came to the Board's attention
etween 1971 and 1980, including *Baby Bare, Bumper Crumpet, Young Danish Girls Uncensored, Girl Masturbation, Natural Swedish Girls, Young Girls' Experiences, How To Seduce And Pick Up Young Girls, Schoolgirl Virgins,* and *Spanking Girls' Bottoms.* While the content of these books, and those by other publishers as shown in Table 4.1, cannot be confirmed as child pornographic, at the very least the titles suggest a testing of boundaries.

In recent years, the Danish pornographer Peter Theander and his company Color Climax have come to the board's attention on a number of occasions. *Teenage School Girls, Teenage Dream Girls* and *Teenage Sex* were all banned in April and May 1997. Considering Theander's career trajectory (see Chapter 1) it is little surprise to see him feature in an Irish context.

The notion that child pornography was in circulation in Ireland, at least among a small community of interested individuals, is given credence by the fact that this type of material was sold with relative ease by commercial dealers throughout Britain during the 1980s (Tate 1990: 75). It is not beyond belief to think that some of the large numbers of Irish men working or travelling in Britain would have got hold of a selection of magazines and videotapes and brought them home. But it seems that this was an enthusiasm that was carefully

Table 4.1 Banned books

Title	Publisher	Date banned
Boy Lover	Beacon Books, New York	21 May 1963
Men Into Boys	Star Distributions Ltd.	9 November 1973
The Boys Who Asked For Sex	Parisian Press	9 November 1973
Teenage Caning	Trident Publications, London	11 January 1974
Older Men Seduced By Teenagers	Venus Publications Ltd., London	11 October 1974
Baby Pussy	Roydock Books Ltd., London	11 October 1974
Little Girl Lovers	Companion Press Inc., USA	7 March 1975
Daddy's Young Whore	Star Distributions Ltd.	31 July 1979
Little Lovers	Eros Publishing, USA	29 April 1980
Little Girl's First Time	Eros Publishing, USA	29 April 1980
Daddy's Tasty Chicken	Not listed	3 February 1981

(*Source*: Censorship of Publications Board 2004)

concealed; as we have seen it hardly registered on the public or political radars.

It was not until the closing years of the twentieth century that there was a clear recognition that the time had come when an emotional response needed to be replaced by a more systematic, wide-ranging and consistent approach. The next step was to translate a general anxiety into a specific piece of legislation. In June 1998 the Child Trafficking and Pornography Act was brought into existence. It prohibited the production, dissemination, handling or possession of child pornography. It also outlawed the trafficking in, or the use of, children for the purposes of sexual exploitation. In the Act, a child is defined as anyone under 17 years of age and child pornography is defined as any visual or audio representation of a person who is (or is depicted as being) a child and who is engaged in (or is depicted as being engaged in) explicit sexual activity or the depiction, for a sexual purpose, of the genital or anal region of a child. (The full text can be consulted at http://www.irishstatutebook.ie).

Thus, despite there being no obvious child pornography problem in Ireland prior to 1998, specific child pornography legislation was introduced. During the 1990s, child sexual abuse became a highly topical issue in public, professional and political life in Ireland. The public and media exerted pressure on the government to address the problem, including updating and implementing relevant legislation. *Dáil* debates referred to child pornography as a possible precursor to face-to-face child sexual exploitation. Pressure was being exerted by the international community to demonstrate a commitment to child welfare. The Internet was gradually increasing its consumer base across the country with its evident potential to be misused to access child pornography. Most significantly, the Dutroux Case and the First World Congress Against the Commercial Exploitation of Children focused attention on the pornographic exploitation of minors and galvanised the EU into motion, resulting in the 1997 Joint Action. As Austin Curry, Minister of State at the Department of Justice, remarked in an address to the *Dáil*:

> While there had been concern about child sexual abuse before that case [Dutroux], for many that concern manifested itself in an abstract way. There may also have been a naïvety in many quarters about the nature and extent of such abuse. The Belgian case changed all that. It opened our eyes to the vileness of paedophile rings and showed us how organised paedophiles are. (*Dáil Debates*, 17 December 1996, Vol. 473, Col. 136)

The Irish government thus had legal – and moral – obligations to fulfil. This meant that when child pornography became a live issue in 2002 as a result of Operation Amethyst, the legal framework to respond was already in place.

Operation Amethyst and its aftermath

Between July 1998 and May 2002 there were very few prosecutions, let alone convictions, for offences contrary to the Child Trafficking and Pornography Act, 1998. Between January 2000 and December 2001, 26 offences were detected by *Gardaí* and criminal proceedings were initiated in 15 of these.

We know a little about the first prosecutions from media reports. In August 1998, one month after the Act came into existence, a 47-year-old separated father of three was charged with the possession of homemade child pornography videos (*The Irish Times*, 29 April 1999). In December of the same year, a 21-year-old German computer programmer, living in Dublin, was charged with downloading child pornography from the Internet. Both men pleaded guilty and both received 18-month custodial sentences (*The Irish Times*, 9 June 2000; *Irish Examiner*, 24 October 2000).

The first case in which Internet child pornography was found to have been distributed from Ireland was in 2000, when a 26-year-old insurance salesman, who was living in Waterford, unwittingly sent images to an undercover policeman in Germany. He was convicted of distribution of child pornography and the possession of over 700 images and movie files involving male adults and very young children, including babies. Some of the images involved animals. He was sentenced to 30 months imprisonment (*The Irish Times*, 31 July 2002; *Belfast News Letter*, 31 July 2002). Child pornography cases were few and far between and the issue received sporadic media attention. Over the nine-year period 1993 to 2001, an annual average of 24 articles were published in *The Irish Times* that included the term 'child pornography'. Many of them were devoted to foreign affairs (for example, the Dutroux case in 1996). This all changed in 2002 when *Gardaí* launched Operation Amethyst (see Box 4.2 below).

Operation Amethyst revealed that Ireland had its very own child pornography offenders. Needless to say, the operation received extensive media coverage fuelled by the fact that a number of the offenders were well known personalities in Irish society. As the cases proceeded through the criminal justice system, interest did not abate and the offenders continued to attract a disproportionate level of coverage. Between 2002 and 2004, *The Irish Times* published, on average, five times more 'child pornography' related articles (115 each year) than during the preceding nine-year period.

Box 4.2: Operations Avalanche and Amethyst

In 1999 a postal inspector in St Paul, Minnesota came across a Web site advertising child pornography. The inspector used his credit card to subscribe to a linked site, which he tracked to Landslide Productions in Fort Worth, Texas. He informed the postal inspection service agent in Fort Worth, who contacted the child exploitation unit of the Dallas police department, and they got together with representatives of the FBI, Customs, and a computer consultant from Microsoft.

Thomas Reedy (37), and his wife Janice (33), set up Landslide Productions in 1997. Essentially this was a service that provided access to a network of 5,700 pornographic Web sites, including numerous child pornography sites. They appeared to be a normal, young couple living with their 9-year-old daughter in an affluent neighbourhood.

Dallas detective Steve Nelson undertook the task of purchasing material from Web sites with names like 'Cyber Lolita' and 'Child Rape'. Using a credit card he subscribed to a dozen of the child pornography sites and saved the images.

Some 50 law enforcement officers raided the Reedys' home and business premises on 8 September 1999. They brought along the computer consultant from Microsoft to provide the technical expertise. More than 70 images of child pornography were found on Thomas Reedy's computer, but much more important was the extensive list of individuals who paid from US$14.95 to US$29.95 a month to subscribe to the different Web sites run by Landslide Productions. The network ran over 60 countries in three continents and over the short time it had been in existence had notched up several hundred thousand financial transactions. Around 35,000 subscribers were resident in the USA with another 7,272 located in the UK. It is not known precisely how many of these individuals were accessing child pornography. The press claimed that the couple were making nearly US$1.4 million a month.

Within minutes of the sites being shut down subscribers began phoning Landslide to ask what had happened. 'Please give us your phone number and credit card number; we'll try to find out what's happening', Detective Nelson told them. This was the beginning of what became known as Operation Avalanche (a play on the name of the company).

Initially released on bail the Reedys protested their innocence and continued trading in adult pornography. They had not been supplying child images themselves, they said, but had only provided a portal

---

to other sites. Thomas Reedy was given the opportunity to work with the FBI to catch other child pornographers in exchange for a 20-year sentence. He opted to stand trial and take his chances in front of a jury. In April 2000, an 89-count federal indictment was returned against the Reedys and Landslide Productions. On 8 August 2001, US District Judge Terry Means sentenced Thomas Reedy to 15 years in jail for each of the 89 images, a prison sentence of 1,335 years. Janice Reedy was sentenced to 14 years. In 2002, the US Court of Appeals decided that when fixing the penalty, Web sites should be counted rather than individual images, so the sentence was recalculated at 180 years (12 Web sites by 15 years). The reduction of more than 1,000 years, of course, has no practical effect; Thomas Reedy will still die in prison.

While the jailing of the Reedys and the dismantling of the largest commercial child pornography enterprise ever uncovered were a massive success for the authorities in the USA, it was only the beginning of what turned into an international criminal investigation. As a result of the trial, INTERPOL was provided with the credit card and bank details of the subscribers to Landslide's Web site. A selection of these were passed on to the Irish authorities. The ensuing investigation, codenamed Operation Amethyst, saw over 500 *Gardaí* search more than 100 homes and business premises in May 2002. A number of men suspected of being abusers rather than just consumers of pornography were investigated and arrested before these raids.

(*Source*: based on Campbell 2005; Douglas and Singular 2004: 292; *Irish Examiner*, 23 June 2005; *Irish Independent*, 1 June 2002; US *Postal Inspection Service* 2001)

Operation Amethyst provided the first real test of the Irish legislation. Overnight more than 100 suspects were brought into the ambit of the criminal justice system. This may have created the perception that Ireland had suddenly developed a child pornography problem. But it is important to remember the time lapse between offending, detection and sentencing. The offenders caught under Operation Amethyst had accessed child pornography Web sites via Landslide Productions in 1998 and 1999; some of them only on a few occasions but others repeatedly. It is difficult to discern a trend from the available official data although there can be little doubt that individuals were accessing child pornography Web sites as far back as the mid to late 1990s when the Internet started to become available in Ireland.

As cases resulting from Operation Amethyst were still proceeding through the system in early 2006, it will take some time before the level of child pornography offending post-Amethyst can be determined.

Media reports indicate that individuals committing offences contrary to the Child Trafficking and Pornography Act, 1998, continue to come to the attention of the *Gardaí*. Between the introduction of the legislation and the end of 2005, the Amethyst cases constituted around half of all known offences of this kind.

The attention devoted to these cases, especially the initial high-profile ones, focused public concern on child pornography. The salacious reporting indulged in by a number of tabloid newspapers fuelled the impression that these offenders were receiving lenient treatment from the courts. This conflicted strongly with the media construction of the child pornography offender as remorseless and predatory, engaging, albeit usually vicariously, in the sexual exploitation of children. Such people were believed to deserve stiff penalties.

This sense of outrage prompted debate regarding the Child Trafficking and Pornography Act, 1998, and how it was being used in practice. It caused the Department of Justice, Equality and Law Reform to commission a study, the results of which are presented next. The emphasis in the remaining sections is on setting out the empirical data in sufficient detail to allow comparative analysis. In the interests of economy the key findings are provided without much adornment. A wider context is provided in Part III.

Police investigations

The Crime Policy and Administration section at *Garda* headquarters identified 177 police officers from around the country who had investigated at least one child pornography case over the five year period 2000 to 2004. Each was sent a questionnaire survey to complete. Between them, these officers had investigated 204 individuals suspected of committing one or more offences contrary to the Child Trafficking and Pornography Act, 1998. Information relating to 142 of these persons was collected, an overall response rate of 70 per cent. Four of the questionnaires were excluded from the analysis. Three related to cases which fell outside the reference period (one in 1999 and two in 2005) and one was returned blank. Accordingly, the following analysis is based on 138 valid returns.

The modest number of cases brought under the Child Trafficking and Pornography Act, 1998, and the high level of attention they received suggest that the recorded crime figures are probably a good reflection of the number of incidents known to the police. There will

Table 4.2 Child pornography
suspects

Year	Number
2000	6
2001	21
2002	104
2003	48
2004	25
Total	204

(*Source*: Figures provided on
request by *An Garda Síochána*)

be an inevitable degree of underestimation because *Garda* counting
rules mean that where more than one crime is disclosed in a single
episode, the one which attracts the greatest penalty is counted for
statistical purposes. For example, in cases involving sexual assault and
possession of child pornography, only the former matter will appear
in the recorded crime statistics. This partly explains the discrepancy
between the figures shown in Table 4.2 (for example, 104 for 2002)
and in the annual *Garda* report on crime (125 for the same year). Also
of relevance is the fact that the annual report is based on offences
while this study focused on offenders.

The key findings from this trawl of police files are set out in Box
4.3.

Box 4.3: Features of child pornography investigations

Offence category
Most of the cases which resulted in police involvement related to
simple possession: 109 (79.0 per cent) involved offences contrary
to Section 6 of the Act only (possession); 11 (8.0 per cent) involved
offences contrary to Section 5 (distribution and/or production); in eight
of these cases the suspect was also investigated for the lesser offence of
possession of child pornography. Three (2.2 per cent) involved offences
contrary to Section 4 (allowing a child to be used for pornography);
in two of these cases the suspect was also investigated for offences
contrary to Sections 5 and/or 6 of the Act. Six (4.3 per cent) involved
offences contrary to Section 3 (child trafficking for sexual exploitation);
in three of these cases, the suspect was also investigated for offences

---

contrary to Sections 5 and/or 6. In nine (6.5 per cent) the offence was not specified on the returned questionnaire.

Number and nature of images
No relevant material was found in 19 cases (13.8 per cent). Where prohibited material was found it was almost always photographic images: 103 cases (74.6 per cent) involved images only. A small minority of cases – around one in eight – involved text or video. Text was investigated in five cases (3.6 per cent); in two more cases (1.4 per cent) text and images were investigated. Video clips/movies were investigated in three cases (2.2 per cent); in a further six cases (4.3 per cent) movies and images were investigated.

The number of images involved was specified on 101 questionnaires and ranged from one to more than 10,000. In two thirds of cases the number of images found was between 11 and 500. There were some extremes. In a few instances the number could be counted in single digits and in a handful there were several thousand.

Number of images recovered by police

Images	<10	11–100	101–500	501–1000	1001–5000	5000+
Cases	11 (11%)	38 (38%)	29 (29%)	6 (6%)	14 (14%)	3 (3%)

The investigating officer was requested to categorise the images involved in each case according to the typology drawn up by the Sentencing Advisory Panel for England and Wales (see Chapter 3). Level 1 involves images depicting nudity or erotic posing, with no sexual activity. Level 2 includes sexual activity between children and solo masturbation by a child. Level 3 portrays non-penetrative sexual activity between adult and child. In Level 4 images the sexual activity involves adult-child penetration and Level 5 concerns portrayals of sadism or bestiality.

Officers described the nature of the images in 106 questionnaires. The most serious level of material identified in each case is shown below. The entire spectrum was involved, with marked concentrations at Levels 1 and 4. It was not uncommon for the contents of an individual's collection to range across several levels of seriousness. For example, everyone who had images at Level 5 also had images at Levels 1 or 2.

Nature of images, ranked according to seriousness

Severity of content	Level 1	Level 2	Level 3	Level 4	Level 5
Cases	47 (44%)	7 (7%)	7 (7%)	40 (37%)	5 (5%)

Attrition

The most important decisions for *An Garda Síochána* involved whether to record a complaint in the first place, whether the matter was deemed to have been detected and what further action was thought necessary. As this study related exclusively to recorded crime it must remain silent on the first question. However, it can shed light on how discretion was exercised in the 138 cases where a determination was made that a child pornography offence should be officially documented.

After a crime has been recorded a decision must be made about whether it can be detected. Generally speaking this means that criminal proceedings can be commenced or a young person can be dealt with under the Juvenile Diversion Programme. Sometimes an offence is detected but a decision not to prosecute is made. This covers instances where the suspect has died, the time limit to initiate proceedings has passed (six months if dealt with summarily) or the public interest would not be served by taking matters further. In the current sample, the crime was detected in 120 cases (87.0 per cent). In the remaining 18 (13.0 per cent) it was not detected due to insufficient evidence of offending when further investigation was conducted. No further progress could be made in these cases.

Of the 120 detected cases, 106 resulted in files being sent to the Office of the Director of Public Prosecutions (DPP). Direction on how to proceed was given by the Office of the DPP over the telephone on one occasion and by the District Officer in a further case. The file was still being prepared in one case when the questionnaires were returned. Files were not sent to the DPP either because there was insufficient evidence of offending when further investigation was conducted (six cases) or the suspect or injured party had left the jurisdiction preventing the investigation from proceeding (five cases).

The flow of cases, from the initial decision to record to the submission of a file to the DPP, is summarised in Figure 4.1. It can be seen that of the 138 cases in the sample, 78.3 per cent (n = 108) proceeded to the next stage of the criminal justice process.

The usual suspects?

In general, very little is known about the characteristics of child pornography offenders. Drawing on the 138 *Garda* files a few things can be said with a reasonable degree of confidence but first some important limitations must be acknowledged. The sample represents

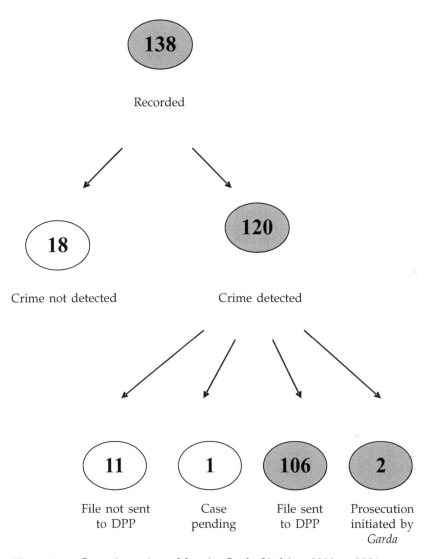

Figure 4.1 Cases investigated by *An Garda Síochána*, 2000 to 2004

all individuals whose activities resulted in police attention, regardless of outcome. In some cases, further enquiries suggested that no offence had actually taken place or that there was insufficient evidence to begin criminal proceedings (for example, upon investigation only adult pornography was found on the suspect's computer).

There is an additional caveat. The characteristics of known offenders may be somewhat unrepresentative as they most probably are the ones who were not skilled (or lucky) enough to evade detection. The Operation Amethyst cases involved individuals who had paid for child pornography up to four years prior to their arrest. It is likely that in the intervening time period awareness of the risks has grown and evasive measures have become more sophisticated. The characteristics of those investigated for child pornography offences are summarised in Box 4.4.

Box 4.4: What do we know about suspects in these cases?

This is an overwhelmingly male pursuit; only one case involved a female and it did not lead to a prosecution. The average age was 39 years, with a range of 15 to 65. This no doubt reflects the inverse relationship between age and computer use. The Central Statistics Office (2006: 34) found that while most people aged between 16 and 44 had used the Internet, this was true for less than one in ten of those aged 65 or above.

Nationality and place of residence
Where nationality was known (127/138 cases), 82.7 per cent were Irish, the remainder coming from Europe (for example, UK and Netherlands) and further afield (for example, USA, South Korea). Those who were born outside the country had generally moved to Ireland to pursue work or educational opportunities.

These individuals were predominantly residing in Leinster and Munster with the other two provinces yielding fewer suspects than would be expected on the basis of their populations. The figures for Ulster relate only to the three counties in the Republic of Ireland (namely Cavan, Monaghan and Donegal). Overall 42.7 per cent were resident in Dublin. This may reflect differential levels of access to the Internet, and availability of broadband, rather than a geographical bias in the propensity to possess child pornography.

Suspects' place of residence

Province	National population (per cent)	Suspects (per cent)
Ulster	6.3	1.6
Munster 28.1	30.6	
Connaught	11.9	4.8
Leinster (excluding Dublin)	25.1	20.2
Dublin	28.7	42.7

(*Source*: population based on 2002 census figures)

Marital status

Similar proportions of those investigated for child pornography offences were single (46.1 per cent) or living with a partner, whether married or cohabiting (46.9 per cent). A small number (7.0 per cent) were divorced or separated. Most (61.4 per cent) had no children. This refers to their status at the time of the offence coming to police attention. It is possible, of course, that as the crime was investigated and became public, relationships came under strain. In a number of cases reported in the media, marriages ended when the offending came to light and fathers were denied access to their children. There were also examples of families rallying around the perpetrator and taking the opportunity to address the underlying problems. Just under half of the individuals who were single were living with their parents while the others lived alone or in shared accommodation.

Employment status

Most were employed at the time of the offence (92 or 66.7 per cent), but more were out of work than would be expected given the buoyant economy (24 or 17.4 per cent). (Unemployment for men in 2005 stood at 4.2 per cent and had changed little since 2000.) In addition, six (4.3 per cent) were students and two (1.4 per cent) were retired. The employment status of 14 individuals (10.1 per cent) was not recorded.

Concurrent charges and previous convictions

In nine out of ten cases (125 or 90.6 per cent) the offences investigated related exclusively to crimes under the various sections of the Child Trafficking and Pornography Act, 1998. In the remainder (13 or 9.4 per cent) there were inquiries into additional matters. Of these, eight individuals were charged with other offences of a sexual nature, including rape.

These were individuals who had seldom come to police attention before: 111 (80.4 per cent) had no previous convictions; 16 (11.6 per cent) had previous convictions recorded against them; seven (5.1 per cent) of these had previous convictions for sexual offences. In 11 cases (8.0 per cent) no information was provided relating to conviction history.

Prosecutorial discretion

The Director of Public Prosecutions decides whether to charge people with criminal offences, and what the offences should be; enforces the criminal law in the courts on behalf of the people; and directs and supervises prosecutions. Criminal cases are divided into two types:

summary and indictable. The former are less serious matters, heard by a judge sitting alone in the district court. The maximum prison sentence that can be imposed for any one such offence is 12 months. Indictable offences are more serious and can be heard by a judge and jury in the circuit court or the central criminal court. Any sentence can be imposed up to the statutory maximum. Some offences can be tried either summarily or on indictment and the law provides for different sentences depending on the method of prosecution. In certain cases, the district court may deal with indictable offences where the accused pleads guilty. (General guidelines for prosecutors are set out in detail in Director of Public Prosecutions 2001. For the view of the DPP himself, see Hamilton 2004.)

Offences contrary to Sections 3 and 4 of the Child Trafficking and Pornography Act, 1998 – trafficking and taking a child for the purpose of sexual exploitation, and allowing a child to be used for pornography – may be prosecuted on indictment only. Offences contrary to Section 5 (production and/or distribution) and Section 6 (possession of child pornography) may be prosecuted either summarily or on indictment. Whether the matter proceeds to a conclusion in the district court depends on the judge's assessment that the available sentencing powers are adequate; if the offence is deemed not to be minor then jurisdiction will be declined.

If a Section 6 case is to be fought it is normally sent before a jury. The view of the DPP is that the damage to reputation involved in a conviction is so serious that if there is not to be a plea of guilty very few cases could be regarded as minor ones fit to be tried without a jury. Where there is a plea of guilty, different considerations arise. Here, the question is whether the DPP should consent to summary disposal and whether the court will accept jurisdiction. The test is whether the sentencing options in the district court are adequate. In forming a view on the adequacy of sentencing options in each case, the following factors are taken into account by the prosecutor.

The personal circumstances of the accused, including:

(a) The number and type of previous convictions.
(b) Has the accused acknowledged a problem and sought treatment?
(c) Did the accused admit the offence and cooperate with the enquiry?

The circumstances of the offence, in particular:

(a) The extent of the offender's involvement, as indicated by: the period of offending; the number of times and frequency with which the offending material was accessed; the means used to obtain the material. Was it paid for? How often were payments made? Was it obtained in a swap arrangement and if so what material did the offender provide?

(b) The material saved and stored, in particular the quantity involved and the nature of the images. At the least serious end are images of children naked or in erotic poses with no sexual activity depicted. A more serious level would depict sexual activity between children or non-penetrative sex with adults. The most serious images are those depicting acts of rape, sadism or bestiality. The apparent age of children depicted is also relevant in assessing seriousness; the younger the children the more serious the offence.

The DPP does not give reasons for his decisions in public. This policy is in place in order to protect individuals from being condemned without a trial. To respect this absolute need for confidentiality, access to files was restricted to an in-house Research Officer in the DPP's office who examined each of the relevant files for the period 2000 to 2004. Before the data were given to the authors for analysis, they were reviewed by the DPP to ensure that all of the information extracted had been rendered completely anonymous. In total, information relating to 153 cases involving offences contrary to the Child Trafficking and Pornography Act, 1998 was provided and the key characteristics of these cases are shown in Box 4.5.

Box 4.5: Prosecuting alleged child pornographers

Charges brought
One hundred and twenty eight cases (83.7 per cent) involved offences contrary to Section 6 of the Act only (possession). Twenty cases (13.1 per cent) involved offences contrary to Section 5 (distribution and/or production); in 16 of these the accused was also investigated for the lesser offence of possession of child pornography. Five cases (3.3 per cent) involved offences contrary to Section 3 (child trafficking and taking a child for sexual exploitation); in all of these the accused was also investigated for offences contrary to Sections 5 and/or 6.

There is a slight discrepancy between the breakdown of cases dealt with by the *Gardaí* and the DPP, as the latter included no breaches of Section 4 (allowing a child to be used for pornography). It may be that

---

such matters were otherwise classified by the DPP after a review of the file or that they were accompanied by a more serious crime of another kind (for example, sexual assault) and categorised accordingly.

How offences came to light
Seventy cases (45.7 per cent) were detected through Operation Amethyst: 61 cases (39.9 per cent) were detected due to information received by the *Gardaí*. This included a tip-off about the accused, a report from a computer repair outlet, a complaint from a manager/colleague (for example, if an office computer was used in the commission of the offence) or intelligence from *An Garda Síochána* or police forces in other jurisdictions. Thirteen cases (8.5 per cent) emerged during an investigation into another matter (for example, an allegation of sexual assault). In nine cases (5.9 per cent) there was no information available regarding how the case was detected.

Attrition

The first key decision made by the DPP is whether or not to prosecute. If the matter is to proceed then a determination must be made regarding the appropriate level of charge. In the files examined for this study the following formed the pattern of decision making:

- In 60 cases (39.2 per cent) the DPP directed a prosecution on indictment. (These included five cases involving offences contrary to Section 3, as these are indictable only. Nine involved offences contrary to Section 5. Forty-six involved offences contrary to Section 6.)

- In 28 cases (18.3 per cent) the DPP directed that the case be prosecuted summarily. (Four of these cases involved offences contrary to Section 5. Twenty-four involved offences contrary to Section 6.)

- In 10 cases (6.5 per cent) the DPP directed that the case be prosecuted on indictment but consented to summary disposal on a plea of guilty. (One case involved offences contrary to Section 5. Nine involved offences contrary to Section 6.)

- In 55 cases (35.9 per cent) the DPP directed that no prosecution be taken. (In six cases the individual had been investigated for offences contrary to Section 5. In 49 the individual had been investigated for offences contrary to Section 6.)

In the first two years the total number of files sent to the DPP was small – 11 in each year – compared with 52 in 2002 and 60 in 2003, as the Operation Amethyst cases moved through the system. By 2004 the number of new files received by the DPP had fallen to 19. The type of prosecution directed is broken down on an annual basis in Figure 4.2. It seems that since 2001 there has been a steady decline in the proportion of cases deemed suitable for summary disposal. Prosecutions on indictment have remained at around 60 per cent of the total. The difference is made up by an increase in the use of summary justice on foot of a guilty plea.

There was a variety of reasons given for why a decision not to prosecute was made in 55 cases:

- In 22 (40.0 per cent) it could not be determined that the accused was knowingly in possession of the images, which were located in temporary files (the location where they are placed when automatically downloaded from the Internet) or in unallocated clusters (the location where they remain when deleted, but not completely erased, from a computer's hard drive).

- In 15 (27.3 per cent) it was decided that a summary prosecution would be most appropriate given the nature of the evidence but it was statute barred (the six month time limit for initiating

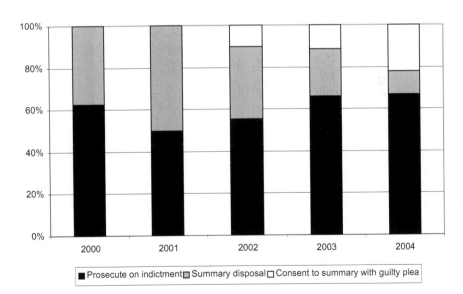

Figure 4.2 Type of prosecution directed by the DPP

proceedings had expired). Two-thirds of these occurred early on in the first major wave of prosecutions: 15.4 per cent (eight out of 52) were out of time in 2002 compared with 3.3 per cent (two out of 60) in 2003.

- In seven (12.7 per cent) the accused did not have sole access to the computer at the time of the offence.

- In four (7.3 per cent) there was uncertainty whether the material found came within the ambit of the Act (namely whether it constituted child pornography or whether it had been accessed prior to the Act coming into force).

- In three (5.5 per cent) those accused were referred to the Juvenile Diversion Scheme.

- One person (1.8 per cent) left the jurisdiction prior to charges being brought and could not be located by the *Gardaí*.

- In three (5.5 per cent) there was insufficient evidence to proceed with a prosecution and further particulars were not available.

The proportion of cases where the DPP directed that no prosecution be taken is shown by year in Figure 4.3. It varies from around a quarter to over half of the total number of cases.

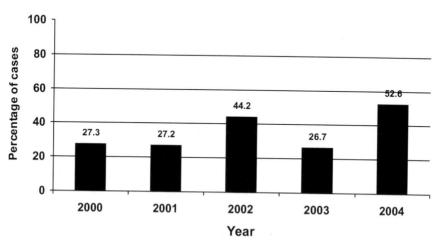

Figure 4.3 Direction by the DPP not to prosecute

Outcomes

In the 98 cases where the DPP directed a prosecution, it is known that:

- 57 (58.2 per cent) led to convictions.

- In eight cases (8.2 per cent) the prosecution was withdrawn. (Three were statute barred due to the six-month time limit for a summary prosecution having expired. These all occurred early on; two in 2000 prior to Operation Amethyst and one in 2002 as the initial cases related to the Operation started to filter into the system. In a further three cases it could not be proved that the accused was knowingly in possession of the material at the time of the offence. It was not specified in two cases why the prosecution was withdrawn.)

- In three cases (3.1 per cent) the accused was acquitted by direction of the judge.

- Two (2.0 per cent) left the jurisdiction and another (1.0 per cent) died before the case was finalised.

- Nine (9.2 per cent) cases were pending.

- In 18 (18.4 per cent) cases the outcome was unknown.

Information relating outcome to plea was available in 55 cases. In 52 of these the conviction followed a guilty plea. Three individuals pleaded not guilty and all three prosecutions failed.

In just under two-thirds of the cases where the prosecution had concluded, information about the sentence awarded was noted on the file (36 out of 57). Where the sentence had a number of components (for example, a suspended prison term and a fine), the most onerous one was counted. The flow of decisions made throughout the prosecution process is summarised in Figure 4.4.

The information on sentencing presented in Figure 4.4 is broken down by offence category in Table 4.3. The popularity of the suspended sentence is clear, especially for crimes of possession. These data relate almost exclusively to the circuit court, as information concerning sentences awarded in the district court is not routinely recorded by the DPP. As far as we could ascertain, only four of the 36 sentences shown in Table 4.3 related to the district court. (A review

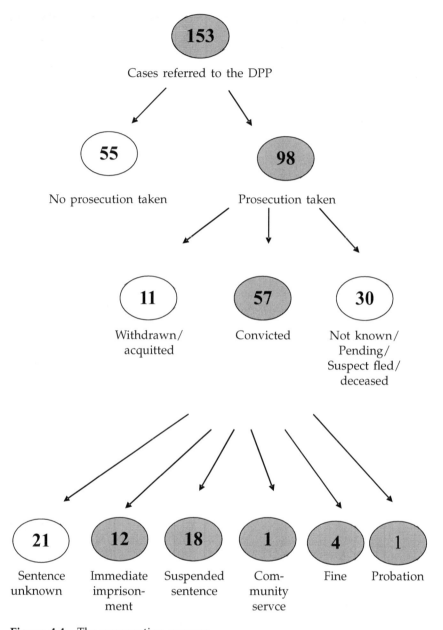

Figure 4.4 The prosecution process

Table 4.3 Sentencing under the Child Trafficking and Pornography Act, 1998

Offence	Sentence	Number
Section 3		
Child trafficking and taking a	Immediate imprisonment	4
child for sexual exploitation	Suspended sentence	0
(n = 4)	Community service	0
	Fine	0
	Probation	0
Section 4		
Allowing a child to be used	Immediate imprisonment	0
for pornography	Suspended sentence	0
(n = 0)	Community service	0
	Fine	0
	Probation	0
Section 5		
Distribution and/or production	Immediate imprisonment	2
of child pornography	Suspended sentence	3
(n = 5)	Community service	0
	Fine	0
	Probation	0
Section 6		
Possession of child pornography	Immediate imprisonment	6
(n = 27)	Suspended sentence	15
	Community service	1
	Fine	4
	Probation	1

of media reports yielded additional information on sentencing, which is summarised in Table 4.5, p. 148.)

To respect concerns around confidentiality it was not possible to track a cohort of cases from their initial investigation through to prosecution and sentence. However, the examination made of police and prosecution decisions shows that most cases dealt with by *An Garda Síochána* resulted in a crime being detected (120/138; 87.0 per cent) and most of these (106/120; 88.3 per cent) resulted in a file being sent to the DPP. In two-thirds of the cases considered by the DPP a prosecution was initiated and most of these led to a conviction.

A small number of individuals pleaded not guilty and each of them was acquitted.

Regardless of outcome, these cases attracted a substantial and sustained level of media coverage, especially around the explanations articulated by judges when determining a suitable penalty. The factors associated with sentencing are addressed next, in particular issues raised in aggravation or mitigation. We also examine the maximum and minimum penalties imposed under the various sections of the Child Trafficking and Pornography Act, 1998.

Judicial perspectives

In order to identify factors associated with different case outcomes, it was essential to probe judges' views in relation to the range and suitability of available sanctions. To this end, interviews were arranged with seven district court and five circuit court judges who had been directly involved with cases taken under the Child Trafficking and Pornography Act, 1998. All but one was male and they had handled between one and six cases involving child pornography offences, the average being 2.6. All had dealt with cases involving possession, while one also handled a case of production and another a case of distribution. The interviews ranged in duration from 25 to 70 minutes (on average 41 minutes).

Clearly, the judges interviewed were not a random sample. In addition, they had different levels of experience; some had handled several child pornography cases while others had dealt with just one. As such, their views are not necessarily representative of all judges. Rather, the following extracts from the interviews serve to illustrate the range of opinions offered to us. The purpose of the interviews was to gain some insights into the sentencing decisions in these cases, in particular how an assessment was made of the seriousness of the offence and the offender's culpability, and what factors impinged on the selection of an appropriate penalty.

Assessing seriousness

Judges were asked to indicate how they assessed the seriousness of an offence of this kind. Two were unable to do so as the case had not proceeded in their court: one was sent forward to the Circuit Court by the DPP, while the prosecution collapsed in the other. The remainder all made reference to the nature of the images as the primary factor (or one of the most important factors) in any consideration of seriousness. Three judges viewed a sample of the defendant's collection while the seven others viewed all the material involved in the case (two judges dealt with a number of cases and viewed either a sample or all of the material depending on the circumstances of the individual case). The judges identified the age of the child and the nature of the activity depicted as the main indicators of seriousness.

> I listened to the prosecuting *Garda* regarding what was on the tapes. Most did not involve penetration or bestiality. Mostly poses and a number involved simulated sexual acts being carried out. You have to go by age. Some were very young, pubescent girls.

Four judges made reference to the Sentencing Advisory Panel guidelines prepared for the judiciary in England and Wales as a means of structuring their approach to this question. Two of these were district court judges who also used the guidelines to help them decide whether to accept or reject jurisdiction. If jurisdiction was declined it was because the matter was deemed likely to require a penalty greater than the maximum at the disposal of the district court (namely 12 months imprisonment on one charge or two years in total).

> The view I took, I think I remember, my cut-off point was at category 3 of the Sentencing Advisory Panel. At 3 I would retain jurisdiction, but 4 to 5, I would refuse.

Three judges said they also considered the circumstances of the offender, including his age, his cooperation with the authorities, willingness to participate in treatment and likelihood of reoffending. One judge particularly stressed the offender's level of criminal activity as evidenced by the degree of engagement with the material. He considered factors such as the time devoted to downloading new material, use of passwords and evidence of trading. However, he also noted that the quantity of material accumulated is not a reliable indicator of engagement, as modern technology facilitates the collection of a vast amount in a short time frame.

> You also have to understand however that you can go from 1 to 100 to 1,000 in a blink.

When asked what effect, if any, a guilty plea should have, there was consensus that it should be met with a discount. A number were strong advocates of substantial discounts and believed that guilty pleas warranted a sentence reduction of at least 20 to 30 per cent. Only one judge queried whether a guilty plea should automatically attract a discount, particularly in cases where there was strong evidence of offending (for example, the credit card transactions that linked individuals to child pornography Web sites in Operation Amethyst cases). However, even this individual concurred that despite this reservation, a guilty plea would still be taken into consideration when sentencing.

> Of course. That's a rule of sentencing and it's quite correct and appropriate ... There are other factors that would also make a difference. In certain circumstances there could be a substantial discount, up to one third. It's a general rule.

> It might mean the difference between a custodial and a non-custodial sentence.

Only two judges indicated how expressions of remorse were taken into account. Both said they were guided by reports (from psychologists and the Probation and Welfare Service) and looked for indications that insight had developed around the nature of the wrongdoing and its impact on the victims. A third judge considered remorse to be implicit in a guilty plea and took it into consideration accordingly.

> Reading the reports initially, [the defendant's] insight was limited. But this is what you'd look for in a psychological report – their awareness that there was a victim at the end of this. Remorse appeared to develop as counselling progressed and insight developed.

> In the second case, yes, and it resulted in a suspended sentence ... the Probation and Welfare told me.

Three judges clearly said they did not take expressions of remorse into account while a fourth noted the difficulty in determining genuine remorse.

> I've a jaundiced view of remorse. A guy who is facing a big sentence is very sorry. There are individuals who get into the

witness box and they're very convincing. It's a dangerous route to go down.

The likely impact of the prosecution on the defendant was discussed. Two judges did not specifically indicate whether they would consider this factor. The remainder were evenly divided.

Very much. You do bear that in mind. There was huge publicity in each case – national and local.

That didn't concern me, not when I viewed the images. How any ordinary person – as these two individuals were supposed to be – could download this revolting material. What I did was little to what happened to them next. They lost their family, their friends, jobs and were placed on the Sex Offender Register.

A number of judges believed that offenders' names should only be published following a conviction due to the media attention these cases attract.

I have made gagging orders ... the media was baying for blood, wanted to make a great story ... there was huge interest ... This is a dangerous area to get into. It could be said by somebody charged with a public order offence that his future is in jeopardy just like somebody charged with child pornography and that their identity should be protected too. This is not a decision to be taken lightly. I might not do it now. I did it then because there was so much publicity at the time, a media frenzy.

[In England] Lord Woolf sought to bring back the ban on publishing the defendant's name. I personally think it's a good proposal. Conviction in the eyes of the public is conclusive. There is no road back for the accused. Their name should be revealed only after conviction.

Judges were asked what weight was given to the likelihood of future offending when deciding on an appropriate sentence. All of those who had sentenced a case said that they had looked for, and been guided by, expert opinion on this matter. Risk assessment reports from psychologists and psychiatrists, as well as Probation and Welfare officers, were consulted and taken very seriously.

I would because it is the future safety of society. If it is a sickness it will re-occur if not treated. If there is a refusal of treatment or denial, I'd be inclined to imprison. If they go for treatment, and not Mickey Mouse but prolonged treatment, for example meeting their probation officer once a week, I'd be inclined not to imprison.

Yes. I believe that if somebody has images ultimately they will want to act out fantasy in real life. In any case like this I would want to get reports always and I would be guided by risk assessments in reports.

The judges were asked whether participation in treatment was an important factor in sentencing. In the vast majority of cases they had dealt with the defendant was receiving treatment. There was overall agreement among the district court judges that participation in treatment was viewed in a positive light when it came to sentencing. A number noted that this did not necessarily imply a clear desire to change as defendants will usually be advised by their lawyer to seek treatment before attending court.

He had participated before coming before the court. Most wise lawyers will anticipate the court's method of approaching a decision. As a defence lawyer you will look for a report to assist the court in determining sentence. It's very important. Culpability, treatment, all aggregate very positively.

Yes, it's important. Defence will advise clients to pre-empt the court's advice to get on a programme.

The circuit court judges did not comment on how important a factor it was in sentencing but in each of the cases they dealt with they had the benefit of reports. One judge noted that the source of the report was important.

It depends on the nature of the report you get, if it's convincing, if you know the institution where it's coming from and how much attention you give it.

Selecting an appropriate sentence

The judges employed the full range of available sanctions, imposing custodial sentences, suspended sentences, community service, fines and probation. They were asked whether the range was adequate. Three judges did not offer an opinion on this topic. Six believed that sufficient options were available.

> It's a discharge up to a good long stretch [in prison] on indictment. It is adequate. We use within the range, let's say.

> I do. You can do everything from nothing to long-term imprisonment. I believe the Sex Offenders Act and the register [convicted sex offenders are required to notify the local police of their whereabouts] is a substantial tool. It allows you to do things that you can't do for any other type of crime. It seems to get a lot of bad press. It's a start. It's limited but there is no other crime where there is even the beginnings of a facility like that. It allows you to suspend part of the sentence on condition that the person attends a social worker for counselling.

Three said they didn't think the range of sanctions was adequate.

> No, I in fact believe, I have a view, probably an extreme one, that all should be indictable, not dealt with in the district court. I'm a great fan of the district court, it's speedy justice for minor offences. Anything involving children and a trespass to their mind or body, should not be given jurisdiction lower than the circuit court.

> No. It's very easy for the criminal justice system to have jail as a sanction or a fine and then turn its back. The literature I have looked at suggests you must endeavour to take steps to ensure that the person is helped. It's easy for me to say to somebody, 'into the slammer and come out when you have finished the sentence'. This is my general criticism.

All judges believed that imprisonment was appropriate for offences of this nature. But generally speaking it was not seen as the default option. Whether to impose a custodial sentence depended on the facts of the case.

> It depends on many different factors. I wouldn't confine it to the seriousness of the offence. There are certain ones which immediately you think this deserves a prison sentence. But there are many other factors – previous record, material involved, whether it's confined to himself or if he's spreading it around. Is

it one isolated incident? It depends on the scale of involvement. You have to look at the person as a person in himself. It's very difficult to look at it in the abstract.

A small minority saw prison as either an extreme option or almost the only option.

More often it is not suitable. If the social workers tell me he is a man who can be left in the community and won't reoffend I would prefer to see him dealt with in the community than in prison.

It would be very difficult to convince me that anything other that a custodial punishment would be suitable.

Over half said they would consider community service an appropriate sanction under certain circumstances.

It would be a good penalty sometimes especially if combined with re-education.

Only two were explicit that community service was inappropriate for offences of this nature.

Get them to do community service work? That wouldn't solve the problem.

Two judges said they would not consider imposing a fine under any circumstances.

I couldn't envisage any circumstances that I would trivialise such material by categorising it as suitable to be dealt with by way of a fine.

The remaining judges, while not completely ruling out financial penalties as a sentencing option, were very cautious of their use in child pornography cases. There was a feeling that they might be seen as inadequate to mark out the seriousness of the activity in question.

A fine is appropriate if there's no risk. You can never satisfy yourself fully but you can have reports done and if everyone is satisfied it's a once-off then you can fine the person. However, taking €30,000 from someone is not adequate. If it's worth that much then it's worth jail.

The vast majority of judges said they would consider putting an offender on probation under certain circumstances. If the risk of reoffending was low, and supervision could reduce it further, this was seen as an option that it was in the public interest to pursue.

If you were of the view that you were prepared to deal with it finally a fine would suffice. If future monitoring of the individual was required then the Probation Service would come into it.

Two judges said they would not consider probation to be an appropriate response.

When asked what they hoped to achieve through the sentence, a number of aims were listed, including to emphasise the seriousness of the crime; express society's disapproval through the court; stop the offending behaviour and prevent a reoccurrence; act as a deterrent; provide rehabilitative opportunities; and punish or shame the offender. A single sentence could be designed to meet several of these aims.

I felt the process itself, counselling and treatment, that there was a rehabilitative process in existence with the accused. It didn't diminish the horror of the crime or the victims either. But you must never forget as a judge either the concept of compassion or rehabilitation. You cannot become case hardened.

Prevention of reoccurrence primarily. Also to mark the seriousness of the offence through a conviction. Public shame. The fact you're convicted of this offence even without a penalty is a serious sanction.

Aggravating and mitigating factors

To supplement the data collected from the agencies of the criminal justice system, and to provide as complete a picture as possible, newspaper coverage in relation to child pornography cases was examined in detail, primarily by searching the archives of the leading national daily newspapers (*The Irish Times*, *Irish Independent* and *Irish Examiner*) and the electronic database *LexisNexis Professional*. Any aggravating or mitigating factors identified by judges during

Table 4.4 Aggravating and mitigating factors identified by judges (listed in descending order of significance)

Aggravating factors	Mitigating factors
1. Nature of the images	1. Guilty plea, especially if timely
2. Effects on children (abuse, exploitation, trauma)	2. No previous convictions
3. Promotion of industry of child sexual exploitation by downloading images	3. Treatment or attempts to address problem
4. Risk of reoffending	4. Cooperation with *Gardaí* (e.g. providing passwords, handing over material)
5. Distribution of material (e.g. installing a broadband connection to trade images)	5. Positive risk assessment (low risk of reoffending)
6. Possible threat to children (e.g. through profession or indicated by other charges)	6. Youth/immaturity of defendant
7. Lack of cooperation with *Gardaí* (e.g. not giving them passwords)	7. Lack of trading/dissemination of material
8. Age of children, especially very young, including infants	8. Social isolation or personal difficulties (e.g. offender experienced child abuse)
9. Breach of trust	9. Remorse
10. Taking photographs of victim	10. Immediate admission of guilt/ accepted responsibility
11. Creation of images as an indication of organised crime	11. Suffering experienced by defendant (e.g. public contempt, media coverage)
12. Lack of remorse	12. Positive psychological reports
	13. Of previous good character (e.g. work, contribution to community, testimonials)
	14. Limited engagement with material (did not download/ participate in chat rooms)
	15. Family present (including effects on family, support by family)
	16. Offences at lower end of the scale
	17. Had not breached or betrayed any trust
	18. Had not come to *Garda* attention since crime
	19. Apparent insight into wrongdoing

(*Source*: review of newspaper content, interviews with judges) sentencing, and reported in the press, were extracted. Combined with the factors identified by members of the judiciary during interviews, a comprehensive list was compiled. In total, 20 judges identified 31 different factors; 12 aggravating and 19 mitigating. These are summarised in Table 4.4. In addition to highlighting a greater number of mitigating factors, these factors were mentioned more often: the 19 mitigating factors were raised on 80 occasions compared with 26 references to the 12 aggravating factors.

The nature of the images was cited as an aggravating factor by a number of judges. Several also noted that any indication of the offender posing a risk to children, or abusing a position of trust, was considered to exacerbate the seriousness of what they had done. Pictures of very young children were viewed with particular abhorrence.

> The individual was a [profession with access to children]. That by any standards is an aggravating factor. The fact that he is a [profession] means that he has access to children when they are vulnerable. I cannot say that the individual was a practising paedophile but the material comes from practising paedophiles.

An immediate acceptance of responsibility, the lack of previous convictions and a willingness to seek professional help were cited most frequently as mitigating factors. Social isolation and immaturity were also seen as factors working in favour of the offender.

> Young age of the defendant. Any sort of social isolation. For example, a young fella with a nervous breakdown stuck in his bedroom. The alcoholic.

> The example given earlier of the loner. I would be worried about that guy. His self-image, own life, so low in terms of self-esteem, worried about what he might do to himself. But good came out of it. If his self-image could be improved through the counselling he was receiving, I would see the threat he posed reduced as such.

Box 4.6 shows how a range of mitigating (guilty plea, cooperation with *Garda*, receiving treatment, low risk, personal difficulties) and aggravating factors (contribution to child abuse, distribution of images, age of children) were weighed up in two sample cases before a decision was made about how to strike an appropriate balance. In addition to the penalty imposed in court, each of the two individuals would have been subject to the notification requirements set out in the Sex Offenders Act, 2001 (see Chapter 6).

Box 4.6: Selecting an appropriate penalty

Prison
B.G. (47) pleaded guilty to possession and distribution of child pornography contrary to Sections 5 and 6 of the Child Trafficking and Pornography Act, 1998. Dublin Circuit Criminal Court heard that 1,244 images and 76 movies involving naked and partially-clothed children, from infancy up to 16, engaged in sexual activities with adults were found on his computer. *Gardaí* also found evidence that he had engaged in 3,000 chat-room sessions with 'like-minded people' and distributed eight images to individuals with whom he had been communicating.

Judge Desmond Hogan, who viewed some of the images in court, refused an application by counsel for B.G. to adjourn the sentence because he was receiving counselling and said on balance he deserved a custodial sentence. The judge said: 'The mitigating factors in this case are that he fully co-operated with the *Gardaí* and readily handed over the results of his activities in the form of floppy discs and other copies of the illegal pornographic materials he had accumulated. He also pleaded guilty. However there is one question that is constant in my mind and that is how could a person contribute to and participate in what is nothing more than the irretrievable loss of innocence of young, vulnerable children for his own sense of voyeurism and sexual gratification. He then distributed material to enable others to continue in the same vein. I must bear in mind that these images and movies were of very young children and in two of the cases I have seen, the children were no more than above infant age.'

Judge Hogan imposed three concurrent sentences of three years but suspended the last one for a period of seven years.

(*Source*: *The Irish Times*, 30 June 2004; *Irish Independent*, 30 June 2004; *Irish Examiner*, 30 June 2004; *Daily Mirror*, 30 June 2004)

Financial penalty
D.R. (23) pleaded guilty to possessing child pornography in Cork Circuit Court. He had used his parents' credit card to purchase material over the Internet.

Judge Seán Ó Donnabháin said he had viewed the images from the defendant's computer and there were very explicit images of very young children. However, there were a number of mitigating factors. These included the fact that he had no previous convictions, that he

---

had not breached or betrayed any trust by his crime, that he wasn't trading in child pornography images and that he had pleaded guilty and co-operated fully with investigating *Gardai*.

Taking these into account, together with a psychiatrist's report that there was minimal risk of re-offending, Judge Ó Donnabháin fined D.R. €1,500.

(*Source*: *The Irish Times*, 17 November 2004)

The vast majority of judges believed a set of guidelines, similar to those devised by the Sentencing Advisory Panel, would be of benefit to Irish judges; especially when experience with such cases was limited.

> I'm in favour of it. They're guidelines only, not prescriptive. They're very useful. They help to clarify one's thinking regarding what is the tipping point between custody and non-custody.

> I have seen them … I would be happy enough. Especially when you start off, it gives you a framework, a skeleton to work off. It allows you to differentiate between the mass of material that you are shown.

Only one judge did not believe they would be helpful, at least at district court level.

> No. You have the maximum in the district court, which is 12 months for any one offence and with a guilty plea you have to give a discount so there's not much room for manoeuvre. Guidelines are not needed, the decision is nearly made for you.

Making the punishment fit the crime

A trawl of newspaper sources yielded coverage of 78 cases. Details regarding sentencing were published in 47 of these. While the interviewed judges provided details of sentencing in 13 cases, they did not disclose the identity of defendants they had dealt with. The same applied to the 36 cases from the DPP where the sentence was known (see Table 4.3, p. 135). As many of these cases overlapped, it is not possible to state with accuracy the total number of cases for which sentencing details were obtained (we know it is between

47 and 96). The following analysis was therefore restricted to the identification of maximum and minimum sentence lengths.

As shown in Table 4.5, for offences contrary to Section 3 of the Act (child trafficking and taking a child for the purpose of sexual exploitation) the sanction range was from six years to two years imprisonment. For Section 4 offences (allowing a child to be used for pornography) the range was six years to two and a half years imprisonment. Neither of these offence categories can be dealt with in the district court. Where the most serious charge related to Section 5 offences (production and/or distribution of child pornography), the range of sentences handed down was three years imprisonment to two years suspended. Although summary disposal in the district court is possible for such cases, all of those which we could trace were sentenced in the circuit court.

The vast majority of offences involved Section 6 (possession) and there was greater variety in the way they were dealt with. In cases sentenced in the circuit court, the range was five years imprisonment (the final two suspended) to 12 months probation. In cases sentenced in the district court, the range was nine months imprisonment (with the last three months suspended) to a €600 fine.

Table 4.5 Range of sentences imposed for child pornography offences

	Circuit Court		District Court	
	Maximum sentence	Minimum sentence	Maximum sentence	Minimum sentence
Section 3	6 years custody	2 years custody	NR	NR
Section 4	6 years custody	2.5 years custody	NR	NR
Section 5	3 years custody	2 years suspended	NA	NA
Section 6	5 years with last 2 years suspended	12 months probation	9 months custody with last 3 months suspended	€600 fine

(*Source*: review of newspaper reports. NR means 'not relevant', NA means 'not available')

Closing observation

Confidentiality requirements meant that it was not possible to link data gathered from the various criminal justice agencies, as the identities of individuals processed by *An Garda Síochána* and the DPP were not known. This had the inevitable consequence that tracking cases from initial recording to final case outcome was not possible, so individual characteristics could not be related to prosecutorial and judicial decisions. Rather we have presented a series of slices of information all relating to the same five-year time period (2000 to 2004) and the same type of crime (offences under the Child Trafficking and Pornography Act, 1998), but the various data sources are not linked.

Despite this limitation, as the preceding analyses have shown, it has been possible to shed light on some important dimensions of how one country's criminal justice system responded to child pornography. These are related to a number of wider themes set out in the third, and final, part of this book, in particular the challenges for police (Chapter 5), the various approaches to prosecution and punishment (Chapter 6), and the ramifications for society of a preoccupation with childhood sexuality (Chapter 7).

Part III
Formulating a Response

Chapter 5

Policing: challenges and consequences

As described in Chapter 1, throughout the 1970s child pornography was legal in some countries and tolerated in others. Although difficult to imagine today there was a surprising lack of concern about the lives that had been shattered to produce magazines and videos that appealed to persons whose preference was for sexual partners who could never give meaningful consent. Even when prohibition was introduced in Europe and the USA there was a period of ambivalence and uneven enforcement. It was probably not until the 1990s that the need for action was universally accepted (with some exceptions such as Japan) and moral abhorrence became fused with the legal imperative to protect children. Today, few would question the value of outlawing child pornography. Legal prohibitions are found at all levels from the United Nations Convention on the Rights of the Child (1989), to the Council of Europe Recommendation on Child Sexual Exploitation (1991) and the European Union Framework Decision on Combating the Sexual Exploitation of Children and Child Pornography (2003). The legislative environment in developed countries now leaves little room for manoeuvre to child pornographers.

As with so many other types of crime, the Internet has introduced a new range of possibilities for offenders. Child pornographers were among the first to see the potential of the technology to facilitate an escalation of their activities. They used the new tools to increase exponentially the trade in images, to widen their appeal and to frustrate attempts at detection. This put police forces all over the world under severe pressure. Not only did they have to respond to a large amount of murder and mayhem in the real world, but virtual reality presented an entirely novel set of challenges.

The sheer size of the Internet, the anarchic way it grows, the lack of any boundaries to its expansion and its disregard for national borders make it a policing environment without parallel. Coupled with the rapidity of change, the rate of technological innovation, the variety of content and the sheer volume of traffic on the Information Superhighway, even the most determined and well-resourced police force will often confront impossibly large obstacles to successful investigation.

The focus in this chapter is on the practical problems associated with carrying out effective investigations. Some of the issues explored are technological and global (for example, the decentralised structure of the Internet) while others relate to law enforcement activities (for example, the problems associated with preserving electronic evidence). Lessons that might be useful for the evolving international law enforcement response are identified.

Police operations

While undeniably complex, law enforcement agencies in a number of countries have launched some impressively successful child pornography investigations. Evidently, the challenges are not insurmountable, as illustrated by the example of Operation Blue Orchid (see Chapter 2), where even countries as ideologically at odds as Russia and the USA showed they were prepared to join forces to stamp out this kind of crime.

Sommer (2002: 180) outlined a number of ways that police can monitor Internet activity. 'Passive scrutiny' is where they observe but do not intervene; their role is simply to gather evidence. 'Active scrutiny' involves a degree of interaction with suspected paedophiles as a way of building a case. The other end of the scale involves deploying software that allows remote access to how a suspect's computer keyboard is used (for example to obtain passwords), intercepting communications and obtaining information about users from ISPs.

Having reviewed media coverage of child pornography offending between 1976 and 2004 with a particular focus on the police response, Krone (2005a) identified four distinct target groups. The first related to individuals who possessed child pornography but were not integrated into wider networks. Typically they came to attention as a result of victim complaints or third parties who obtained access to an individual's computer and became alarmed by what they found.

The second was the covert group. Sometimes one individual came to attention for the reasons outlined above but the ensuing investigation generated new names. On other occasions the police learned of the existence of the entire group (for example through an ISP) and used forensic techniques to identify individual members. These groups communicated using all of the popular Internet resources (for example email, Usenet, IRC). Varying levels of security were employed. Krone's third category related to Web site subscribers. These involved commercial arrangements whereby interested parties used credit cards to purchase access to material. This could involve a one-off payment or a regular subscription. Finally there were police sting operations. These involved either the active monitoring of communications between offenders or the creation of a scenario where police attempted to lure the unsuspecting into their clutches.

It has been estimated that around one-in-four of all arrests for Internet sex crimes against minors in the USA involve traps set by investigators posing as minors (Mitchell *et al.* 2005). These traps have led to many successful prosecutions despite the fact that the suspects had not victimised a child but were arrested in situations where they believed they were meeting a minor for a sexual encounter. Almost half (41 per cent) of the offenders apprehended in this way were found to possess child pornography. Some had histories of child sexual assault (ibid: 260). (For a UK perspective on some of the legal difficulties associated with proactive Internet policing see Gillespie 2002.) Another strategy is for law enforcement authorities to mail child pornography to suspects and then arrest them when they seize the bait (for a discussion of how such strategies blur the line between creating and catching criminals, see Chin 2006).

There are two main reasons for the blanket ban on child pornography in the USA, despite the constitutional protection for free speech. These are that the production of such material usually involves child sexual abuse and that the dissemination of the material constitutes a separate and continuing harm against the children portrayed in it. The latter argument poses a serious problem for undercover operations involving the distribution of child pornography. Anglin (2002: 1092) makes the interesting point that the practice of sending photographs and videos as part of sting operations 'exposes federal agents to potential civil liability and undermines the integrity of the criminal justice system'. The injury is actionable by the children involved, whose right to privacy has been violated, and the system is brought into disrepute because the innocent are harmed to catch the guilty. Although no lawsuits have yet been filed against law enforcement personnel, Anglin argues that there are good grounds for believing that they would meet with success.

Difficulties in policing child pornography

Current approaches to law enforcement are based on a number of assumptions about victims, offenders and the relationships between them. Brenner (2004) highlights how cybercrime erodes a number of these assumptions. For example, in the real world the perpetrator and victim must be physically proximate, the scale of offending is typically modest (usually one victim at a time) and the planning of the offence carries a risk of identification or apprehension (for example, being captured on CCTV while reconnoitring a bank with a view to a later robbery attempt). By contrast, in cybercrime the offender can be on a different continent to the victim, enjoy perfect anonymity, leave no fingerprints or DNA and victimise a number of people simultaneously. This allows for a much greater volume of undetectable criminal activity than is ever possible in the real world.

In a similar vein, Jewkes (2003) discerned four major problem areas that confront police forces when they attempt to tackle cybercrime. The first relates to the sheer volume of material in question, the inevitably global scope of the problem and the difficulty applying laws across jurisdictional boundaries. Jewkes gives the example of the Love Bug virus which took only two hours to affect an estimated 45 million computer users in 20 countries, causing untold damage. The FBI established that the virus writer was a computer science student in the Philippines, who could not be punished because he had broken no domestic law.

The second relates to underreporting. Like all forms of criminal activity there is a large 'dark figure'. This may be more significant for cybercrime if victims are unaware of what constitutes illegal activity and unsure where to direct a report. The problem is exacerbated by the lack of standard procedures for recording crimes of this kind. While international comparisons are fraught for crimes in general, they are well nigh impossible for computer crime.

The third concerns police culture. Inertia and a reluctance to innovate, combined with inadequate training, mean that traditional methods of policing are simply not up to the challenge. There is also a feeling that dealing with the virtual world will keep police officers at their desks and submerge them in procedures and red tape. For an aspiring 'thief taker' this is not real detective work.

The fourth relates to limited resources. The potential for cybercrime is so enormous it could consume a budget of almost any size. Police forces must determine how to ration the finances at their disposal, based on some objective assessment of the problems they face. In this context the lack of good quality information on the amount of cybercrime means that it is difficult to decide about the size of an appropriate allocation. Finally the kind of expertise required for the forensic examination of computers and the investigation of crimes in cyberspace is expensive to buy in. This has obvious implications for a manager conscious of remaining in the black at the end of the financial year. (Sommer (2004) makes the additional point that police officers who have the requisite skills might find that being tied to their computers causes them to miss out on acquiring the broader managerial experience required for promotion. This may increase the attraction of better-rewarded opportunities in the private sector.)

Jewkes's points relate to the whole gamut of cybercrime from identity theft to fraud, virus writing and hacking. In their investigation of child pornography offences police officers can be hampered by all of the above, and more. The Internet has allowed offenders to network, even with people they have never met and whose identities they may be unsure of. Dealing with the almost inevitable cross-border angle presents police with one of the first difficulties: the lack of an agreed definition of child pornography or obscenity and the likely impossibility of ever arriving at one given differing, and shifting, value systems.

Grant *et al.* (1997: 174) believe that international agreement about the definition of child pornography will not be resolved quickly: 'Policy makers will continue to address the issue but should do so with consideration for its many complexities. These include cross-national variations in matters relating to consent, complications of perception and reality, the relevance of context, and the importance of differing moral, religious, social economic and cultural factors'. While the pursuit of a universally accepted definition is ultimately futile given the considerable variation in attitudes, norms and practices regarding what are acceptable representations of children, the effort to identify areas of consensus may be worthwhile in order to introduce greater clarity about the issues at stake and to promote better cooperation across borders.

Add to this picture different law enforcement structures including wide variations in the age of consent, prosecution systems, counting rules and language barriers, and the task becomes even more fraught. Where the policing function is spread across a number of national and regional bodies (for example there are 43 constabularies in England and Wales and more than 50 legal systems in the USA), and other regulatory authorities (for example industry associations and hotlines), the coordination of effort is further complicated. More prosaically, communication can be hampered by problems in translation, software compatibility and computer settings, especially when non-Roman alphabets are used. Different time zones create further challenges. If it happens that real-time abuse is observed during the working day in one country, it is essential that swift contact can be made with the relevant authorities in the host nation, regardless of the hour. While serious impediments to effective policing exist they are not insuperable, as illustrated by Box 5.1.

Box 5.1: You can't fool all of the people all of the time

A 34-year-old married man in Canada was arrested soon after sexually abusing a child live on the Internet. He was a small-town photographer with a home studio who occasionally made calendars to sell at the local mall. He had been under investigation for a number of months after he allegedly shared child pornography images with an undercover officer. However, there was insufficient evidence at the time to arrest him. A month prior to the live assault he had once again sent images to an undercover officer.

A member of Toronto's child exploitation unit said he was shaken to the core when the suspected paedophile he was chatting with online began sexually assaulting a preschooler and sending images of the attack over the Internet in real time. 'You think you see everything, or you think you can deal with everything, but at that moment, what I recall is my heart racing out of control, sweating, and feeling like I was going to throw up, to be honest,' he told a news conference in Toronto. 'We see these images. Unfortunately we see a lot of them, many times a day even. But to see this child, you know, and look in that child's eyes and realize that that child was live somewhere and that we had the possibility to save her ... right then, it's difficult to describe. It was a bit odd, and I'm getting the same feeling right now talking about it.'

The undercover officer continued to chat with the offender online while setting in motion the police response. He was tracked down by tracing his IP address through his Internet provider and was arrested within an hour and 25 minutes of the offence being witnessed. The young girl was returned to her family and police seized two computers and about 100 CD-ROMs and floppy disks. The man faced 11 assault and pornography charges.

Detective Constable Krawczyk said the incident was indicative of how paedophiles are becoming emboldened by the anonymity provided by the Internet. 'They're getting more daring because the Internet allows them to talk about their conquests and allows them to discuss with like-minded people,' he said. 'You couldn't go down the street 30 years ago and say, "I'm a paedophile and who else is here?" Now you can go down the street known as the Internet and say who else here is a paedophile and talk about it and set up places where you can meet and talk about it and normalize it.' Detective Constable Krawczyk also issued a warning to any paedophiles operating online. 'To all paedophiles or people who want to sexually exploit children on the Internet, we are on the Internet 24/7. We know where you are, and we're there too. We will find you, and we will arrest you, and we will rescue the children that you are exploiting,' he said.

(*Source*: *The Globe and Mail*, 2 November 2006; 3 November 2006)

The intensity with which a country polices Internet child pornography offences depends on the priority given to the problem by the government, competing demands on law enforcement resources and the extent to which Internet access is easily available. As noted by Healy (1996: 3): 'In developing countries, the reality of child pornography is dwarfed by the magnitude of other problems such as poverty, infant mortality, illiteracy, hunger and disease and often there is little reliable data on the subject'. Thus, available information tends to show a bias towards those countries (usually better off ones) where police actively pursue child pornography offenders and where police action is publicised (Carr 2001). The degree to which international obligations exist further complicates matters. Not all nations have entered into the kinds of legal arrangements, such as extradition treaties, that are necessary to ensure that mutual legal assistance can be arranged swiftly and effectively.

Where images have been accessed through the Internet it is rare for a victim to be identified and it can be very difficult to ascertain the age of a child unless the victim's identity is known. Thus, investigators are regularly faced with the often impossible task of determining whether an individual is legally a 'child'. Exacerbating this problem is the fact that many well-developed 14- and 15-year-olds could pass as adults. As a result, in the words of one commentator, 'the police have tended to focus on pubescent or pre-pubescent images' (Gillespie 2004: 363). It is reasonable to assume that when the age of the individual is ambiguous (they could be an adult or at least have reached the age of consent) and where there is no other evidence, the matter will attract a low level of interest. In the theme paper for the Second World Congress on Commercial Sexual Exploitation of Children, Carr (2001: 16) spelled out the consequences of these investigative challenges in the following terms:

> Because of differences in legal definitions between countries and the perceptions of local police forces, it is increasingly thought that, operationally, the only types of cases where it is likely that there will be no potential legal obstacles to cooperation between national law enforcement agencies are those where the young people involved in the pornographic depictions are very obviously below the age of the lowest common denominator.

Carr suspected that this scenario was also being played out within many national jurisdictions with the result that, in practice, any child pornography victims who had pubic hair, well-developed sexual organs or mature breasts would be treated as if they were adults, denying them the benefits of child protection laws.

In addition Grant et al. (1997) argued that laws drafted for photographic and print media may not be adequate in the digital age. The rules of evidence vary across jurisdictions and contraband that exists in the form of electromagnetic impulses on a computer disk may be insufficient in places where evidence is required to take a more tangible form. Even in this technological era a printed picture is probably of greater value to a prosecution than a digital archive. It somehow seems more 'real'.

Another potential problem for law enforcement is that printing off an image and showing it to investigators, judge or jury is likely to constitute an offence in the absence of explicit legal protection. In Ireland, impeachment proceedings against a circuit court judge began when a prosecution on child pornography charges failed due to an invalid search warrant. To allow members of parliament to possess, print or distribute material allegedly taken from the judge's computer, without committing an offence, required a new piece of legislation, the Child Trafficking and Pornography (Amendment) Act, 2004. These proceedings were discontinued when the judge took early retirement on the grounds of ill health as soon as it was possible for him to do so without losing all of his pension entitlements (*The Irish Times*, 14 November 2006).

The investigation of computer-related crime is extremely resource-intensive. Even to establish that no offence has been committed requires a significant amount of effort. The yield, in terms of successful prosecutions, is poor. For example, while Operation Avalanche generated 35,000 suspects in the USA, only a few hundred were ever arrested (Campbell 2005). The time-consuming nature of forensic examinations of computers is illustrated by Wilding (2003: 1) who describes one instance where a seized computer contained nearly 12,000 deleted images – not a large stash – which had to be retrieved:

> The ensuing extraction and analysis of the offending graphics files, video clips and Internet cache took four working days. The analysis of the correspondence, uploads and downloads in the chat-room used to distribute many of the offending pictures took another working day, while a further analysis ... of digital images alleged to have been from the defendant's camera, required a further two working days. All of which amounted to seven working days expended to achieve the most *basic* examination of a *single* computer. (emphasis in original)

Offenders are versatile and continue to refine their technical skills, becoming more sophisticated in their manipulation of Internet services in order to evade detection. A smart cybercriminal will never send a traceable message. It is easy to exchange messages using remailers that anonymise communications and then forward them to their destination. Some offenders have even gone so far as to abuse their own children in order to minimise the risk of apprehension (see, for example, Operation Hamlet, Box 2.3, p. 53).

Child pornographers are making use of more sophisticated security measures to evade detection. Encryption techniques (known in the trade as steganography) make it possible to hide an illegal image within an otherwise innocuous file. Astrowsky (2000: 2) fears that 'this will allow those who traffic in or are aroused by this illicit material to transmit or receive images and possess this material without alerting the attention of investigators'. Tremblay (2006: 153) gives the example of one individual who, when arrested, had a large collection of pictures but was so confident of how well he had covered his tracks that he gave permission to a detective to examine his computer. The detective searched but uncovered none of the concealed contraband.

In 2006 the UK's Home Office initiated a consultation exercise on the introduction of powers to compel individuals to make intelligible, electronic information that they had protected. Failure to do so could result in a prison term of up to two years. These provisions had been included in Part III of the Regulation of Investigatory Powers Act, 2000 but were not implemented. Views were also invited on the specific issue of whether the maximum penalty should be increased in cases involving child pornography images. It was felt that child pornographers were taking advantage of the available technology to reduce the likely impact of the law should their activities be uncovered.

As the Home Office (2006: 5) expressed it: 'an offender who may face up to ten years imprisonment for possession of indecent images or pseudo-images, if their protected information is rendered intelligible, may readily accept a sentence of two years imprisonment for failing to disclose protected information or the key to that information'. This concern was based on a number of cases where police inquiries had been frustrated by individuals who possessed encrypted files that they declined to open or who claimed to have forgotten their passwords. Just as the facility to allow secure storage of financial particulars and customer details is essential for online business, it offers a new layer of protection to the Internet criminal.

Take the case of the Shadowz Brotherhood. On 2 July 2002, police in seven countries arrested 50 people suspected of crimes involving child abuse and child pornography, in Operation Twins. The investigation centered on a high-tech paedophile group that called itself the Shadowz Brotherhood. This group of around 100 individuals employed advanced encryption software to avoid detection and maintained a 'star' rating system that indicated what level of access certain members had. Operation Twins began in early 2001, when Swedish intelligence discovered the club. Europol coordinated the year-long investigation. At one point before the July raids, British investigators flew to the US state of Georgia to rescue a young girl who was being raped by her father. Police forces in several countries arrested 50 people in connection with the Shadowz Brotherhood. Sixty-two Internet Service Providers were ordered to remove material related to the group from more than 240 Web sites (retrieved 3 June 2006, from http://www.criminaldefenseassociates.com).

Jewkes and Andrews (2005) highlighted the ease with which suspects could confuse investigating officers by using arcane technical jargon. Recognising the scale of the cybercrime problem and the need for an informed police response, universities have become involved and courses in computer forensics, Hi-Tech investigations and information security have become increasingly popular, especially across the USA. In Ireland, University College Dublin has established a postgraduate programme in forensic computing and cybercrime investigation. Exclusively for police officers, it covers topics such as disk and file system forensics, Internet and organisational networks and automation of digital evidence analysis. There are a growing number of academic publications that deal with the more technical issues associated with extracting information from personal computers and the Internet (see for example the *International Journal of Digital Evidence* at http://www.ijde.org and the *International Journal of Cyber Criminology* at http://www.cybercrimejournal.co.nr). Like other types of offender, those with an interest in producing or collecting child pornography are not inexorably drawn to this activity but respond to perceived costs and benefits. If they are thought of as rational decision makers there is scope for applying the techniques of situational crime prevention to this form of criminal conduct (Wortley and Smallbone (2006) have made a start on this project).

There is one final consideration here and it is that investigators can find themselves subjected to campaigns of harassment including death threats, disturbing telephone calls, and legal counterclaims. There have been instances when an investigator's airline tickets were cancelled by computer, when an off-duty police officer was videotaped and the video circulated to militant groups, when personal details of investigators such as home address, vehicle registration and name of spouse were posted to bulletin boards (Ferraro and Casey 2005: 101–3). While intimidation by suspects is a possibility in any criminal investigation it takes on an added dimension when carried out by a technologically astute offender. A brick through the front window is less worrying than a threat to one's children by a suspected child molester and his online allies, especially where they remain faceless and nameless.

Lessons from a national case study

The Republic of Ireland had no discernable child pornography problem at the end of the twentieth century. Nevertheless, a complex piece of legislation designed to respond to just such a problem came into existence in 1998. As we saw in Chapters 1 and 4, this was largely a consequence of international developments such as the Dutroux case in Belgium, a desire to show leadership while the country held the presidency of the European Union, and a certain amount of free-floating anxiety about child sexual exploitation at the domestic level.

At the same time as this legislation was being introduced an investigation was beginning in Texas into the activities of Landslide Productions (see Box 4.2, pp. 119–20). This evolved into what became known as Operation Avalanche and established two things with brutal clarity: that the demand for images of sexual violence against children knows no jurisdictional boundary; and that the human appetite for perversion may be impossible to sate. Anyone with a credit card and access to a computer could source material, the possession of which would earn them the opprobrium of civilised society, moral condemnation and a harsh legal response. Despite these risks the trade in images was brisk.

Avalanche led to a series of subsidiary investigations in other countries. The Irish edition, codenamed Amethyst, took place in the summer of 2002. In a very short period of time a cluster of cases came within the ambit of the Child Trafficking and Pornography Act, 1998. This provided an opportunity to study how the legislation was interpreted and applied, especially how it guided decisions made by police, prosecutors and judges, and how these decisions were reported in the press.

What has been described in the preceding chapter is essentially a case study of how the organs of the state responded to the shock wave of sexual deviance on a scale, and of a nature, that had not previously been encountered. This was amplified by the exposure of the perverse preferences of a number of formerly law abiding, and even outstanding, citizens. It occurred against a backdrop of revelations about hidden child sexual abuse involving fathers, sports coaches and clergy. This was one of the defining themes of the 1990s.

We have learned something about how police in Ireland grappled with the investigation of child pornography allegations, and where they encountered operational difficulties. In addition, it is possible to identify a number of potential future obstacles based on experiences in other jurisdictions. Some of the problems that have beset police forces elsewhere, such as a variety of legislative formulae governing obscenity and child abuse, the communication challenges that exist when there is a multiplicity of police forces, and the sheer scale of the problem, do not apply in Ireland. This is due to the existence of a single piece of legislation, a statutory definition of the crime in question and a national police force.

The quantity and nature of evidence

The biggest obstacle facing any police force attempting to tackle child pornography is the huge commitment required in terms of time. To some extent this touches on issues previously mentioned, such as the architecture of the cyber-environment. The strengths of the Internet, in particular its invulnerability to centralised control, and the rapidity with which it changes, make it peculiarly difficult to grapple with. When this is combined with the huge volume of information transmitted every minute, routine surveillance becomes enormously expensive and highly inefficient. Even narrowly targeted surveillance is problematic on account of the easy availability of advanced encryption software and private communication channels. The sheer amount of content and the exponential rate at which it grows and can be securely hidden make detective work painstaking and often fruitless. Unlike conventional policing the crime scene cannot be sealed off and made sterile until its possibilities have been exhausted.

A forensically aware offender will be difficult to catch and even a naïve one will take time to prosecute successfully. At the most basic level, the investigation of a single case requiring examination of a single computer is enormously laborious. Wilding (2003) observed that to eyeball the contents of a picture takes around three seconds. On this basis an extremely efficient and non-stop review of a collection of 100,000 pictures (not excessively large in this context) would take more than two full working weeks, with barely time to blink. This is only the start of the process. Much more time is required where the image is unclear or encrypted or there is doubt about the subject's age or whether the content is actually illegal under the terms of the prevailing legislation. The need to make judgments of this kind means that this is not a task which computer software can be designed to execute. Even more time is required to explore the degree of engagement with the material, whether the suspect has been involved in production and distribution and so forth.

In a number of cases that have come before the courts the defendants possessed adult pornography as well as child pornographic images and their collections were stored on a variety of devices. Investigating officers needed to analyse the entire archive in order to present to the court the extent of the offender's involvement in crime. It is highly probable that, on occasion, members of *An Garda Síochána* have devoted their time to trawling through large amounts of adult pornography before concluding there was no illegal material present. Such cases are just as resource-intensive and time-consuming as those where child pornography is actually found.

Similarly, police may receive a tip-off from a concerned (or vindictive) co-worker or spouse about suspicious images they came across, only to discover upon investigation that the 'child' was in fact over-18 or the images were not actually illegal (for example, topless under-18-year-olds). An example of the latter is the computer electronics graduate who was arrested as he took photographs of the legs of young majorettes at the St Patrick's Day Parade in Limerick city in 2003 (*Irish Independent*, 14 June 2006). Although unsettling, such behaviour is not contrary to the law, but clearly its investigation requires police time in terms of locating the images and determining if their content is illegal. In this case the inquiries led to the discovery of a cache of child pornography, but if the individual's interest had stopped with children's legs it is difficult to see how he could have been prosecuted, unless his behaviour was deemed to constitute a breach of the peace.

Perhaps more frustrating for law enforcement personnel are those cases where credit card transactions were recorded but no material was discovered upon investigation. Of course there are incidents where there was genuinely no illegal activity on the part of the suspect. For example, Landslide Productions provided access to many more adult than child pornography Web sites and a number of prosecutions failed in Britain when it was successfully argued that the defendant had in fact exclusively sought adult material (Campbell 2005). Again, the computer needs to be thoroughly analysed before the investigation can be closed. The other explanation, of course, is that the suspect removed the offending material prior to a search warrant being executed. In one case when *Gardaí* arrived to search a suspect's house they found he had thrown incriminating items (two computers and credit card documentation) out with his rubbish, and analysis of his PC revealed software called 'Evidence Eliminator' which had been used the day after he attempted to pay for sex with a child (*The Irish Times*, 22 January 2003). The clever offender will ensure that he wipes his traces clean and the aficionado will file his material so thoroughly that when found there will be little doubt about the level of involvement. It is the careless, or novice, offender who is most at risk of discovery by not properly discarding – or securely storing – images. Box 5.2 illustrates the lengths to which individuals will go in order to conceal their wrongdoing, whether motivated by regret or fear of the consequences, and the lengths to which determined police officers need to go in order to recover evidence of offending.

Box 5.2: Fishing for evidence

On foot of information from US authorities, *Gardaí* questioned C.J., a father of five, concerning allegations that he had downloaded images from a Texas-based Web site. C.J. told them the laptop computer that should have been in his office was no longer there and suggested that someone must have taken it. He then changed his story and said that he had thrown it into a river. Detectives accompanied him to the water but it quickly became apparent that there was nothing to be found. C.J. changed his story again, this time saying that he had given the computer to his son, so the investigation moved to the son's house. The detectives were informed when they arrived there that the laptop had been broken into pieces by the son and thrown into the sea. *Garda* divers needed just five minutes to recover the evidence.

Wicklow Circuit Court heard that the damage done by waves and water did not stop officers retrieving 1,068 images from the computer's hard drive. They featured children as young as six or seven engaged in sex acts with adult males, or posing with genitals exposed. It was stated that 65 per cent of the collection featured sex acts while 35 per cent involved poses. Judge Groarke remarked that the pornography found in the defendant's possession was graphic, detailed and grossly obscene, as well as being a serious abuse of the children photographed. The implication was that the defendant had assisted in the abuse of children, though at a far distance. 'This is not a victimless crime,' stated the judge.

The prosecution accepted that the pictures had been acquired for C.J.'s own use and there was no evidence that he distributed them to anyone else. A report from the Granada Institute suggested that he was rated a low risk for re-offending. The judge was in no doubt that the defendant felt significant guilt for what he had done. He sympathised with C.J.'s family who were present in court to witness his humiliation. He also expressed concern for those who had to sift through the images found on the computer and said, after viewing just a small selection, that he felt abused himself at having to look at them.

(*Source*: *The Wicklow People*, 16 December 2004)

Another obstacle to progress involves situations where a computer has multiple users. In certain cases illegal images may be easily accessible but identifying the offender can prove impossible in an open office environment, a university computer laboratory or an Internet café. For example, in November 2003 a Dublin college reported that child pornographic material had been saved on one of its computers to which hundreds of students had access. The police were notified and although it was eventually shown that only one computer in the laboratory had been used to access illegal material, the entire facility had to be closed for a time so that all of the computers could be analysed and their memories cleared. A college spokeswoman said the possibility that the material had deliberately been left on display as part of a student prank could not be ruled out (*The Irish Times*, 11 November 2003). If true, this highlights how police resources can be depleted unnecessarily.

The integrity of evidence

In every criminal investigation it is crucial to ensure that the integrity of evidence is not compromised. In the UK the Association of Chief Police Officers (ACPO) has drawn up a set of best practice guidelines for computer-based electronic evidence. The principles underlying these guidelines are summarised in Box 5.3. They emphasise the need for caution, planning, meticulous record keeping and clear lines of accountability. The key objective is to ensure that evidence is not contaminated. Ideally this will involve making an image of the entire target device so that examination of the material does not cause damage or deletion. The main problem with digital evidence is its volatility. Turning a computer on, viewing but not altering files, and then shutting down will cause many files on the hard drive to be written to. Great care is required to ensure that the process of investigation does not jeopardise the success of any prosecution. Digital information needs to be preserved swiftly but securely.

Box 5.3: Collecting evidence from suspect computers

Principle 1   No action taken by law enforcement agencies or their agents should change data held on a computer or storage media which may subsequently be relied upon in court.

Principle 2   In exceptional circumstances, where a person finds it necessary to access original data held on a computer or on storage media, that person must be competent to do so and be able to give evidence explaining the relevance and the implications of their actions.

Principle 3   An audit trail or other record of all processes applied to computer based electronic evidence should be created and preserved. An independent third party should be able to examine those processes and achieve the same result.

> Principle 4   The person in charge of the investigation has overall responsibility for ensuring that the law and these principles are adhered to.
>
> (*Source*: Association of Chief Police Officers 2006: 6)

The ACPO guide reminds investigating officers that electronic evidence is subject to the same rules that apply to documentary evidence and the onus is on the prosecution to show to the court that what is produced is no more and no less than when it was first taken into the possession of the police. (For a detailed overview of the logistics of evidence recovery and preservation from personal computers and the Internet, see Ferraro and Casey 2005: chapters 7, 8 and 11.)

While obtaining reliable and valid evidence is inherently problematic, just as it is for more traditional forms of criminal activity, in some of the biggest operations the problem has been the sheer volume of material that confronts investigators. Too much intelligence can place an inquiry under strain. While it is unlikely that future investigations will throw up greater numbers of suspects, lessons can be learned from Operation Amethyst's equivalent in the UK – namely Operation Ore. Here investigators were provided with the names of over 7,200 individuals who had paid to access pornography Web sites through Landslide Productions. Police forces were faced with the unusual situation of having too much information and many were overwhelmed by the enormity of the task before them (Jewkes 2003).

A triage system was introduced in an effort to manage the workload, with top priority given to persons on the list who were convicted sex offenders or had immediate access to children. People in positions of authority, such as police and magistrates, were processed next while those who had no apparent involvement with children were accorded the lowest level of emphasis (Krone 2004). While this ranking was of some assistance, it was not possible during the first year of the operation to search the homes of more than a minority of those who had come under suspicion.

Notwithstanding these difficulties, the way evidence is presented in court can have a dramatic impact on the outcome of a prosecution. Duncan Campbell appeared as an expert witness in a number of Operation Ore cases. By studying archived versions of Web pages associated with Landslide Productions he was able to demonstrate that the way cases were constructed against the accused gave undue emphasis to the links to child pornography. This was exacerbated by a close media involvement, at the behest of the police, in the operation as it unfolded. In Campbell's (2005) view, this combination of exaggeration and media frenzy led to 'systematic injustice'. To this can be added the probable lack of technological expertise on the part of the judiciary, who by virtue of their age are unlikely to have acquired a deep knowledge of the whys and wherefores of information technology, and on the part of juries, where expertise will be unevenly spread.

Sommer (2002: 176) reinforces the inherent dangers with strong words of warning: 'Potentially, we face a dangerous combination: a set of offences around the sexual abuse of children which cause widespread repugnance and where there is great demand for determined law enforcement action; and uncertainty about the forensic quality of evidence that may be being adduced. Such combinations have been behind some of the great miscarriages of justice of the last 25 years' (see, for example, Box 7.1, p. 211). Although no convictions for child pornography offences have been overturned in the Irish courts to date, it is appropriate to sound a cautionary note at this early stage in the country's attempts to grapple with the political, legal and social consequences of the problem.

Growing availability and better concealment

The substantial increases in home computer ownership and the growing popularity of the Internet make more contact with child pornography inevitable. As users become increasingly adept at exploiting the potential for anonymity offered by the Internet, the activity will become more difficult to eradicate. There will be less overt organisation and the fellowship of dedicated enthusiasts will bury its traces more deeply in the recesses of cyberspace.

In 1998 when the Irish men who were later to be apprehended as a result of Operation Amethyst were purchasing access to child pornography from Landslide Productions, only 5 per cent of households in Ireland were connected to the Internet. This had risen to 45 per cent by 2005 (Central Statistics Office 2006: 27). It would be extraordinary if such an increase in access did not result in an increased level of child pornography viewing, possession and exchange. An indication of the huge amount of material in circulation was revealed during an investigation by Austrian police in 2006 of a Web site in Russia, that allowed access for a small fee (US$89; €68 for three months), to what was reported in the press as more than 8,000 gigabytes of child pornographic files; about 470 hours of broadcast-quality video (*The*

Irish Times, 8 February 2007). Yet the *Garda* annual statistics show the opposite trend: 32 offences contrary to the Child Trafficking and Pornography Act, 1998 were recorded in 2005 compared with 125 in 2002. This hardly reflects a decrease in offending but rather shows how difficult it is to police this form of criminal activity.

The downward trend in the number of cases known to *An Garda Síochána* since the glut of Operation Amethyst investigations in 2002 (see Table 4.2, p. 122) suggests that the discovery of child pornography is becoming more difficult. Given the ever-increasing stock of pictures available in cyberspace, increasingly cheap and easy production methods, growing broadband availability and greater awareness of encryption techniques, it is unlikely that fewer people are accessing this material. The truth is probably that offenders have become more cautious and computer literate as a result of well-publicised police raids that have taken place over the past five or six years. Viewers are more risk-aware and better at covering their tracks; more people are looking but fewer are being caught.

This notion finds support in the rising number of reports to the Hotline, an anonymous reporting service for members of the public that was set up in 1999. In its third report, published on 27 February 2006, the Hotline recorded 5,102 communications from the public of suspected illegal material between July 2003 and December 2005 (http://www.hotline.ie). This compared with 1,792 reports between July 2001 and June 2003. Even allowing for the longer time period this still marked a substantial increase. Almost nine out of ten (87.6 per cent) concerned child pornography.

In a quarter of cases the content referred to was not found by the Hotline. This included situations where insufficient, or incorrect, details were provided by the reporter, the Web server was unavailable, or the content had already been removed by the Internet Service Provider. In the majority of cases where child pornography was suspected and the Hotline located the reported content, it was determined to be adult pornography. On a few occasions reports referred to images of children that were deemed not to be illegal under the Child Trafficking and Pornography Act, 1998. There were 1,033 reports where the target content was assessed as probably illegal; 908 were child-related.

Not only had the number of reports increased but it seemed that the language used on the sites in question had become more offensive and the level of child abuse displayed in openly accessible images had increased in severity. Hotline analysts observed a 'marked increase in pay-sites offering images depicting children in more sexually explicit situations, often directly involving adults and photographed in "run down" settings. In some more extreme cases the children have appeared malnourished and even some with visible physical injuries'.

The Hotline reported that the area causing greatest concern to it was the *lack* of reporting about suspected illegal content on peer-to-peer file sharing services. This stood in marked contrast to the obvious potential for such activity to bring computer users into contact with child pornography. What's more, none of the reports determined to relate to 'probably illegal' material referred to material either hosted or distributed from Ireland. All were traced to locations outside the jurisdiction. Of these, the majority were apparently located in countries where no national hotline existed, thus making it more problematic to forward the queries for action. These observations further underline the necessity of international cooperation in any attempt to combat this type of crime. Box 5.4 gives an example of the Hotline's *modus operandi*.

Box 5.4: The Hotline in action

A report was received citing a Web site on the private pages of a major Italian ISP. It claimed that a series of related Web pages were advertising videos for sale. The site included many still shots of the video which the reporter suspected were child pornography. Hotline staff successfully located the site. The content was verified as advertising videos which were available for purchase by credit card. Still images purporting to represent examples of the video content were used on the site. These showed a girl estimated to be about 10 years old in explicit poses and engaging in sexual activity with an adult male.

As there is a hotline in Italy (Stop-IT) a standard forwarding report was prepared and submitted to it. Details of the activity were completed in the Hotline database and the case was closed in www. hotline.ie. Stop-IT pursued the matter in conjunction with Italian law enforcement agencies and the site was taken down.

Within a few weeks the identical material was again reported to www.hotline.ie but it had now moved to servers which were apparently located in South Korea. A similar process occurred when the Hotline reported it to Internet119, its Korean equivalent, which resulted in the site being removed in that jurisdiction. It has since come to the attention of other Hotlines in a number of other countries around the world.

(*Source: Second Report of www.hotline.ie* 2004: 37)

Three days after the Hotline published its third report, newspapers reported a series of raids on businesses and private residences that were part of a new police operation, codenamed Iron. This involved up to 80 individuals who had used their credit cards to purchase child pornography online from Belarus. The details had been passed on to *An Garda Síochána* from the USA where they had come to attention during a wider investigation – Operation Falcon – being carried out by customs agents (*Irish Examiner*, 2 March 2006; *Irish Star*, 2 March 2006). Operations such as Amethyst and Iron show how dependent police in any one country are on their colleagues in other jurisdictions. Without the intelligence provided by the USA in particular, child pornography in Ireland would have remained a very private vice.

It is not all bad news for police services. As ever the emergence of new types of crime can be used as a tool for attracting additional funds. Sommer (2002: 176) noted that following Operation Cathedral (see Box 2.1, pp. 38–9) penalties were increased, further police resources sought and new training schemes initiated. In his words: 'Cathedral also provided impressive "mood music" to the arguments about increased and updated police powers which eventually led to the passing of the Regulation of Investigatory Powers Act 2000'.

But the mood music can change and the public's attention is easily diverted to the crime of the moment. The *Daily Telegraph* editorial of 15 January 2003 echoed this sentiment when it declared: 'Nobody denies that the sexual abuse of children is a revolting crime, or that those who pay for child pornography encourage that abuse. But many may think that, while burglaries and muggings are on the increase, the police have more pressing work to do than hunting for those who surf the Internet in search of filth'. It is a difficult balancing act for the police. If they do not place sufficient emphasis on rounding up child pornographers they cause dismay among the public, but if their attention to this type of crime means that they are distracted from other policing duties they are subjected to criticism.

The limits of traditional policing

It is recognised that the responsibility for creating a safe, and legal, Internet environment is widely spread. This is too big a task for the police alone. The active cooperation of ISPs, businesses and other institutions, as well as individual users, is essential if there is to be any prospect of success. Campaigners for Internet safety have widened their attention to embrace more general regulatory issues. In particular, self-governance of the Internet has become a focal point. As Akdeniz (2001: 249) observed:

> The Internet is a complex, anarchic and multi-national environment where old concepts of regulation, reliant as they are upon tangibility in time and space, may not be easily applicable or enforceable and that is why the wider concept of governance may be more suitable.

Akdeniz suggested that the optimum approach is a layered governance system which includes a mixture of national and international legislation coupled with self-imposed regulation by the ISPs and online users.

ISPs received a wake-up call in 1998 when Felix Somm, the former president of the German ISP, CompuServe, was given a two-year suspended prison sentence and fined DM100,000 (€51,100) for failing to block Internet access to child pornography. Somm's conviction received widespread condemnation with even the prosecutors calling for his acquittal. It was argued that the decision turned ISPs into scapegoats (Bender 1998). In recent times the majority of ISPs have worked in close cooperation with law enforcement agencies and have made significant efforts to eradicate child pornography from their servers. In Ireland, the law recognises that ISPs can only be held responsible for child pornography distribution if it is 'knowingly' facilitated.

Reflecting a growing awareness that Internet services can place children at risk, AOL and Microsoft shut down their free, unmoderated chat rooms in 2003. While welcomed by child protection organisations, others attacked the move as reckless, suggesting that it would send chat room users 'underground' where they might be more vulnerable (*BBC News*, 24 September 2003). This highlights the difficulties associated with creating safer online environments even with major institutional backing.

In 1998 the EU approved a four year Action Plan (1999 to 2002) on promoting safer use of the Internet by combating illegal and harmful content on global networks. An evaluation in 2003 rated the Action Plan very positively and it was extended on two further occasions, most recently to cover the period 2005 to 2008. The objectives of the programme were widened to encompass new and emerging communication technologies that could influence children's use of the Internet (for example, 3G mobile telephones which allow high-speed wireless Internet connection and video streaming). The Action Plan supported a self-regulatory approach by ISPs and Article 3 set out a number of initiatives to this effect, the most important of which were:

1 Promotion of industry self-regulation and content-monitoring schemes.
2 Encouraging industry to provide filtering tools and rating systems, which allow adults to select content appropriate for children in their care, while leaving them free to decide what legal content they wish to access, and which take account of linguistic and cultural diversity.
3 Increasing awareness of services provided by the industry among users, in particular parents, teachers and children, so that they can better understand and take advantage of the opportunities of the Internet.
4 Activities fostering international cooperation in the above areas.

One of the major achievements of the Action Plan was the establishment of a European network of hotlines to which citizens can report illegal content such as child pornography. INHOPE, the International Association of Internet Hotlines, was formally established in 1999. The organisation has since grown to include 24 member countries from Europe, the USA, Australia and Asia. Hotlines do not themselves attempt to block or remove illegal content; this is the duty of the ISP. Nor do they attempt to track the purveyors of prohibited material; this is the duty of the law enforcement agencies. Their role is to act as a conduit for Internet users so that their concerns can be highlighted and passed on to the relevant body for action. Between March 2003 and February 2004, INHOPE's members processed more than 250,000 reports. Over one third of these related to child pornography, child trafficking and sex tourism (INHOPE 2004).

The Internet Watch Foundation (IWF) discharges the hotline function in the UK and faces the same range of practical challenges as its counterparts in other countries in terms of successful international collaboration. Recent intelligence from the IWF revealed that some Web sites containing child abuse content hosted abroad remained accessible for up to five years, despite being reported to the relevant authorities. A fifth of all Web sites hosting child abuse content on the IWF database were accessible at the start and end of a six week period. One Web site, first reported in 1999, was reported on a further 96 occasions and the details were passed on by the IWF to the relevant authorities 20 times. Still it remained available (IWF Press Release, 20 July 2006).

A similar service but with a wider remit, the CyberTipline, was established in the USA in 1998 and is run by the Virginia-based National Center for Missing and Exploited Children (NCMEC). It operates in partnership with a range of agencies including the FBI, the US Postal Inspection Service, US Customs and the Secret Service. During its first year the CyberTipline received 3,267 reports of suspected child pornography. By 2004 this had risen to 106,119. The NCMEC attributed the exponential increase to the availability of new technologies such as digital cameras and peer-to-peer networking, as well as increased public awareness and a duty under federal law for ISPs to report incidents of child pornography to the CyberTipline (NCMEC Press Release, 27 January 2005).

The other important element of the international legal context is the Council of Europe Cybercrime Convention. The Convention entered into force on 1 July 2004. It was signed by Ireland on 28 February 2002 but as of September 2006 had not been ratified. A number of non-member states of the Council of Europe, notably Canada, Japan and the USA, were involved in the drafting of the Convention and became signatories to it.

This was the first international treaty on crimes committed via the Internet and other computer networks, dealing particularly with infringements of copyright, computer-related fraud, child pornography and violations of network security. Its main objective was to pursue a common criminal policy aimed at protecting society against cybercrime, especially by adopting appropriate legislation and fostering international cooperation. Parties to the Convention agreed to three main objectives:

1   To ensure that national law establishes a number of criminal offences in relation to: unauthorised access to and illicit tampering with systems, programmes or data (for example hacking), the content of communications (for example pornography), fraud, forgery and copyright infringements. (The committee drafting the Convention discussed the possibility of including other content-related offences, such as the distribution of racist propaganda through computer systems. However, consensus could not be reached on the criminalisation of such conduct due to strong concerns expressed by some delegations about the implications for freedom of expression.)

2   To ensure that such legislation facilitates certain basic procedural requirements which will allow police to investigate crimes in a volatile technological environment, where huge quantities of evidence may be altered, moved or deleted in seconds. The provisions relate to the expedited preservation of stored computer data.

3   To ensure that such legislation establishes a framework for international collaboration. In the case of crimes committed by use of computer systems, there will be occasions in which more than one party has jurisdiction over some or all of the participants in the crime. For example, many virus attacks, frauds and copyright violations committed through use of the Internet target victims located in many states. In order to avoid duplication of effort, unnecessary inconvenience for witnesses, or competition among law enforcement officials of the states concerned, or to otherwise facilitate the efficiency or fairness of the proceedings, the affected parties are to consult in order to determine the proper venue for prosecution. In some cases, it will be most effective for the states concerned to choose a single venue for prosecution; in others, it may be best for one state to prosecute some participants, while one or more other states pursue others.

A number of independent Internet monitoring groups, set up and run by volunteers, predated the establishment of the official hotlines. The oldest of these is Cyberangels which came into existence in 1995. Based in the USA it has an international reach. Others include Pedowatch and Ethical Hackers Against Pedophilia, both established in 1996. The latter is a 17-member secret society dedicated to identifying and closing down the producers of child pornography. They do not reveal their methods and while they refuse to admit breaking the law, do not feel constrained by it either. In September 1998, Pennsylvania resident William H. Prugh, was charged with 15 counts of possessing and disseminating child pornography which he had posted and downloaded from the newsgroup alt.pictures. erotica.pre-teen. He used the nickname RAMM@intothewall, which he thought was untraceable. Ethical Hackers Against Pedophilia discovered his identity and assisted the police in collecting evidence for his arrest. Kelly and Regan (2000: 26) observe that the activities of these groups are not always welcome and that ironically, 'the hackers appear to cause more distress to sections of the industry and its supporters than the sexual exploitation they are trying to expose'.

Providers of adult content have increasingly sought to distance themselves from illegality. In the USA a number of them have joined forces to help eradicate child pornography by certifying legitimate adult sites, providing information about child protection and operating a hotline through which consumers of adult material can report child pornography that they find on the Internet (see http://www.asacp.org). The industry has become increasingly acceptable in polite society and the study of adult pornography as a distinct genre of filmmaking has begun to emerge as an area of scholarly interest (see Lehman 2006 and Lee 2005, for accounts of the way that child sexual abuse is presented in popular culture, particularly film).

The fact that online adult pornographers have joined forces with vigilante groups, regulatory bodies and more traditional law enforcement authorities shows how complex and multifaceted Internet policing has become. Against a background of increasingly detailed national laws and international treaties, a continuously evolving Internet environment, and overwhelming volumes of information, responding effectively is a mighty challenge even where the issue is prioritised and heavily resourced. Different considerations arise when individuals are apprehended and brought to justice. The pitfalls experienced by prosecutors and some of the controversies around sentencing and punishment are addressed in Chapter 6.

Chapter 6

Prosecuting and punishing

The focus in this chapter is on how to follow effective investigations with successful prosecutions. Some of the issues explored concern the scope of the law (for example, should there be a prohibition on the possession of computer-generated images that did not involve children in their production?) while others revolve around the interpretation of legislative provisions in a variety of countries including Canada, Ireland, the USA and the UK (for example, how to determine if an individual 'knowingly possessed' material found on his computer hard drive or how to establish if this material was intended for a 'sexual purpose'). The difficulty in finding a balance between punishment and public protection is particularly important in this type of crime and the role of sex offender registers (increasingly popular in North America and the UK as an additional control mechanism) is examined below.

To begin with, we return to some of the lessons learned from the findings presented in Part II of this book. According to the annual reports of the DPP the most common reason for a direction not to prosecute is insufficient evidence. This was the explanation given in 74 per cent of all cases between 2002 and 2004, which provides a good point of comparison with the data collection period for the national case study. In the same three years, 5 per cent were referred to the Juvenile Diversion Programme and in 8 per cent the time limit had expired, thereby precluding any further action. There was no progress in the remaining cases for considerations to do with the public interest (5 per cent), on sympathetic (1 per cent) or other (7 per cent) grounds (Director of Public Prosecutions 2005: 37).

The rate of non-prosecution in child pornography cases was not out of line with the overall pattern of case management in the Office of the DPP as shown in Table 6.1. In other words it would appear that the DPP exercises no more caution handling these cases than when dealing with other matters. But the distribution of reasons for not initiating a prosecution in cases involving child pornography was slightly different in that none were discontinued on account of public interest or sympathetic considerations. This reflects the narrower range of criminal activity involved and its level of seriousness compared with other matters dealt with by the DPP (for example theft) where public interest factors could play a more influential role. A greater proportion were time expired (27 per cent) and a similarly small number (6 per cent) were referred to the Juvenile Diversion Programme. In the remainder there was no further action because of doubts about whether the suspect had knowing possession of the images or unique access to the computer in question, or the material satisfied the definition of child pornography as set out in the legislation.

Why prosecutions failed

Most child pornography prosecutions led to a conviction (see Figure 4.4, p. 134). A small number of individuals whose files were reviewed for this study pleaded not guilty and each of them was acquitted. But we know from media reports that there were also occasions when juries convicted. These may have been cases which had not been dealt with to a conclusion by the time the research for this book ended or that took place outside the main study period (2000 to 2004). For

Table 6.1 Case management by the Director of Public Prosecutions (per cent)

Direction	All cases 2002–2004	Child pornography cases 2000–2004
No prosecution	40	36
Prosecution on indictment	30	39
Summary disposal	29	24

(*Source*: based on Director of Public Prosecutions (2005: 36) and findings reported in Chapter 4)

example, in May 2006 a computer technician who had what *Gardaí* described as 'the vilest and most horrendous ever' images of child pornography was found guilty after trial. The verdict of the jury was unanimous. Having viewed some of the images the judge said that they depicted sadism and bestiality on toddlers and imposed a three-year prison sentence (*The Irish Times*, 2 June 2006).

To knowingly possess

A burden is placed on prosecutors by the use of the word 'knowingly' in relation to possession under Section 6 of the Child Trafficking and Pornography Act, 1998. This can raise particular problems when images are found on computers in homes or workplaces where persons other than the accused also have access. Although clearly stated protocols can limit computer misuse in an office environment these are certainly not foolproof. Individual user passwords are often shared with colleagues or easy to deduce. Not all employees will lock their system every time they leave it unattended. System administrators or supervisors will generally be able to override password protection.

Even if only one person had access to the computer on which illegal images were found, there is still the question of establishing that the accused was 'knowingly' in possession of the images. Consider the case of F.S. who was acquitted by direction of the trial judge, despite acknowledging that he had paid for and viewed child pornography (Box 6.1).

> **Box 6.1: Unknowing possession**
>
> Dublin Circuit Court was told that F.S., a 36-year-old solicitor, had used his credit card in 1999 to access child pornography. F.S. said the images were of children aged seven years and older in 'disgusting' sexual positions but that he had cancelled his subscription to the Web site as he had 'an immense guilt complex'. He entered a not guilty plea.
>
> When shown images which had been retrieved during forensic analysis of his computer F.S. told *Gardaí* that he had never seen them before and was surprised at their existence as he 'never did any downloading'. F.S. said that he did not actively search for child pornography on the Internet but that it would appear when he was accessing other sites. He said he would look at free preview tours but never stored or downloaded images. The court was told that 71 images of child pornography were found in temporary Internet files and that

21 of those were larger than 'thumbnail' size. Addresses of a number of sites containing child pornography were also found in the Internet history files.

Sergeant Michael Moran said that he felt the Internet files on F.S.'s computer were indicative of the type of browsing which was being done by the user of the computer. He said that the full size images would not be found on the front page of a Web site or appear as a result of a 'pop up'. A 'pop up' is usually a marketing tool which appears at the direction of a Web site rather than the user. He said he would 'always see large images as [indicating] further use of a site'. Sergeant Moran said that child pornography sites were hard to find. 'In my experience a child porn Web site "pop up" would never appear behind an adult porn site as it would be commercial suicide.' He said that while anything was technically possible, the images on F.S.'s computer were 'very unlikely' to be there as the result of a virus. Detective Sergeant John Finan of the *Garda* Computer Crime Unit said that he had never seen a virus go to the lengths required to change an Internet history file, which automatically records the address of a site visited to ease future browsing of the Internet by the user of the computer.

The jury heard that F.S.'s computer was stored in the locker of a *Garda* station for four months before it was forensically examined. Counsel for the defence said a 'Trojan virus' was found on his client's computer and suggested these were notorious for spreading unwanted pornographic images.

On day ten of the trial Judge Yvonne Murphy directed the jury to acquit F.S. She found insufficient evidence that F.S. was knowingly in possession of images in the temporary Internet folder of his computer. She said he made verbal admissions to *Gardaí* that he accessed a child pornography Web site a few years earlier and had since viewed similar images while browsing the Internet, but had not sought such images. The judge said while there was evidence of child pornography on the computer, it had not been established it was in a mode accessible to F.S. on the date on the indictment. She said her judgment did not imply there would have been sufficient evidence to convict if the date on the indictment had been widened.

(*Source*: *The Star*, 8 December 2004, 10 December 2004; *The Irish Times*, 10 December 2004; *Irish Examiner*, 16 December 2004; *Irish Independent*, 21 December 2004)

It is possible that somebody could unwittingly store images of child pornography on their computer. When a Web page is viewed a copy is stored in a folder known as the cache; the individual files within it are known as temporary Internet files. When a previously viewed

Web page is revisited the cached file is retrieved. This allows it to be displayed more quickly than if it was acquired again from the Internet (for an informative overview of caching and retrieval processes see Howard 2004: 1229–31). This means that viewing child pornography online, which is not in itself prohibited by Irish legislation, causes a trace to be left on the user's hard drive and it thereby comes into their possession.

It sometimes happens that a computer user is involuntarily exposed to a series of Web sites or his screen is taken over by cascades of pop-up advertisements that can only be interrupted by shutting down the system. Ferraro and Casey (2005: 281) describe this as the 'mousetrap' scenario and argue that it can be used persuasively as a defence in child pornography cases when the evidence is located only in temporary Internet storage, the number of images is few and they are thumbnail-sized. How can possession be 'knowing' if the computer automatically stored the images in its cache without any instruction to do so on the user's part? Such a position is given added weight if the individual does not know what a cache is or has little computer expertise. Under these circumstances, and in the absence of other evidence, it seems unlikely that criminal charges would be brought. If, on the other hand, there are numerous full size images and they have been saved or searched for by a user who can be shown to have knowledge of the internal workings of computer systems the defence is less credible.

So while an individual may have inadvertently stumbled upon contraband material, not being aware in advance that it was child pornography, and deleted it as soon as he realised what it was, he is still in possession of child pornography. This is true even if he considered the image horrific and genuinely thought that all traces of it had been wiped from his disk. If the offence were one of absolute liability there would be potential for injustice in such cases. The requirement that the possession be 'knowing' allows some room for manoeuvre. An unwelcome 'pop up', or a file with a misleading name that was opened and immediately discarded when the content became known, would not necessarily lead to criminal charges – but it could. According to Howard (2004: 1239–53) courts in the US have treated cache possession in different ways. A majority have determined that a cached image is enough to show knowing possession but some have rejected this view and others have simply noted the issue. This is an area where it is important to allow a measure of prosecutorial discretion.

While most computer users might view them as entirely distinct activities, involving widely different levels of commitment and intent, viewing and downloading are inextricably intertwined, and downloading equates with possession. The courts in England and Wales have taken matters one step further by finding in two cases in 2002 (*R v. Bowden* and *R v. Jayson*) that downloading an image to view on one's screen or printing an image from the Internet means 'making', as distinct from simply 'possessing', the material. Gillespie (2005) argues that these judgments have blurred the lines between two types of offending which differ in terms of seriousness. He recommends the introduction of new legislation to redraw the boundaries between personal access (including downloading) and the creation of images.

It is also possible that an individual's credit card details could be used, without their permission, to purchase illegal material online. But as in purchasing more generally the rule of *caveat emptor* ('let the buyer beware') applies. When A.D.'s home was raided during Operation Amethyst he was found to be in possession of 120 images of naked girls aged between 3 and 14 with adult males. His solicitor told the court that A.D. received the folders on his computer under the guise of adult pornography and did not know what was in them until they were downloaded and opened, whereupon he did his best to delete them. A.D.'s credit card details had been hacked after he used it for other sites, and on two occasions his bank accepted that the number had been used by someone else and refunded money to him. By searching for pornography to purchase he had exposed himself to the risk of criminal victimisation. The judge rejected this version of events stating, 'he knew what he was downloading and used his credit card for that purpose'. A.D. was sentenced to a prison term of six months, suspended for two years on condition that he entered into a €1,000 bond to keep the peace. An order was made for the confiscation of his computer and the destruction of the images (*The Irish Times*, 3 July 2003; *The Meath Chronicle*, 12 July 2003).

In a similar set of circumstances Y.A., a restaurateur, pleaded guilty to possession of 128 images of child pornography on a laptop computer in his home in May 2002. Y.A. denied that he was the person who had downloaded the material but said he was taking responsibility as he had 'not kept his eye on things'. Dublin district court heard that Y.A. left credit cards for his business, a Chinese restaurant, lying around his home. He allowed employees to stay with him and he claimed that it was one of them who used the credit card to pay for the images. The judge took into account that Y.A. was not the person involved in downloading the images. He sentenced the defendant to three months imprisonment but suspended it on condition that he pay €5,000 to a local hospice (*Irish Independent*, 4 December 2003). Just as there was no doubt that Y.A. and A.D. were in possession of child pornography – indeed they both pleaded guilty – it was also accepted by the court that their credit card details may have been used unlawfully by others. While this did not allow them to escape conviction, it seems to have mitigated the punishment.

It is also possible that an innocent person's credit card could be used to purchase child pornography leaving no trace on their personal computer. There have been such cases in England. Thompson and Williams (2004: 116) give the examples of the teacher taken into custody under Operation Ore whose credit card details had been taken by a colleague and used to purchase over 140,000 images, and the garden centre employee who had made a note of customers' credit card numbers and used them to fund his online purchasing.

We saw above, and set out in more detail in Chapter 4, how frequently the decision not to prosecute was based on the difficulty of establishing that the accused was knowingly in possession of material (usually found in temporary files or unallocated clusters). Removing the requirement that possession be 'knowing' would certainly increase the prosecution rate. But taking away this vital element of discretion would render liable to prosecution individuals who had stumbled across prohibited material inadvertently and deleted it at once. Even if such cases did not proceed to a conviction the stigma associated with involvement in the criminal process for the innocent, or careless, computer user greatly outweighs the possible return in terms of increased prosecutorial activity.

Procedural irregularities

A review of prosecution files and media coverage of child pornography cases revealed a number of reasons why prosecutions failed due to avoidable action on the part of *An Garda Síochána*. Sometimes cases fell because of administrative oversights such as not executing a warrant in good time.

The most high profile child pornography case in Ireland collapsed due to a defective warrant. A circuit court judge pleaded not guilty to possession of child pornography after his home was raided during Operation Amethyst. It was alleged that some 280 pornographic images were taken from the defendant's home computer, many of which were said to be deleted files that had to be restored by *Gardaí*. The DPP further alleged that the material contained images of children engaged in explicit sexual activity, or involved depictions of the genital or anal region of a child. The case collapsed and the defendant was acquitted by direction of the trial judge when it became clear that the search warrant had expired prior to its execution. Judge Carroll Moran said he had no alternative but to find that the evidence seized was inadmissible. He admonished the prosecution, noting: 'The law is crystal clear. The issue could not have been simpler and it was wrong for the prosecution to bring this case to trial when they knew, or ought to have known, that this finding would be the inevitable result' (*The Irish Times*, 19 December 2003; 24 April 2004).

Another case collapsed because the warrant had been signed by the wrong judge. G.S. (26) denied 15 counts of possession of images of female children engaged in sexually explicit activity stored on his home computer on various dates between 1999 and 2002. At trial his defence successfully argued that the warrant used to search G.S.'s house was defective because it had been signed by a judge outside the jurisdiction where the offence was alleged to have taken place. As a result the trial judge ruled that certain evidence was inadmissible and directed the jury to find G.S. not guilty (*The Irish Times*, 25 March 2003; 18 November 2004).

A final reason why no prosecution took place was that the police took too long in seeking directions. This meant that the six-month time limit for a summary prosecution had expired before a decision could be made by the DPP. If the case was not suitable to be dealt with on indictment this was the end of the matter. This difficulty is easy to rectify and, as we saw in Chapter 4, it became less significant as the experience of handling such cases broadened.

Potential challenges to successful prosecutions

In addition to the areas outlined above, which have already posed problems for police and prosecutors, there are a number of stumbling blocks that may emerge in the coming years. These have yet to be fully tested in the courts in Ireland but have been problematic in jurisdictions where similar legislation is in place. The most significant of them, as far as can be discerned from an examination of developments in other countries, are outlined next.

Trojan Horses

A Trojan Horse is a computer program, usually a virus, that is hidden or disguised as another program or an email. The individual unwittingly downloads what they believe to be safe and instead finds something designed to harm their system. According to Brenner *et al.* (2004: 8–9) the 'Trojan Horse Defence' (also known as the SODDI defence – 'Some Other Dude Did It'!) was first used in a case involving possession of child pornography in England. A forensics expert found a Trojan Horse program on the accused's computer and concluded that it was responsible for the images present on his hard drive. The charges were dismissed because the prosecution could not be sure, beyond reasonable doubt, that the accused was responsible for downloading the images. A few months later another man, on whose computer were found 172 indecent images of children and eleven Trojan horse programmes, used the same defence and achieved the same result.

A defendant in the USA went further, albeit in a different context. When charged with masterminding an attack on the computers of the port of Houston, Texas he argued that unspecified others had placed a Trojan on his machine and launched the attack without his knowledge. When forensic examination revealed no trace of a Trojan he argued that it must have completely erased itself. Despite the prosecution's claim that no available technology would allow this, the jury acquitted after a short period of deliberation (Brenner *et al.* 2004: 5–7). It is difficult to eliminate the SODDI possibility once it has been raised, especially given the reality that an unwary computer user can lose control of their machine and it can become a destination for illicit materials. They might find, for example, that pornographic Web sites had been added to their list of bookmarks.

The possibility that such inadvertent corruption can happen to anyone at anytime must impact on juror decision making. Brenner *et al.* (2004: 52–3) see this as a variation on a well-established theme, namely, 'the defense's use of complex, arcane technology to unsettle jurors and lead them to find reasonable doubt where there is none'. Part of the solution, they argue, is for prosecutors to better understand the technological issues 'thereby helping the jury understand that the mere possibility that something *could* have happened is not, in and of itself, enough to establish reasonable doubt in a criminal trial' (original emphasis). There may be a parallel earlier in the criminal process whereby offenders use their superior knowledge of computer technology to confuse police investigators or to lead them astray with abstruse jargon and complicated explanations. The third of the ACPO principles, regarding an audit trail that can withstand independent scrutiny (see Box 5.3, pp. 168–9), is important in this regard. The possibility of a Trojan Horse Defence has been raised in Irish courts on at least two occasions (see Box 6.1, p. 181–2) but in each case the prosecution failed before the defence could be tested.

Defining sexual purpose

The Child Trafficking and Pornography Act, 1998 defines child pornography as 'the depiction for a sexual purpose, of the genital or anal region of a child' (Section 2.1.c). Establishing that 'purpose' has been the cause of controversy in Canada where the same requirement applies, on the grounds that it forces the court to adopt the perspective of the paedophile and attempt to infer his motivation. In the view of Danay (2005: 158) this test 'imports a dangerously subjective element into prosecutions stemming from child pornography'. It requires the judge to establish not only that the accused has such material in his possession but to imagine its desired effect.

Danay (2005: 158–9) gives the example of the case of *R v. Nedelec* (2001) where one of the photographs in the possession of the accused was of a 3- or 4-year-old girl opening Christmas presents with her nightgown bunched up above her waist. The judge found that this picture was collected for a sexual purpose and as such constituted child pornography. He elaborated that: 'However innocently the picture was taken, the clear and prominent depiction of the little girl's genital area is startling'. Danay's contention is that if the image was really an innocent snapshot there should be nothing startling about the fact that the child's genitals happened to be exposed. When, after forensic examination and judicial consideration, such an image is defined as pornographic this reinforces the notion that children, in even the happiest and most unthreatening of domestic circumstances, can be considered as sexual objects.

Legislation based on obscenity is plagued by difficulties of definition and interpretation. This is exemplified by US Supreme Court Justice Potter Stewart's much cited observation in an obscenity case decided in 1964 (*Jacobellis v. Ohio*) that, as regards hard-core (adult) pornography, he might never be able to produce an intelligible definition of what constituted such material, 'But I know it when I see it'. The problem is, of course, that people see it from many different perspectives; what counts as 'indecent' or 'obscene' is a judgment open to individual interpretation. (For a critique of the vague and elastic nature of the obscene, and its role in the subordination of women, see Itzin 1992.) Similar difficulties are raised with the introduction, in legislation dealing with child pornography, of a subjective dimension around the purpose to which prohibited material might be put. While these provisions have yet to be tested in the Irish courts they seem open to disputation and appeal.

Anatomical focus

Under Section 2 of the Act, images identified as illegal (namely, those depicting the genital or anal region of a child or depictions of a child engaged in, or witnessing, explicit sexual activity) seem to exclude material involving naked children which shows breasts and buttocks but no more. This means that many images, which would be found in offenders' collections, and probably considered by the public to constitute child pornography, and by psychologists to contribute to the readiness to offend, would not come under the definition of the Act.

Take for example, a photograph of a well-developed topless 14-year-old girl in a typical 'glamour model' pose. Or a 9-year-old in skimpy lingerie. An individual who has a collection of thousands of such images, carefully filed and catalogued, does not appear to be committing an offence under the Act. While these images might have a sexual purpose, and the person in possession of them might pose a threat, the prosecution will not succeed if the focus is anatomically incorrect. The extent to which this presents a significant problem has yet to be revealed.

Age

Even if the material is unambiguously pornographic it must be established that a 'child' is involved. This can be problematic, particularly in borderline cases, when images depict individuals in their mid-teens. Considering the infrequency with which victims of child pornography are identified, clear evidence of age (such as a birth certificate) is scarcely ever available. Interestingly, under the Irish legislation the burden of proof is reversed here. If the individual in the image is deemed by the court to be aged under 17, the onus is on the defendant to prove to the contrary (Section 2.3), a task that would surely be impossible in most cases.

There is no doubting the popularity of the 'barely legal' and 'teen' genre of adult magazines that deliberately blur the adult/child distinction. Lane (2001: 125) also gives the example of Web sites that publish photographs of girls on their eighteenth birthdays. In his words: 'So long as accurate records are kept, the product is legal, and the closer that customers believe the models are to 18, the heavier the demand'. Taken 24 hours earlier the picture would be illegal but now it is fair game. The man who downloads such an image and emails it to his friends for their sexual gratification is committing no crime. A day earlier and, in law, he would have been part of a paedophile ring and a distributor of 'vile' material whose actions placed his good name and liberty in jeopardy. If convicted he would become a registered sex offender. The marketing of such materials as 'barely legal' no doubt provides viewers with an extra frisson of excitement.

An exposé in a tabloid newspaper revealed that one of the stars of what was described as Ireland's first series of hard-core pornography films, *F****d in Ireland*, was 16 when the films were made (*Sunday World*, 7 May 2006). This immediately transformed the films from legal adult fare to child pornography. Given the nature of the industry this may well have led to an increase in demand and additional profits for the manufacturer. It is difficult to imagine better publicity than a front-page story in Ireland's biggest selling Sunday tabloid. (A check of The British Girls Adult Films Database the week after the story appeared revealed that the movie was available on the Rude Europa label for purchase as a DVD (STG£20.95/€30.86) or to be viewed online over a broadband connection (STG£6.99/€10.30).)

Computer graphics

Section 2.1 of the Act defines child pornography broadly to include 'any representation, description or information produced by or from computer-graphics or by any other electronic or mechanical means'. If software is used to generate or modify an image so that the 'predominant impression conveyed is that the figure shown is a child' this satisfies the legislative definition, even if some of the principal characteristics shown are those of an adult (Section 2.2). This raises a question about the extent to which it is appropriate for the law to become involved in punishing conduct (for example, viewing computer-generated images) that involved no harm to a child. This issue, hotly contested in the USA, has not yet been raised in Ireland.

There are further complications when consideration moves, for example, to sexualised representations of cartoon characters, private textual records of fantasies, and literature or films of recognised artistic merit. In the latter case the Act exempts from prohibition any book or periodical that has been examined by the Censorship of Publications Board and deemed fit for circulation and, similarly, any film or video that has been granted a certificate.

The scenario described in Box 6.2, based on a Canadian case, could just as easily arise in Ireland given the similarity of the legislative environments. Precisely what child pornography is, as well as what it is not, may not be explicitly defined in a given jurisdiction. This can create problems for an international traveller who possesses material that is legal in his country of origin but not in his destination.

Box 6.2: Comics in Canada

A Canadian man received 18 months probation and 100 hours community service for possession of child pornography. Gordon Chin pleaded guilty but claimed he was unaware that the content was illegal in Canada. His collection was made up of child pornography cartoons, including cartoon images of naked, tied-up children and babies being raped with pistols. There were also sexualised images of popular TV cartoon characters (e.g. naked Pokemon). His court appearance was the culmination of a 10-month investigation that began when customs officials found explicit comic books in a package destined for Chin's home. Child pornography cartoons are technically legal in the United States (where a real child is required to make the material illegal), as well as in Japan where the content originated. Yet Canada's description of child pornography includes the 'visual representation' of children.

'Why would anyone want to look at stuff like this?' asked Judge David Tilley. 'I don't think this is the kind of filth that should be available to the public.' Defence Attorney D'arcy Depoe claimed Chin was ignorant of Canadian law and said there was nothing to suggest he was ever going to do anything with it other than look at it in the privacy of his own home. Chin was banned from owning a computer or using the Internet during his probation, and his name was added to the sex offender registry for five years.

(*Source*: retrieved 20 October 2005 from http://www.xbiz.com/news)

The production of child pornography does not always require a technologically sophisticated approach. Scissors and glue can lead to the same end result. For example, in one case heard at Dublin District Court a 49-year-old security man pleaded guilty to possession of child pornography at his home. He had cut out pictures of naked children from a naturist magazine and glued them into an adult pornography publication. The judge opined that the case came in at the lower end of the scale so imposed a fine of €500. The accused made a €3,000 donation to a children's charity (*Irish Independent*, 11 November 2006).

Bona fide research

Under Section 6.3 of the Act it is a defence for the person accused of possession of child pornography to prove that this was 'for the purposes of bona fide research'. This affords the protection of the law to the work carried out by the COPINE project in University College Cork (see Chapter 1). This possibility has not been raised as a defence yet, but it may well be in the future. It is likely that the chances of success in this regard will be slim. There have been a number of cases in England when the accused maintained that the material in his possession had been collected for research purposes, most notably the musician Pete Townshend (see Oswell 2006). According to Lanning (2001: 83) 'research' is an excuse regularly raised by paedophiles. This may serve psychological as well as legal purposes, being an exercise in rationalisation as well as a courtroom tactic.

Choosing an appropriate penalty

In August 2002 the Sentencing Advisory Panel (SAP) in London published its advice to the Court of Appeal on sentences for indecent images of children. It related the choice and length of sentence to the nature of the material and the degree of engagement with it. The following were suggested as appropriate starting points for an adult offender, found guilty after a trial, with no previous convictions for similar offences (the five levels are described in the closing pages of Chapter 3):

Fine	where the material was purely for personal use and consisted of a small quantity of Level 1 material or the collection consisted entirely of pseudo-photographs.
Community penalty	where there was a large amount of Level 1 material and/or a small number of images at Level 2 and the material had not been distributed or shown to anyone else.
Custody	where any of the material had been shown or circulated to others or where there was a moderate or large amount at Level 2 or above.

A short custodial sentence (up to six months) was deemed appropriate where there had been limited distribution of material at Levels 1 or 2 or possession of a small number of level 3 images. Sentences of more than three years were reserved for cases where images at Levels 4 or 5 had been shown or distributed or the offender was actively involved in the production of such images or had commissioned them. The English Court of Appeal accepted the advice of the SAP in November 2002 in the case of *R. v. Oliver*.

The sentencing exercise is more loosely structured in Ireland than in England and Wales and the idea of a variety of different thresholds, or, indeed, a tariff of any kind, does not apply with the same force. O'Malley (2004) outlined five sentencing principles that are particularly relevant to the Irish context when the punishment of child pornography is being considered. It is worth setting them out at some length.

First of all, that there should be a presumption against the imposition of a custodial sentence in cases of mere possession, including possession which has resulted from use of the Internet. This presumption may be rebutted where there is an unusually large number of images and where a reasonable proportion of them show actual children being subjected to sexual abuse or being treated in a particularly degrading manner, or where the children shown are very young. In deciding if the presumption has been rebutted, the court should have regard to the impact which the adverse publicity attaching to the conviction will have on the offender and the fact that the possession of the images is remote in time and place from the commission of the abuse itself.

Second, it is only in the most extreme and exceptional case that a custodial sentence should be imposed when all or most of the images are computer-generated or when they are in some other way pseudo-images of children.

Third, a custodial sentence may be appropriate when the offender has been involved in distributing, exchanging or trading in child pornography. If, however, that involvement has been slight, a non-custodial option or suspended sentence should be considered.

Fourth, there should be a presumption in favour of a custodial sentence when the offender has been engaged over a period of time in distributing child pornography, especially if the pornography in question shows children engaged in sexual acts or portrays them in a degrading fashion.

Fifth, and finally, when a court decides that a custodial sentence is merited, it should have regard to the sentences which have been imposed for offences involving the kind of behaviour reflected in the pornographic images in question and should then make appropriate reductions in light of the remoteness of the offender from the infliction of the abuse in question.

One difference is immediately apparent. This could perhaps be described as a more parsimonious attitude towards the use of custody. The advice to the English courts invokes this option more readily and applies it more widely. For example, any element of distribution, even of images at the less serious end of the scale, is likely to result in a period of incarceration.

When applying the above principles, O'Malley (2004) observed that the following may be treated as aggravating factors:

- The images have been distributed to one or more children.
- The offender has traded in child pornography for profit.
- The offender has previous convictions for child pornography or child abuse offences.
- The images show very young children being abused.
- The images have been posted on the Internet in such a way as to be reasonably accessible to the public.

He added a number of mitigating factors that could come into play:

- A plea of guilty.
- Evidence of remorse.
- Cooperation with the police and other law enforcement agencies (especially if the offender had furnished information which facilitated the detection of persons or organisations involved in the distribution of child pornography).
- The personal circumstances of the offender (for example, previous good character, absence of prior convictions, having made a useful contribution to society, the adverse social and economic consequences following on from a criminal conviction).

These factors are among those put forward by judges in interviews and summarised in Table 4.4 (see p. 144). Many of them were highlighted by the Court of Criminal Appeal in Dublin when it considered an appeal against sentence severity from a man convicted of possessing child pornography (*The Irish Times Law Report*, 15 May 2006). We have seen that judges were quicker to identify mitigating than aggravating factors. It is interesting to speculate why this might have been the case. One possibility is that they found it easier to pathologise the behaviour in question and this meant that they could see a much clearer role for treatment. These were offenders who could sometimes be seen as yielding to temptation rather than deliberately planning and perpetrating a criminal enterprise. Another factor is that the defendants in these cases were unfamiliar with the courts. Only one in eight had a previous conviction (see Box 4.4, pp. 126–7) making it easier to see their lapse as 'out of character'. This meant that the consequences for their lives were more dramatic and more immediate than in many of the cases that routinely come before the judiciary and involve young men from disadvantaged areas who are wearyingly familiar with the criminal justice system.

In the main, child pornography offenders had further to fall. It is possible that the cumulative impact of public exposure, stigma, and sex offender registration made them more pitiable. For some individuals the prosecution process was so damaging that the sentence of the court hardly mattered. In cases where imprisonment was not the clear-cut option, such considerations may have tilted the balance in the defendant's favour. Add to this the somewhat remote nature of the victims and the variation in the degree of engagement with pornography, and it is not surprising that judges regularly explained their decisions with reference to themes such as risk reduction rather than retribution.

The interviews conducted with judges for this study showed universal abhorrence for the crimes in question but also an occasionally striking confidence in the ability of the individual to change, and a willingness to accord significant weight to risk predictions offered by psychiatrists and psychologists. Many could separate the criminal from the crime and all gave careful thought to matching the penalty to the characteristics of the offender. They did not subscribe to the view that such men were incorrigible or inevitably deserved heavy punishment. This is not to say that they were lenient. As we saw in Table 4.5 (see p. 148) the full range of sentences, from probation to the maximum sentence of five years imprisonment, was used for the most common offence of possession. For more serious offences involving production, distribution or allowing a child to be used in pornography prison sentences were invariably imposed. They were usually fairly lengthy and seldom suspended.

The nature of the material is central to the consideration of an appropriate penalty. The SAP recommended that sentencers take the time to look at the images. The principles outlined by O'Malley are also based on a judgment about the content of the material (for example, victim age). Box 6.3 shows how the judicial perspective can alter after images have been viewed at first-hand. The reporting psychologist believed M.J. was a low risk but had not looked at the images found to be in his possession. The judge seemed to concur initially but when he saw the pictures in question he was outraged and reversed his initial inclination to spare the defendant from custody.

Box 6.3: Perspectives on risk

M.J., father of a two-year-old child, pleaded guilty to possession of child pornography after his home was raided during Operation Amethyst. Navan District Court heard that M.J. had more than 100 disturbing images, including girls as young as four in various sexual poses. There were also images with elements of rape, attempted rape and bestiality involving dogs.

Eight months previously Judge John Brophy adjourned M.J.'s case in order to allow him continue with treatment at the Granada Institute. He noted from reports that the defendant seemed to be progressing well and indicated that if further reports were as favourable, 'I may take a certain course and not record a conviction' [i.e. apply the Probation Act]. The follow-up report was very favourable with a therapist from the Granada Institute describing M.J. as a 'low risk offender' who had no interest in abusing children. However, she admitted that she had not seen the images.

Judge Brophy's intentions were revised when he viewed the offending material. 'I cannot say in my lifetime I have ever seen anything so revolting and disgusting and degrading for the children involved,' he told the court. He described the case as one of the most difficult he had encountered in his career and likened it to the Marc Dutroux case in Belgium. 'I physically felt like getting sick. That's how badly it affected me. It's one of the most difficult cases I have dealt with in thirteen-and-a-half years on the bench. At this point in time, I should have refused jurisdiction and sent him to judge and jury,' he said. 'No ordinary person in their right mind could look at this material. I felt sickened and revolted. You do not look at a little four or five-year-old girl with a giant Mastiff [breed of dog] attempting to have sex with her. That is out of the norm.' The people that were hurt were the innocent children M.J. had paid to see, who would have been sold to paedophiles or kidnapped and forced to carry out disgusting acts, he said.

Defence counsel said his client's life had been turned upside down as a result of the court case, which forced him to give up a well-paid job and move home. He had admitted his guilt at the first available opportunity and knew his behaviour was despicable, but had made every effort to address it. Rejecting a plea for leniency, the judge said

---

anyone prepared to give their credit card number and download the material he saw could only be described as a paedophile. He sentenced M.J. to six months in prison and placed him on the Sex Offenders Register for the mandated period.

(*Source*: *Irish Independent*, 25 March 2004)

Little comparative data is available regarding sentencing practice. In a study carried out several years before the SAP review, Edwards (2000) found that judges failed to recognise what she felt was the 'dangerousness' of persons convicted of possession or distribution. In her view sentencing reflected a notion of child pornographers as 'benign' and the sentences passed were 'derisory', with judges and magistrates reluctant to impose fines or prison terms commensurate with the seriousness of the offence. Looking at cases of possession sentenced by magistrates in 1997, around one in six led to imprisonment. Those convicted of taking indecent photographs who were dealt with by the crown court were most often jailed, but sentences tended to be relatively brief. Edwards (2000: 17) concluded that the courts were 'exceedingly lenient' with this category of offender. This is a surprising finding, especially given that the general experience in England and Wales since the early 1990s is of a growing willingness to use prison, and for longer than would have been considered conscionable in the past. It may be the case that a follow-up study would reveal an upward drift in the size of fines and the length of prison terms. It is also possible that the consistency of approach ushered in by the SAP guidelines would reduce the likelihood of apparently extreme outcomes.

The range of penalties varies dramatically across countries. Yar (2006: 116) contrasts the sentencing options in the USA and Greece. In the former country, the federal Child Protection and Sexual Predator Punishment Act, 1998, prescribes between ten and twenty years imprisonment for a first time offender, and thirty years to life for a recidivist. Under Greek law, the punishment for the same production and distribution offences is a fine and not more than one month in prison.

But even within the USA, where the overall level of punishment is high, there is extreme variation. Arizona man Morton Berger probably received the longest sentence ever imposed for possession of child pornography. In 2004, Berger was convicted on 20 counts of this offence. Under Arizona law each image was treated as a separate offence and because each depiction was of a child aged under 15 years the sentences had to be served consecutively. Taking account of the fact that Berger had no previous convictions, he received the maximum allowable mitigation which reduced the penalty per offence to ten years. This translated into two hundred consecutive years in custody, without any possibility of parole or pardon. Berger appealed to the Arizona Supreme Court on the grounds that the sentence violated the US Constitution's Eighth Amendment protections against cruel or unusual punishment. His conviction was upheld in May 2006. An appeal to the US Supreme Court failed in February 2007, meaning that the middle-aged father of four and former high school teacher will spend the rest of his natural life behind bars. (He got off lightly. The prosecutor had been seeking a 340-year penalty on the basis that the presumptive term for each crime of this kind is seventeen years. Under the least favourable circumstances he could have been given the maximum sentence of twenty-four years per image, a total of 480 years. This is evidence of the punitive obsession at its most stark, and most pointless.)

Looking at the situation in New South Wales between 2000 and 2003, Krone (2005b) found that for possession, a sentence of immediate custody was the exception (imposed in 13 per cent of cases). Most of those convicted were placed on a bond, given a suspended sentence or ordered to perform community service. For those dealt with for the offence of publishing child pornography, only one out of the 11 cases in the sample resulted in imprisonment (for three months). Five were placed on a bond, one was fined, two received suspended sentences and two were given community service orders. The range of sentences handed down in Irish courts appears to be broadly in line with what has been observed in England and Australia, but it seems that the courts have not been as reluctant to consider terms of imprisonment that stretched to several years (see Table 4.5, p. 148). Given the sketchy nature of the available data, contrasting legal environments and different time periods studied, this observation is made tentatively.

The totality of punishment

The Sex Offenders Act came into force in Ireland on 27 September 2001. Its central purpose is to impose a requirement on individuals who have been convicted of certain sexual offences to notify *An Garda Síochána* of specific information. The Act also provides for a new civil court order against sex offenders whose behaviour in the community gives the *Gardaí* reasonable cause for concern for the public's safety.

It creates a new offence for sex offenders who seek or accept work involving unsupervised contact with children without informing the employer of their conviction.

All sexual offences committed against children come under the provisions of this Act. Accordingly, individuals convicted of offences contrary to sections 3, 4, 5 or 6 of the Child Trafficking and Pornography Act, 1998, are subject to notification requirements. (The data collected from *An Garda Síochána* revealed that seven of the men who came to attention for offences under the Act had previously been convicted of sexual offences. In one case the date of the conviction was not available. In the other six it was prior to 2001, so no notification requirements applied.)

Registered individuals must notify *An Garda Síochána* of their names and addresses and any changes to their details to ensure that records are kept fully up to date. They are required to inform the *Gardaí* of any address where they stay for seven days or more. The duration of the notification requirement depends on the length of sentence, as shown in the following scheme:

- Indefinite if sentence imposed is imprisonment for more than two years.
- Ten years if sentence imposed is imprisonment for between six months and two years.
- Seven years if sentence imposed is imprisonment for six months or less.
- Five years if sentence imposed is non-custodial, including a fully suspended sentence.

Offenders who are subject to a lifetime notification requirement are given the option of applying to the court, not less than ten years following their release from prison, to be relieved of their obligation to notify the *Gardaí* of changes to their name or address. The court can so relieve them if it is satisfied that the common good is no longer served by their continuing obligation to keep the authorities appraised of their whereabouts. (The finite periods are halved in the case of offenders who are under 18 at the time of sentencing.)

While the registration requirement is not intended as an additional punishment, it clearly carries some punitive weight and constrains an individual's freedom of movement even after their sentence has expired. This has been recognised by the courts. In 2002, in *DPP v. NY*, the Court of Criminal Appeal described registration as 'a real and substantial punitive element, to which the court is entitled to have regard' when deciding on an appropriate sentence. The court's view was that the 'stigma' associated with the requirements of the Act was a relevant consideration, especially when sentencing an offender who was not considered to pose a continuing risk. The case in question involved a young man who had pleaded guilty to two counts of rape and had been sentenced to two concurrent terms of three years imprisonment, with the last nine months of each suspended unconditionally. His appeal against the severity of this sentence was successful, and given that he had already served seven months in prison, the balance of his sentence was suspended.

If it is acceptable to take account of the likely impact of registration when sentencing a rapist, it would be reasonable to assume that this consideration would carry even greater weight in the case of an individual convicted of possessing child pornography, especially if the offence was at the lower end of the scale of gravity. However, this is an area where the jurisprudence remains somewhat unclear. The day before the judgment in *NY*, the High Court, in *Enright v. Ireland*, took a contrary view, concluding that many ancillary penalties, including sex offender notification orders, were non-punitive in nature (see O'Malley, 2006: 95–100).

In addition to the notification requirements there is also the possibility of post-release supervision. The Sex Offenders Act, 2001 obliges the court to take account of public protection, crime prevention and individual rehabilitation when considering whether the sentence should incorporate an element of supervision after the custodial component ends. The combination of custody plus supervision cannot exceed the maximum term of imprisonment available for the offence. For child pornography cases this ranges from five years for possession to fourteen years for production or distribution. Conditions can be attached, such as participation in treatment or a prohibition on specified activities. The conditions can be varied or discharged at any time. While designed to reduce the risk posed by released sex offenders, the effect of these arrangements is to place restrictions on freedom post-release. Again, while not acknowledged as a penalty, supervision is clearly burdensome. It adds another layer of restrictions that magnify the intensity of the original sentence.

Non-compliance with notification requirements, or supervision conditions, is a summary offence carrying a penalty of up to 12 months imprisonment or a fine or both. The same sanction applies to any breach of an order made under the Act to prohibit specified activities. Individuals who conceal their conviction in an attempt to find work with vulnerable groups commit an offence that can be dealt with summarily or on indictment. If prosecuted on indictment the maximum penalty is five years imprisonment. In 2005 proceedings were taken on 18 occasions under the Sex Offenders Act. This compared with four in 2004, one in 2003 and none at all in 2002.

Eroding disparities

As highlighted throughout this book, the public is very sensitive to publicity devoted to child sexual exploitation. Couple this with a tendency for the media to sensationalise any suggestion of the abuse of a child and the result can be inaccurate or exaggerated reporting. The flipside of this argument is that some of the abuse has been so horrific that exaggeration would add little to the shock value. A simple statement of the facts is as much as the reader can be expected to bear.

Nevertheless, the public make threat assessments and form opinions based on what they learn from media reports. When the Operation Amethyst cases began their slow passage through the courts a perception of judicial leniency was communicated through the media. This gave way to a view that there was an unacceptable level of disparity in the way cases were treated. But media coverage does not always move beyond the initial court decisions. Later developments tend to be accorded a lower level of significance. The following pair of vignettes illustrates how incomplete reporting can distort public perceptions.

L.C., a 52-year-old Texan living in Dublin, was convicted of the possession of 175 child pornography images. Despite having pleaded guilty he received the maximum sentence of five years imprisonment, the last two of which were suspended (*Evening Herald*, 13 May 2005; *The Irish Times*, 11 February 2006; 15 May 2006). The previous year, a 55-year-old former mathematics teacher pleaded guilty to one count of gross indecency on a male person under the age of 17 and to the possession of cannabis resin for sale or supply. The Dublin man, who could not be named in order to protect his victims' identities, also pleaded guilty to the possession of child pornography in the form of a videocassette of himself performing oral sex on a young child. When *Gardaí* raided the man's home they found a 'minor cinema' in his attic with a camera and television and over 900 pornographic videos. They also discovered a number of sexually explicit sketches and postcards of naked men exposing their genitals to young boys.

201

The court heard that the man gave drugs to young boys when giving private lessons and made them watch the videos. When *Gardaí* seized videos of him performing indecent acts, he gave them the names of three victims, only one of whom was willing to make a statement. The accused protested that he did not sell the cannabis but gave it out free to young boys because he enjoyed their company. He said he bought pornographic videos from a man he met in a sex shop near Dublin city centre. The defendant avoided custody because he was the sole carer for his 92-year-old mother and received a four-year suspended sentence (*The Irish Times*, 28 January 2004).

On the face of it the handling of these cases suggests a gross disparity in how seriously the offences were viewed. The perpetrator of the crime that would be considered more serious by most people walked free, while L.C. received the maximum penalty allowed by law with no discount for his guilty plea. But this situation was later reversed. L.C. successfully appealed the severity of his sentence and in February 2006 it was reduced to one year's imprisonment. Because of the time he had served L.C. was released immediately. The teacher had his suspended sentence activated because he failed to abide by its conditions, having come to police attention for being drunk and disorderly. In other words the final outcome imparted a sense of balance. Given that the outcome of appeals results in little publicity, and that few would be aware of the fact that a suspended sentence was activated, the way that the original sentences changed would not have impinged on the public's awareness.

The erosion of disparities as a result of the decisions of superior courts, or the behaviour of convicted persons initially given the benefit of the doubt, would be known to few. In this way the checks and balances that are built into the system can be rendered invisible.

Also, the media can get it wrong. On occasion this fuels discontent or a perception of a system that is out of kilter with public sentiment or even at odds with justice. Consider the case of the celebrity chef referred to in Chapter 4, who was reported to have been fined €40,000 for possession of child pornography. This greatly annoyed the public who believed the man's wealth had bought him his freedom. But this was a misrepresentation of the facts. In reality he received a heftier punishment than some others who had engaged in criminality to a similar extent; namely, 240 hours of community service in lieu of a nine-month prison sentence. What was described as a fine was in fact a voluntary donation to charity.

Judges recognise the unbalanced handling of these cases by the media, especially the tabloid newspapers. Some of those interviewed for the study described in the second part of this book believed that it should be possible to prohibit publication of a defendant's name prior to conviction given the huge stigma associated with involvement, however peripheral, in child pornography. On a number of occasions judges went so far as to impose gagging orders on the media. In February 2006 such orders were deemed unconstitutional by the High Court as they breached the requirement that justice be administered in public. This decision was on foot of an action initiated by all of the national broadsheets (*The Irish Times*, *Irish Examiner* and Independent newspapers) and the national broadcaster (RTÉ). The legal team for the individual in question – a Church of Ireland clergyman – did not appeal this decision to the Supreme Court and he was duly 'outed'. He had been on bail since the order not to name him was made in July 2003 (*The Irish Times*, 16 February 2006; 18 February 2006).

Concluding comment

The Child Trafficking and Pornography Act, 1998, is regarded by some local commentators as 'one of the leading pieces of legislation in this area in the world' (Hotline 2004: 8). But this may be because by the time cases get to it, after a process of weeding out the weakest, guilty pleas are almost always entered. To date there have been few robust challenges to the legislation in the courts. Given that it remains largely untested, such optimism regarding its international significance is premature.

But, in any event, the effectiveness or otherwise of particular legislative formulations is only part of the picture. There is a wider issue to consider here. This is the extent to which a preoccupation with child pornography and abuse is a distraction from more pressing concerns. Furedi (2005: 107–125) shows how the conceptualisation of childhood as a particularly dangerous time has led to a dramatic erosion of freedom (for children) and a sometimes crippling sense of insecurity (for parents). Children, within the middle classes especially, are no longer allowed to walk to school unaccompanied, or to wander the fields or urban streetscapes without adult supervision. They are encouraged to consider any stranger as a potential threat and to view the world through a lens of suspicion and even hostility. An attitude of trust and openness is seen as evidence of vulnerability. More time is spent at home playing with electronic toys or living vicariously through television programmes. This restricted and sedentary lifestyle has negative implications for health and well- being. As Furedi puts it, childhood has been reorganised around the precautionary principle, that is, taking no unnecessary risks, however remote the possibility of harm.

This means that lives are willingly constrained to avoid the miniscule chance of being abducted or killed by a predatory stranger. But the inevitable consequence of such cosseting is more time on the road or at home, places where there is a greater likelihood of injury and harm. In a world that seems to be moving too fast and too unpredictably, our desire to protect the innocence of children has taken on a new edge. Just as a well-intentioned concern for the safety of children can reduce their life chances, so too can the response to child pornography have adverse consequences for society. It is to this paradox that we turn our attention next.

Chapter 7

Where to from here?

In the previous two chapters some of the challenges posed by the child pornography trade for criminal justice systems were reviewed. Here the focus shifts to the implications for society more generally of a fixation with stamping out sexual abuse. While this signals a laudable concern for child protection, it brings in its wake a number of unintended pernicious consequences. In particular, by its emphasis on the sexualisation of children, it aggravates the problem that it sets out to address.

When child pornography was legal, or its status was unclear, whatever media coverage it attracted had limited impact. The newspaper reader who learned of PIE or NAMBLA in the 1970s and wanted to find out more had to invest a significant amount of time and energy in making contact with the organisation. The curious but uncommitted reader was unlikely to have taken matters further. Now that the boundaries are unambiguously defined there is a great deal of coverage. News stories relating to child pornography attract disproportionate attention. All of it is adverse but it has the unfortunate side effect of piquing the interest of potential offenders. The audience is now global rather than national and the Internet means that further particulars are just a click away. The formation of a Dutch political party promoting paedophilia in 2006 (see Chapter 1) resulted in an entry in Wikipedia, the online encyclopedia, the same day. Anyone who wanted to learn more did not need to know the identities of those involved in the organisation or their location, nor did they need to jeopardise their own saftey by attempting to get in touch. All that was required was to switch on their personal computer and google the four letters 'PNVD'.

Any consideration of the criminal justice implications of child pornography needs to be alive to the broader relationship between child pornography (which is almost universally condemned) and childhood sexuality (the exploitation of which remains an important marketing tool). Today's society holds strong views on what constitutes an appropriate age for sexual behaviour with many countries only permitting young people to consent to sexual activity when they reach their mid- to late-teens, usually several years after they are deemed to be criminally responsible. For example, the age of consent in Denmark, France, Greece, and Sweden is 15; in the UK, the Netherlands, Finland and Belgium, it is 16. Laws concerning sexual activity between adults and children tend to be strict and, in general, penalties are severe. In this regard we should remember that the concept of childhood sexual innocence is of relatively recent provenance.

This notion of children differing from adults, and requiring specific protection in law, although not unwelcome, has not always existed. Historically, girls in particular have been considered ready for marriage from a young age, typically the onset of puberty. The idea that children are pure, chaste and innocent is somewhat novel. Historians, such as Philippe Ariès (1962), have argued that before the seventeenth century children were essentially viewed as miniature adults, and were therefore given the freedom to travel, work and have sex with little protection or meddling from their elders. They were exposed to coarse language and sexual innuendo. They drank and brawled and fornicated with great gusto.

Contemporaneous accounts of the early childhood of Louis XIII of France (1601–1643) show that he enthusiastically displayed his penis whenever an opportunity arose, to the great entertainment of his parents and servants, who were encouraged to touch and kiss the royal member. His first erections were a source of amusement to the Court as he described his 'drawbridge' and demonstrated how he could make it go up and down. Ariès (1962: 103) suggests that, 'There is no reason to believe that the moral climate was any different in other families, whether of nobles or commoners; the practice of associating children with the sexual ribaldries of adults formed part of contemporary manners'. From the vantage point of the early twenty-first century, such intimacies strike us as abnormal and even perverse. (Elias (1939/2000: 142–60) charts how, gradually, sexual behaviour became associated with shame and embarassment and was considered something from which children should be shielded.)

Pearsall (1969: 290) described the common practice of young children prostituting themselves in English cities during Victorian times, aided by the law which set the age of consent at 12. The extent of trafficking in children for sexual purposes was highlighted by W.T. Stead in a series of lengthy articles appearing under the title 'The maiden tribute of modern Babylon' in the *Pall Mall Gazette* in July 1885. The trade in young teenage virgins was particularly brisk. While street sex workers would rarely be this young today in developed countries (although, as Brown and Barrett (2002) show, the problem has not disappeared) their ready availability in places like Thailand and the Philippines has contributed to a thriving sex tourism industry.

Childhood as we know it did not exist in the past. Nor did adolescence as a buffer zone between childish incapacity and the burdens of adulthood. The *Oxford English Dictionary* shows that the word 'teenager' originated in the USA in the early 1940s. Before the Second World War, it would seem, children became 'grown ups' without a lengthy intervening stage during which this transition was negotiated. In most respects a 15- or 16-year-old girl today has no more rights than a 5- or 6-year-old in terms of sexual autonomy. This is despite the fact that biologically she is ready for motherhood and had she been born in a previous century to working parents she would have been in service or otherwise employed.

One consequence of the attenuation of childhood is that the vulnerability, innocence and dependence on others that it implies have been extended across a much wider age range than heretofore. In the name of child protection a conflict zone has been created around children and the expression of their desires. The extent to which youthful sexual allure both repels and attracts is a theme running through this chapter.

A modern malaise and an unforgiving response

Lee (2005: 14) notes that in 1975 an American psychiatry textbook estimated that one in a million children were sexually abused but that within a decade the figure was revised upwards to one in a hundred. By the end of the twentieth century the rate was put at one in four (Lanning and Burgess 1989; McGee *et al.* 2002). This fraction gained widespread acceptance and One in Four was adopted as the name of campaigning groups established in Ireland, the UK and the USA to give voice to the concerns of this (largely) silent minority.

The chances of winning the lottery, or being struck by lightening, remained at more than one in a million, but the odds of child sexual abuse were so reduced that to emerge from childhood unscathed seemed to now require a measure of good fortune.

Although there is a tendency to state that child abuse was 'discovered' in the 1970s and 1980s, this is perhaps a shorthand way of describing what was essentially a shift in mentality. The rape and sexual exploitation of children by parents and strangers are as old as time. What in fact happened in the late twentieth century was that there was a formal recognition that sexual activity perpetrated by adults against children was widespread and had unequivocally negative consequences. As the century drew to a close, the media 'discovered' the existence of the 'paedophile'. Nash (1999: 1) has described the 1990s as:

> The decade of the predatory sex offender, at least in terms of constructing a demon. Across the world a range of legislation has been set in place which seeks to single out this group of offenders for greater punishment, fewer rights and potential exclusion from society.

In an analysis of articles published in six leading British newspapers (*Guardian, Independent, Telegraph, Daily Mirror, Daily Mail, Times*), Soothill *et al.* (1998: 882) found nothing less than 'an explosion of interest in the topic among all these newspapers since 1996'. A similar analysis of the Irish newspaper of reference, *The Irish Times*, revealed a slightly earlier 'explosion', coinciding with the Fr Brendan Smyth scandal in 1994 (see Chapter 4), which for sub-editors provided the perfect coupling of 'paedophile priest'. A photograph of Smyth's scowling face as he appeared to lunge towards a cameraman outside the Four Courts in Dublin regularly accompanies stories about controversial sex abuse cases, even years after his death (see for example, *Irish Independent*, 1 June 2006). There was another surge of interest in 2002 when Operation Amethyst got underway (see Table 7.1).

It is interesting to note that photographs of Smyth taken while he was serving a prison sentence in Northern Ireland created a flurry of interest in that jurisdiction in 1995. The priest was shown wearing a prison uniform and collecting rubbish, said to be other prisoners' excrement, under the headline, 'Penance for a Pervert' (Greer 2003: 77). It seems that the combination of sex, sin, punishment and repentance is difficult for journalists to resist.

Table 7.1 Search of *The Irish Times* for 'paedophile' or 'paedophilia'

Start date	End date	Number of hits
1/6/1992	31/12/1992	2
1/1/1993	31/12/1993	8
1/1/1994	31/12/1994	241
1/1/1995	31/12/1995	181
1/1/1996	31/12/1996	231
1/1/1997	31/12/1997	185
1/1/1998	31/12/1998	161
1/1/1999	31/12/1999	151
1/1/2000	31/12/2000	98
1/1/2001	31/12/2001	93
1/1/2002	31/12/2002	229
1/1/2003	31/12/2003	108
1/1/2004	31/12/2004	81
1/1/2005	31/12/2005	119

(*Source*: LexisNexis)

There can be a striking contrast between lurid media headlines of remorseless predators and the lived reality of many offenders. The former is exaggerated, the latter is minimised, but all are demonised. How to address the needs of the pathetic lonely man who seeks solace in masturbating to images of children but finds only self-loathing and the detestation of his peers is seldom the focus of media attention. Greer (2003: 66) analysed the tendency for coverage of sex abuse cases to concentrate on events rather than wider issues such as aetiology, treatment, prevention and appropriate legal responses. He located this in organisational constraints such as tight deadlines and limited resources in newsrooms as well as in certain values that inform the construction of crime narratives, such as dramatisation, immediacy, personalisation and speculation. Greer further argued that this tendency has become entrenched in recent years with the result that 'press representations are becoming ever more impoverished in terms of their informative content' (p. 89). It seems that there is an inverse relationship between the amount of reporting and the dispassionate assessment of the issues; the more we read the less we really know.

Society's acceptance of adults who display a sexual interest in children, while marginal a generation ago, was somewhat benign (as evidenced by the emergence of groups such as PIE and NAMBLA in the 1970s). This has since decreased to the point of zero-tolerance. The label 'beast', 'monster' or 'fiend' becomes a complete description of the individual. There is little room for nuance. It seems impossible to countenance the possibility that a collector of child pornography could also be a loving parent, an enthusiastic sportsman, an accomplished musician, or a generous contributor to charitable organisations. The individual's personality is collapsed into a single criminal category in a destructive process of simplification. While there is an acceptance that, by and large, criminals can put their past behind them (or be seen as having acted out of character or in response to particular situational cues) this does not extend to the paedophile. There might be ex-offenders but never ex-sex-offenders.

Danay (2005: 164) quoted a Canadian member of parliament who told the House of Commons that: 'the recidivism of paedophiles is almost 100 per cent, if not 100 per cent'. Danay observed that this perception of paedophiles, while commonly held, was grossly inaccurate. He noted that the recidivism rates of child sex offenders are among the lowest in the criminal population. Such a view finds support from reconviction studies carried out in Britain and the USA (see for example Friendship and Thornton 2001).

The shame and stigma associated with being prosecuted for child pornography take a powerful toll. O'Malley (2006: 297) points out that these collateral hardships can sometimes be lethal: by early 2005 at least 33 persons questioned in connection with Operation Ore in the UK had committed suicide and in late 2004, in the course of a single week in Australia, six suicides directly connected with child pornography investigations took place. Campbell (2005) described the pressure associated with these criminal investigations – even when the suspect was exonerated – as 'toxic' and observed that, 'If any one of these people [suspects] has not been broken by the experience, no-one I know is aware of them'. In France, four child pornography suspects took their own lives in one five-day period. In the wake of these events, the deceased were described as involved in 'the legally minor – but professionally and socially devastating – crime of possession of videos portraying scenes of sex with children' (*Independent* (London), 23 June 1997). An example of the poisonous and enduring nature of a wrongful accusation is given in Box 7.1.

Box 7.1: The burden of 'unproven guilt'

On 16 April 2003, Toronto's police chief Julian Fantino held a news conference. The names of six men accused of using their credit cards to buy child pornography were released to the media. Five had already been apprehended and a warrant had been issued for the arrest of the sixth. Fantino explained the background: 'These Project Snowball arrests involve offenders from all walks of life, who live in every corner of the city. They only have one thing in common, and that is the criminal approach to their relationship with children'. The flawed investigation was to have tragic consequences.

According to Bob LeCraw, his brother James was 'on top of the world' prior to Project Snowball. 'He had a great job. Everything was going well for him.' All this changed when LeCraw was publicly named as a suspect. He lost his job as managing director of a non-profit agency that provided computers to schools. He had to take out a second mortgage to manage his increasing debt. His friends shunned him and his reputation was destroyed.

Despite the charges being withdrawn, he never recovered from the associated stigma. The once outgoing man became withdrawn. James LeCraw gave an interview the following year when he declared his innocence and called for changes in the way people accused of particularly offensive crimes are treated by the police and the media. After learning he was not going to be reinstated in his job, LeCraw made his feelings known in an email he wrote to his brothers: 'To be honest, I'm melting down with the inability to handle the anger, betrayal and frustration. So I guess there is no real innocence, just unproven guilt'.

James LeCraw committed suicide on 19 July 2004. He left behind a letter accusing Chief Fantino of issuing an irresponsible public statement that ruined his life. He asked his family to seek the legal redress he could not afford himself.

Of the five other suspects named at the 2003 news conference, only one was convicted and he has since applied for a new trial. One was never charged while three had the charges against them withdrawn.

(*Source*: CBC News, 10 January 2005, 14 March 2006; *The Globe and Mail*, 29 November 2004)

To refer to the loss of a child pornographer's life as a 'waste' or a 'tragedy' might cause hackles to rise in some quarters given the widely-held view that such offenders' crimes are so heinous they have squandered any right to mercy or forgiveness. That more latitude is extended to murderers and terrorists shows how the possessors of child pornography are seen to have plumbed the depths of depravity to such an extent that there is no way to resurface. Some judges in Ireland were sensitive to these hardships and, as we have seen, on occasion attempted to prohibit publication of defendants' names in the media. As one of them described it: 'I am also swayed by the basic unfairness that at any time until the arraignment the case against him can be withdrawn. I am not satisfied that the presumption of innocence gives him sufficient protection' (*The Irish Times*, 9 October 2003).

O'Malley (2004: 5–6) made the point that: 'The judicial punishment imposed on certain offenders is often less onerous than the prolonged hounding to which they are subject usually, though not exclusively, by the tabloid media'. The extremes to which this can lead are illustrated in an interesting case study by Cross (2005). This describes the release, in England, of 68-year-old Robert Oliver after serving a sentence for the rape and murder of a 14-year-old boy. Oliver was so reviled that even the suggestion he was present in a community was enough to mobilise angry public demonstrations. Newspapers were quick to publish photographs of him and to inform readers of his whereabouts. His life appeared to be in danger. Indeed, one of his known associates was shot dead at home shortly after being released from prison.

The solution was to offer Oliver accommodation in a special unit *within* the grounds of Nottingham prison. Although legally a free man he was required to give 24 hours notice if he wished to leave the unit and had to be accompanied by uniformed police officers while outside. Even this was not enough. The prison officer community was outraged and leaked information to the local newspapers about how public safety was being compromised. Although elderly and behind bars, the level of revulsion and fear was such that the threat was perceived to remain high and constant. This is an inevitable consequence of the social construction of the paedophile as a monster from whom the public can never be fully protected but against whom they must unite in horror and condemnation. Few people will have sympathy for Oliver's predicament, and remaining impartial is difficult given the awfulness of his crimes. Nonetheless the hue and cry led by the media inflamed public passions and denied Oliver the possibility of resettlement after release. It also demonstrated to potential vigilantes the willingness of certain elements of the media to find common purpose with them.

In many cases it is the conviction rather than the sentence that produces the greater quantum of punishment. Even somebody who does not lose their liberty still stands to lose their family, friends, job and standing in the community. Depending on the severity of the sanction they may be required to register as sex offenders for the rest of their lives. These are burdens not borne by other offenders, some of whom have been convicted of more serious offences. Consider the notoriety and celebrity that has been won by, for example, the Kray twins in England and 'Chopper' Read in Australia. These men, and many others, have become feted for their extreme violence and have inspired a series of books, movies and merchandise. Sometimes they are depicted as role models; men who, while indisputably 'forceful', are operating according to a recognised code of honour. The murderous Read has even starred in award-winning television commercials produced by the Pedestrian Council of Australia as part of an anti-drink-driving campaign. It is difficult to imagine any released paedophile coming to play such a role in public life.

Danay (2005: 153) believes that in an effort to mask our interest in sexualised children, and to allow the prurient consideration of child sexual abuse in the legal process, society has constructed a myth of the 'salivating paedophile', an incorrigible sexual predator, who lurks wherever children are found, poised to destroy innocence. This is the quintessential 'monstrous offender' which holds out such symbolic value to criminal justice systems, and allows a harsh and visceral response (see Kennedy 2000). The image of Fr Brendan Smyth, referred to above, has fulfilled this role in Ireland just as Moors murderer Myra Hindley did in the UK.

The scapegoating of certain classes of criminal serves a deeper purpose in terms of defining the boundaries of acceptable conduct and promoting social solidarity. But the boundaries are narrowly defined. The complexity of paedophilic sexuality is denied along with the inevitability that not all non-consensual sexual contacts between adults and children will cause irreparable damage, and the fact that many paedophiles remain abstinent for extended periods, sometimes throughout their lifetimes. (On the extent to which positive life changes can follow sexual assault, see Frazier et al. 2001.) Reflecting on these often unacknowledged aspects of the challenge posed by paedophilia, Schmidt (2002: 477) remarked, bravely, that: 'In view of the pedophile's burden, the necessity of denying himself the experience of love and sexuality, he deserves respect, rather than contempt'.

Perhaps the greatest fall-out from police operations against child pornography was that they challenged stereotypical notions of sex offenders and confronted the public with an unpalatable reality, namely that almost anyone could have an interest in viewing child sex. There was a shocking realisation that the nature of this criminal activity allowed offenders to live in harmony among their community and conduct their offending in the privacy of their homes. The identification of a number of high-profile figures awakened the public to the covert nature of child pornography offending. As O'Malley (2004: 11) expressed it:

> More than most other areas of the criminal law, child pornography offences have proved to be the great leveler. For most run-of-the-mill offences, it is usually those from less advantaged social groups who end up in prison. But the criminalisation of child pornography possession has repeatedly brought about the downfall of the great and the (formerly) good.

Previous studies have shown that those prosecuted for child pornography have a different profile to the young, working-class men found in courtrooms the world over. They come from all walks of life, vary widely in age and are often married and gainfully employed (see Chapter 3). This group of offenders has another distinguishing characteristic: a willingness to seek out treatment. This is a type of crime where individuals are seen to need psychological assistance and to be amenable to it. This distinguishes it from other sex crimes where the paramount concerns are punishment and victim impact. In Irish courts, at least, there is a focus on pathology and treatment; on dealing with offenders as individuals rather than punishing them as undifferentiated members of a criminal class.

There is an interesting contrast here. On the one hand these are seen as sick men who are given credit for seeking treatment to reduce the risk they pose. On the other they are seen as dangerous recidivists against whom we must always be on our guard. This polarisation is problematic and neglects a wider context that it is uncomfortable to acknowledge. It is that there are fewer degrees of difference than we might like to imagine between the man whose preference is for child pornography, the man who enjoys 'barely legal' content, and the man who is unperturbed (or perhaps even titillated?) by the way children are portrayed in advertising and the music industry. It is to the wider implications of a preoccupation with childhood sexuality that we now turn our attention.

Mixed messages

In 1980, the Calvin Klein clothing company launched a series of magazine and television advertisements for jeans showing child star Brooke Shields, in the guise of a sexually attractive woman, uttering the slogan, 'What comes between me and my Calvins? Nothing'. Despite its clearly sexual connotations, there was little adverse comment and sales of the jeans rocketed. In a thought-provoking article, Adler (2001a) argued that the obsession with child sexuality is illustrated by the changing response to advertising campaigns by Calvin Klein. She noted that the public's reaction to the next campaign was radically different. In August 1995, Calvin Klein's new multimillion-dollar jeans campaign was launched on television and on the sides of buses. In Adler's (2001a: 252) words:

> The campaign looked like fetish photographs of a pedophile. In one image, a pubescent girl spreads her legs to reveal white cotton panties under her short skirt. In the TV ads, the teenagers seem to be tricked into auditioning for a part in a pornographic movie. A critic called it 'the most profoundly disturbing campaign in TV history'.

A legal investigation into child pornography was initiated but the models proved to be adults. Nevertheless the advertising campaign was withdrawn amid a public outcry, even as sales of Calvin Klein jeans soared. By 1999, tolerance for any hint of child pornography had vanished as illustrated by the reaction to a third Calvin Klein advertising campaign launched in February of that year. This time the focus was on two young boys (aged about 4 or 5) who were shown jumping on a sofa in their underwear. The company said the advert showed 'children smiling, laughing and just being themselves' (*New York Daily News*, 1 March 1999 – quoting Calvin Klein). The public unhesitatingly perceived the advert as child pornography and the outrage was so vociferous that it forced the withdrawal of the campaign within a day.

Advertising campaigns of this kind do not emerge spontaneously. They are carefully assembled to make a strong emotional appeal. In 1988, Calvin Klein commented that 'I've done everything [in my advertisements] I could do in a provocative sense without being arrested' (cited in *The Guardian*, 16 April 2003). Adler (2001a) argues that the differing reactions to such campaigns are symptoms of a more worrying development. She claims that the cultural fascination with child abuse, driven by the media and increasing attempts to legislate child pornography out of existence, have conditioned society to search for signs of sex in very ordinary portrayals of children. The image of two little boys jumping on a sofa could have been taken from any family album yet it led to public shock and dismay. Adler (2001a: 256) described this transformation in the following terms: 'Child pornography law has changed the way we look at children. I mean this literally. The law requires us to study pictures of children to uncover their potential sexual meanings, and in doing so, it explicitly exhorts us to take on the perspective of the paedophile'.

Writing for *The Irish Times* (20 December 2003), Breda O'Brien echoed this concern at the growing tendency among adults to adopt the paedophile's gaze:

> On a bus journey into the city centre of Dublin the other day, I noticed that Benetton's windows currently feature huge posters of a blonde toddler, naked except for a pair of angel wings. I was disturbed both by the picture and by my reaction to it. I wondered was it another Benetton stunt, like the pictures of operations and car bombs which they used for shock value a few years ago? In a climate where child abuse is continually in the news, are they being deliberately provocative? Then I wondered what had become of us, that a picture of a beautiful child should arouse such suspicions? … It is not so much the innocence of children which is being stolen, but the innocence of parents.

It is hardly surprising that adults are confused by their reaction to certain images, bombarded as they are on a daily basis by media reports that give mixed messages about approaches to child protection. Parents are regularly warned about the increasing dangers of predatory paedophiles and could be forgiven for believing that their children are at significant risk of abduction or online seduction. Yet, the majority of child sexual abuse incidents involve acquaintances or family members and the Internet plays no part. In addition, tabloid newspapers have increasingly adopted the role of moral crusaders and, supposedly in the public interest, have run a number of notorious campaigns to 'out' paedophiles so their neighbours can take 'appropriate' action. Editors claim that they have a duty to inform their readers and that their actions are in the best interests of child welfare and community safety.

It is common in the USA for residents to be notified if a convicted sex offender moves into their neighbourhood (see Zevitz and Farkas 2000). They are typically provided with information including a photograph, a physical description, a criminal history and details of how victims are targeted. In 1990, the state of Washington was the first to enact a sex offender community notification law. Four years later, similar provisions were introduced in New Jersey, when a 7-year-old girl, Megan Kanka, was raped and murdered by a violent sex offender living anonymously across the street. This was rapidly followed by new federal legislation requiring states to maintain registers of sex offenders released from prison and to make information available to communities.

There is a deeply pernicious consequence here: while newspaper sales and television ratings shoot up so too does the risk to children. Vigilantism makes it more difficult for agencies to work with offenders in the community, increasing the risk of them becoming socially isolated, 'going to ground' and abusing more children. It can be counterproductive in other ways too. For example in south Wales, a female hospital doctor fled her home because locals confused 'paediatrician' with 'paedophile' and daubed her property with the word 'paedo' in the middle of the night (*The Guardian*, 30 August 2000). The farcical, but dangerous, extremes to which this concern can be taken are evidenced by the front-page story in a Scottish newspaper that a vigilante group had equipped itself with night-vision viewers and a blacked-out van so that it could patrol the streets of Edinburgh and force known sex offenders out of the city (*Daily Record*, 29 December 2006). A shocking case of vigilantism involved 20-year-old Stephen Marshall who visited Maine's online sex offender register and researched the names and addresses of at least 34 people. He then took his father's pickup truck and three firearms and began to call to the locations on his list. In four cases there was no one at home when he knocked on the door. In two others he found his target and shot him dead. Marshall took his own life before he could be apprehended (*The Globe and Mail*, 25 April 2006).

More disturbing are the ways in which the same media outlets that hound paedophiles blatantly push the boundaries of what is legal. While the front page may scream for retribution for a convicted sex offender or more usually 'kid porn perv' (even one who has served his sentence), turn to page three and a young woman (often barely over the age of consent) is shown topless while another few pages on readers are encouraged to dial premium rate numbers to chat with 'Lolita' (for example, *Weekly Sport*, 3 November 2005). As Polly Toynbee, writing for *The Guardian* newspaper (13 March 2001) observed:

> Hypocrisy is far too weak a word for the *News of the World* [leading UK Sunday paper]. It is their world that has ensured 'innocent' children are surrounded by sexual imagery, pert page three nipples, saucy sexy questionnaires, bonking on every page, a universe grotesquely distorted. Nine-year-olds deep into soap plots on Aids and incest are sold glittery boob tubes for pre-boob girls and bump and grind to rap artists slapping their bitches up. But wait! Here is the *News of the World*, defender of the innocents, riding out to protect them from the awful danger of a handful of snaps of a mother's naked children [reference to Julia Somerville, see further below].

Even socially 'acceptable' depictions of children can leave many feeling uncomfortable. For example, it is common practice for child models and actors to wear full makeup. Couple this with pre-pubescent children modelling underwear in popular clothing catalogues and suddenly the boundaries of acceptability are no longer clear-cut. The Council of Europe (1991: 4–5) drew attention to 'Lolita' fashions and the eroticisation of children in commercial advertising. They noted that: 'Advertisers, in particular, have recently begun to rely on the impact of juvenile seduction, using it in the same way as "conventional" erotic advertising. In so doing, they may have the effect of encouraging those who wish to widen the choice of sexual partners by means of overtly paedophile propaganda.' The Council recommended discouraging and preventing any abuse of children's pictures and voices in an erotic context. This plea for restraint has had little impact. Children and sex are sometimes juxtaposed to create a 'humorous' effect. Elliott (1992: 217) describes the mass produced greeting card which carries the words 'I hate to bother you with my little personal problem' over a picture of two-year old girl. Inside, the child is shown sitting in her nappy under the caption, 'But I'm horny!!!'

In the name of entertainment, children's identities are being subsumed within adult fashions. Gillespie (2004: 362) commented on society's 'schizophrenic approach to the issue of child sexuality'. He noted how those labelled paedophiles are castigated at the same time as the sexualisation of teenagers is big business. He cited the example of the Russian pop-group *t.A.T.u.* who hit number one in the UK and Irish charts in 2003 with a song where both teenage band members dressed as schoolgirls and, in a provocative video, danced with and kissed each other (the band's name is a Russian acronym for 'This Girl Loves That Girl'). A spokesperson for the band said that they were aiming for the 'pervert market'. Gillespie interpreted this as a 'tongue-in-cheek' remark but other commentators suggest a sinister marketing strategy. In February 2003 *The Sun* newspaper quoted the band's manager as follows: 'I got the idea of Tatu from market research. I saw that most people look up pornography on the Internet and of those, most are looking for underage sex. I saw their needs weren't fulfilled. Later, it turned out, I was right. This is the same as my own desires. I prefer underage girls.' The newspaper went on to allege that the manager, a former child psychologist, had slept with one of the singers when she was 14.

There is nothing new about popular culture exploiting the pervasive latent interest in sexualised children. In 1975 Playboy Press published nude photographs of 10-year-old Brooke Shields. The photographer, who took them with parental consent, described his subject as 'the first prepubescent sex symbol in the world' and prints of his portraits soon became highly sought after and very expensive (Crewdson 1988: 248).

In 2003, the major retail outlet British Home Stores (Bhs), was criticised for selling padded bras and branded briefs in its Little Miss Naughty range, aimed at girls aged 10 and under. A spokesman for Bhs described the underwear as 'harmless fun' (*BBC News*, 26 March 2003). The previous year the retailer Abercrombie & Fitch came under fire in New York for offering pre-teens thong underwear with the words 'eye candy' and 'wink wink' printed on the front (*CNN News*, 22 May 2002). Marketing companies had found a new and lucrative niche, which they called KGOY (Kids Getting Older Younger). This trend arrived in Ireland a couple of years later when the National Parents' Council protested at the sale, in Penneys department store, of padded bras for girls aged 9 and 10 and knickers for the same age group carrying the message: 'This chick bites back'. The store defended the sale of these items arguing that the bras were 'moulded rather than padded items and they are made that way for modesty rather than shape enhancement purposes' and that the slogans were age appropriate (*Irish Independent*, 21 August 2006).

To push this argument further take the extreme example of JonBenet Ramsey. The 6-year-old Beauty Pageant Queen was murdered in Boulder, Colorado, in December 1996. Numerous theories circulated about the circumstances of her death, including the possibility that she was accidentally killed while attempts were being made to photograph her pornographically (Singular 1999: 212). It was not until August 2006 that an arrest was made when 41-year-old American schoolteacher, John Mark Karr, came to the attention of the authorities in Bangkok and admitted to the killing (*New York Times*, 17 August 2006). Karr told police that he was with JonBenet when she died, but stated that he loved her and the death was accidental (*CNN.com*, 17 August 2006).

Despite the time that had elapsed since the killing and the fact that the murder had taken place on a different continent, this arrest made the headlines immediately in Europe and became a global news story. Within days Karr was returned to the United States to face the rigours of the law. When basic forensic tests were carried out, it was quickly concluded that his 'confession' was the ranting of a fantasist, obsessed – like so many of his fellow Americans – with the death of a beautiful child from a rich family. All charges were abruptly dropped but Karr remained in custody because authorities in Northern California asked that he be sent there to face child pornography charges. In October 2006 all the remaining matters against Karr were struck out because crucial evidence had been lost.

There is a disturbing angle to this tale. The country that was baying for Karr's blood because of his interest in underage sex was the same place where, aged 19, he was able to take a 13-year-old as his first wife (*The Killing of JonBenet: An Evil Twist*, 5 December 2006, Channel 4 Television). This marriage was annulled and several years later Karr married again, this time a 16-year-old pregnant with his twins. It is difficult to imagine a better example of the coexistence in a society of confused attitudes to children's sexuality and child protection.

JonBenet's pageant pictures are widely circulated on the Internet. It requires little imagination on the part of the viewer to see how they might appeal to adults with a sexual interest in children. Consider the following description of two of her costumes (Singular 1999: 46):

> In one photograph, she was vamping in a tight black leotard, her skirt flung over her shoulder, her hand placed provocatively on her thigh, and her feet and ankles tied with black straps. In another, she wore bright red lipstick and a white dress, imitating the signature style of America's greatest sexual icon. A large button on this outfit read, *Hello, I'm Marilyn Monroe.*

Footage of this kind was broadcast repeatedly after JonBenet's death leading CBS news anchor Dan Rather to condemn the television industry for airing pictures that 'border on kiddie porn' (cited in Adler 2001a: 254). But this is an area where standards are somewhat elastic. The Ramsay summer residence in Michigan was included on tours of the area's finer homes. In the parents' bedroom visitors could see a photograph of JonBenet 'with a provocative expression on her face, wearing nothing but make-up and a feather boa snaking around her torso' (Singular 1999: 160).

But is this overlapping of prurience and innocence really so unique? Not if we consider footage of the young Britney Spears's performances – big voice, big hair, pouting lips, short skirts; an image that helped her to achieve international superstardom. As her biography on a number of music Web sites notes: 'From the outset, Spears's sex appeal was an important part of her image; the video for her debut single, 'Baby One More Time', outfitted her in full Catholic-school regalia, and sent her well on the way to becoming an international sex symbol.' For a long time, Spears's management achieved a remarkable balancing act. She portrayed a wholesome innocence which endeared her to legions of young female devotees, even going so far as to swear chastity until marriage. However, her provocative and uninhibited sexuality enticed many male fans, and made her a pin-up for all ages.

Britney's Dublin concerts were a sell-out in 2004 despite criticism of her overtly sexual on-stage performances. One daily newspaper gave its readers a tantalising glimpse of what they had missed: 'Britney mimed more than just songs, she also worked her way through a costumer's Kama Sutra ... Towards the end, dancers in skin-toned underwear, on beds, were throwing shapes which shocked and horrified those parents who took their youngsters to the show' (*Irish Examiner*, 3 June 2004). Another observed: 'SEX SELLS. Just ask Britney Spears. Simulated fellatio, eye-popping, figure-hugging outfits and more lingerie than you'd find at an Ann Summers girlie party are the controversial trademarks of her Onyx Hotel Tour. The tour, which ended its Irish leg last night, may have been the most sexually explicit ever performed by a mass-market pop star in this country. But the sex-obsessed stage show didn't hinder ticket sales' (*Irish Independent*, 7 June 2004). While journalists stoked up the controversy, the concerts attracted full houses every night and there were no reports of parents marching out in protest. In an environment where innocence, youth and sexual fantasy are wrapped up to sell music and fashions, and where the public quivers with indignation at any hint of improper sexual interest in children, it could be argued that the demand for child pornography has risen in proportion to the condemnation directed towards its users.

The story of Thea Pumbroek, with which we closed Chapter 3, forces one to confront the wrecked child behind the movie 'star'. Thea's purpose was to sexually arouse adults and for this she paid with her life. A natural response to such a tragedy is to see it as an isolated incident. This is comforting but misleading. At first glance it would be ludicrous to compare Thea with modern-day pop starlets. However, they are points on a continuum. There can be little denying the blatantly sexualised image which child entertainers are sometimes forced to adopt in order to compete in the cutthroat industry that is show business. This link is laid bare when managers cynically declare that they are aiming for the 'pervert market'. Some might put this down to 'changing times', as the alternative is too difficult to stomach. This raises, in a pointed fashion, the question of whether society has sanitised the child pornography trade and offered back to us the all singing, all dancing, lip pouting, seductively posing, child star.

A dangerous distraction?

The foregoing should not be taken to imply that nothing is being done to protect children. The opposite is true. Never before have children received so much attention from legislators, policy makers and concerned citizens. The past twenty-five years have witnessed a global tsunami of laws and promises. As child pornography became recognised as sexual abuse and exploitation, rather than a matter of personal choice and sexual preference, it became defined exclusively as a criminal justice issue. Since then, child pornography law has taken on a life of its own. New technologies (for example camera phones) and new crimes (for example online grooming) have ensured that the legislation is under regular review. Constant vigilance is seen as a small price to pay to protect the innocence of children and few have disputed the necessity of an unambiguous legal response even if in reality its impact will, at best, be slight.

This is symbolic politics *par excellence*, which is not to say that it is not valuable, merely to be realistic about its likely impact. As outlined in chapters 5 and 6, there are enormous practical difficulties policing, prosecuting and punishing a crime that often involves the transmission across borders of encrypted images directly between two like-minded individuals. Sometimes major breakthroughs lead to mass arrests but as the child pornographers learn the latest law enforcement tactics they revise their *modus operandi* to stay one step ahead. Some of them are foolish, others careless and a few become complacent or arrogant. They may be caught and brought to justice. Many more will not be. The attempt to protect victims is Sisyphean.

Returning once again to Adler (2001a: 213), she is not so sure about the value of privileging a formal legislative response and argues forcefully that child pornography law has paradoxical consequences. As she explained:

The growth of child pornography law has opened up a whole arena for the elaborate exploration of children as sexual creatures. Cases require courts to engage in long, detailed analyses of the 'sexual coyness' or playfulness of children, and of their potential to arouse. Courts have undertaken Talmudic discussions of the meaning of 'pubic area' and 'discernibility' of a child's genitals in a picture at issue. But even when a child is pictured as a sexual victim rather than a sexual siren, the child is still pictured as sexual. Child pornography law becomes in this view a vast realm of discourse in which the image of the child as sexual is preserved and multiplied.

Elaborating on Adler's arguments, Danay (2005: 163) highlighted several examples of close judicial engagement with the graphic details of child pornography images. For example, at a sentencing hearing for an individual convicted of possessing child pornography in Canada (*R. v. Hardy* 2002), the judge described some of the material in the following terms: 'A little girl is shown being mounted by a German Shepherd. Children are shown masturbating each other. Children are shown in bondage ... The toddler is heard crying "No No." Another picture shows the rape of a handcuffed and hooded child.' Danay's argument is that this excerpt (heavily censored for inclusion here) demonstrates how condemnations of hard-core pornography can become virtually indistinguishable from the salacious description of the impugned material. Similar comments might bring the author into conflict with the law if found among their private jottings. But they are a legitimate part of the legal discourse when articulated in open court. This has a further unintended and unpleasant consequence. Descriptions of real-world situations, such as court transcripts from child sexual abuse cases, are sometimes exchanged between prisoners for sexual titillation (Sampson 1994: 92). In this way the deliberations of the courts can feed into the sexual gratification of the very individuals whose conduct is being denounced.

So too can the actions of some of the organisations that have been set up by purportedly well-intentioned citizens to hunt down sexual predators on the Internet. One such group styles itself Perverted Justice. Its members adopt an underage persona and then visit chat rooms where they wait to be approached by adults who express a sexual interest in children. The transcripts of the ensuing conversations are posted to the organisation's Web site (http://www.perverted-justice.com) along with other material, such as video footage of men masturbating in front of their Webcams to an audience that they mistakenly believe to be a child whose interest they have aroused. Instead an explicit record of their actions is passed on to law enforcement authorities before being made available on the Internet.

The organisation claims that between June 2004 and the end of 2006 it was responsible for 121 convictions of sex offenders. The paradox is that some of the material available on the Web site is so graphic that it would doubtless be a source of fantasy material to the very people whose conduct is of such concern. The transcript of the conversation between Sadlilgrrl (a 23-year-old volunteer posing as a lonely 13-year-old) and Fleet Captain Jaime Wolfe (a 34-year-old man arrested when he went to meet his new conquest at a video store) involves highly explicit talk of anal sex, bondage, sadism and bestiality. It is a shocking record of the extent to which some computer users will go to corrupt minors. It also raises real concerns about the roles adults are prepared to play, and the fantasies they are quick to stimulate and endorse, in the name of child protection. It has been decided that no purpose would be served by reproducing it, or a similar transcript here, other than to commit the error that we are concerned to highlight.

As an aside, it is interesting to note that the report of the US Attorney General's Commission on Pornography (*Meese Commission*) published in 1986 contained a lengthy appendix of excerpts from adult literature and descriptions of pornographic films. According to Lane (2001: 107) this made it 'one of the decade's most sexually explicit works', a somewhat ironic outcome given its emphatic denunciation of the harms caused by pornography. To add insult to irony, many religious bookshops refused to stock the report for fear that it would offend their customers, whose concerns it had been designed to assuage.

Accordingly, the strategies intended to eliminate child pornograp
may in fact be creating a bigger market for it. Campaigners constant
beseech us to be vigilant, to be on the lookout for potential exploiter
And as we strive to protect those who are too young to look afte
their own interests, we become finely tuned to detect any threats
So finely tuned that a well-meaning pharmacy assistant in the
UK reported ITN newsreader, Julia Somerville, to the police for
attempting to develop pictures of her 7-year-old daughter in the
bath. The assistant acknowledged that the child 'was smiling and
didn't seem miserable or worried' but what alarmed him was that
there were 28 photographs which was 'too many' and a duplicate
set of prints had been requested (Furedi 2005: 75). A celebration of
childhood innocence and fun had been reinterpreted as a possibly
criminal perversion.

Ms Somerville and her partner were questioned for a number of
hours by the police and there was extensive media intrusion into
their private lives, to say nothing of the effect on their daughter. The
case was dropped after four weeks. Reflecting on the matter a few
years later, in the context of a wider analysis of art and censorship,
Polly Toynbee wrote that:

> This is the legacy of paedophile hysteria. Children do take
> their clothes off, do run about gardens and beaches and are
> photographed by parents to capture just such never-again
> innocence. But the current obsession with child sex forces
> everyone to view the world through paedophile eyes. The
> abhorrent aberrant has won, making us all dirty voyeurs by
> proxy ... but that lets paedophiles set the standard for what is
> normal. Their warped vision of immature genitals now has to
> be imposed upon us all. Nude and rude adults can be thrust
> obscenely everywhere, but children's bodies must be shrouded
> as if they were indeed sexual. This is the world upside down –
> the paedophile's view, not ours. (*The Guardian*, 13 March 2001)

Photographs do not always speak for themselves. Viewers react
to them and this determines the force of their emotional impact.
Edwards (1994) juxtaposed erotic images of naked American children
(taken by well-known photographers Robert Mappelthorpe and Sally
Mann) with a photograph of a partially clothed child prostitute in
Dhaka, Bangladesh. Mapplethorpe's subject is a blond boy depicted
sitting on the back of an armchair, facing the camera with legs
spread. The chair seems to be positioned beside a fridge in a normal

225

stic setting. The boy looks directly at the lens and his genitals
early exposed. Mann's portrait is of her own daughter, shown
rontal. The background is black; there is no context. Her hands
laced over her non-existent breasts and her gaze is averted. Like
plethorpe's boy her expression is enigmatic. The child prostitute
ontrast appears to be smiling. She wears a skirt and jewellery
her arms are folded across her stomach. She is pictured on the
t. Behind her stands a man grabbing his crotch. In all three cases
subject of the photograph is clearly pre-pubescent.

is likely that viewers will be less disturbed by the picture of
child who is raped for pay than the well-fed Americans whose
grity is not intentionally under threat, although their images may
used to satisfy paedophilic lust. This says something about the
dity of our concerns: the child who most obviously demands
ipathy and protection ceases to move us while snapshots of nude
dren taken by their parents cause outrage.

The drive to eradicate child pornography is a distraction from
iportant issues such as child poverty, discrimination, early school
eaving and marginalisation. These factors diminish children's life
chances and render them vulnerable to a myriad of harms, including
sexual abuse. These child victims are more plentiful and easier to
identify than those whose abuse is captured on film. By placing child
pornography centre stage these subtler harms are downplayed. This
is a disturbing example of how a society can be blind to the factors
that predispose its junior citizens to victimisation while at the same
time serving up a substantial measure of righteous indignation for
the small number of offenders who are brought to justice.

The 'paedophile' is a convenient vessel into which a society
can pour its fear, uncertainty and guilt. If this emotional energy,
and the resources that follow it, were directed instead towards
the enhanced protection of children exposed to neglect, poverty,
inadequate nutrition, environmental contamination and premature
death, the social benefits would be substantial. In this regard it is
salutary to remember that, despite significant advances in medicine,
more than 10 million children die each year and the vast majority of
these deaths are preventable with current technology (Lopez 2000).
Diarrhoea continues to place young lives in jeopardy in developing
countries but is inconsequential elsewhere. Also a child's life chances
in a poor country can be severely restricted by afflictions that are
easily remedied in Western nations (for example blindness, cleft lip
and palate). This is to say nothing of the risks faced by child soldiers
and slave labourers.

Child protection is about changing the political arrangements tl allow such harms to persist. This message can sometimes get lc in the alarm about child sexual abuse. Kincaid (1998: 290) expresse this well when he made the striking comment that, 'our franti babble over outrages to the sexual being of children is a mask fo. our lack of concern, our willingness to overlook the battered and the starving, the impoverished and ill-educated, those without comfort and without hope'. Indeed it is precisely these poor and undervalued children who become targets for the citizens of wealthy countries who travel to their poorer neighbours to rape and film with little prospect of apprehension. Even if a criminal prosecution ensues under such circumstances, economic realities can come into play to affect the outcome.

When 61-year-old Gary Glitter was accused of child rape in Vietnam in November 2005 he faced a possible death penalty. The payment of STG£1,100 (€1,600) in 'compensation' to each of the two alleged victims' families resulted in them writing letters to the court asking for the case against him to be dropped (*The People*, 1 January 2006). Nguyen Van Xung, deputy chief prosecutor, said: 'It will not affect the investigation and the trial process, but the court may consider it as a factor to lessen the sentence' (*The Herald* (Scotland), 29 December 2005). Glitter still faced charges of sexually assaulting the girls (one of whom was only 10 at the time) and risked re-arrest on his return to the UK on sex tourism charges. In March 2006 he was sentenced to three years imprisonment with the possibility of parole after serving one. The court ordered the destruction of his laptop computer's hard drive on which police had found 2,231 pornographic images of children and 31 'paedophile films'. This was not the first time that Glitter had been accused of an illegal interest in children (we noted in Chapter 3 that he had been jailed in 1999 for possession of child pornography).

Despite the hysteria that has accompanied the debate on child pornography over the past decade it would seem that not all of a nation's children are cherished equally. As we have seen, underlying the high level of expressed rage at the destruction of innocence there is an ambivalence regarding some aspects of childhood sexuality which are seen as cute rather than criminal. In addition it would seem that some instances of abuse receive far less attention than they deserve given the harms in question. Victim empathy seems to have a hierarchical quality. Consider the following example.

In 2004, a middle-aged single man, who had been considered a 'pillar of the community', was imprisoned for producing child graphy. He admitted that he had paid young boys to undress masturbate for his camera. Sometimes he masturbated the en himself. One notable facet of the way this case was ted was the apparent lack of concern for the victims, five of n had been identified and approached by police. There were no for political action to protect vulnerable children, no cries of n that this type of child sexual abuse had taken place in a public . As far as can be told only one newspaper article referred to case and it did not contain a single sentence expressing outrage children could be molested so openly (*The Irish Times*, 25 uary 2005). Even the language used in court tended to minimise harms caused. The admitted sexual abuse of vulnerable young ple was described a 'sordid business' involving images 'not at more serious end of the scale of child abuse'. All of the victims e members of the Travelling community, a highly disadvantaged, much discriminated against, subsection of Irish society (see reatnach 2006). One hardly needs to wonder if their plight would ive attracted more interest had they been the sons of lawyers, loctors or university professors.

Few people are suggesting that the adverse consequences of child pornography legislation are such that it should be repealed in its entirety, although there are some calls (for example White 2006) for an uncensored Internet. The horrors of a less repressive approach in the 1970s are still too fresh. It is not going too far to say that one inexorable consequence of this liberal context was the death of Thea Pumbroek and the creation of an archive of magazines and videos that has been avidly sought ever since. Child pornography legislation is important even if it leads to few arrests, because it demonstrates society's denunciation of the activity and acknowledges the experience of victims.

But it is arguable that the legislation is overbroad. Analysing the Canadian situation, Ryder (2003: 109) distinguished between images that involve harm in their production and what he terms 'harmless representations of the sexuality of children and youth'. There is a widespread consensus that possession of the former creates a market for further abuse and degradation and that involvement in the creation, distribution or use of such images should be heavily penalised. But Ryder argues that the latter category, which includes paintings, drawings, stories and sculptures as well as visual records of lawful sexual activity engaged in by teenagers, requires different treatment and, generally speaking, should be no concern of the criminal law. To this could be added the category of pseudo-photographs in countries where they are prohibited. Williams (2004) makes a similar argument with regard to the UK.

One of the difficulties with the elastic nature of the definition of child pornography is that it brackets men who film themselves raping children for profit with men who use computer graphics to produce fantasy material for their private viewing pleasure. It is possible that in some of the latter cases the imaginary scenarios provide a sexual outlet for individuals who might otherwise seek a flesh and blood victim. Some of the former will involve men whose behaviour demands long-term incarceration. Grouping them together is dangerously misleading. The trend has been for the law to extend its reach so that even material that did not involve harm in its production can be proscribed. This marks a shift of emphasis from protecting children to punishing thoughts. To illustrate this problem, Adler (2001b: 941–2) asks us to consider two different photographs:

> The first is horrible: It depicts a naked ten-year-old girl being fondled by an adult. The child had been kidnapped, imprisoned by an underworld child sex ring, and used to make pornography. The pornographers sell the picture to pedophiles around the world. Now imagine a second photograph: It is taken while a ten-year-old girl wearing a bikini plays on the beach with her mother. Unbeknownst to either the girl or her mother, a man far away on the beach has a camera with a telephoto lens. He takes a picture of the little girl, zooming in on her genitals, which are covered only by her bathing suit. The girl and her mother never see the man; they never know the photo has been taken. The photographer, who finds the resulting picture sexually stimulating, keeps the photograph to himself, in his secret stash of 'child pornography'. He never shows it to anyone else.

Adler's point is that US child pornography law was intended to combat the first kind of photograph but that its boundaries have been expanded to encapsulate the second as well. While we might feel uneasy about an individual who took sexual pleasure from photographs of children playing on beaches, it is clearly the case that such photographs are not based on an underlying act of abuse, and arguable that this makes them qualitatively different from child pornography and deserving of a different legal response.

But how can we hope to arrive at a consensus about what is meant by child pornography when there is such variation in the range of permitted sexual conduct? Two court cases, occurring in the same year in different European countries, show widely differing responses toward sexual activity involving teenage girls. In November 2005, a circuit court in the west of Ireland heard an appeal from the district court against an 11-month prison sentence imposed on a 19-year-old for 'unlawful carnal knowledge' of his 15-year-old girlfriend (the age of consent being 15 for boys but 17 for girls). By the time the appeal took place the couple were engaged to be married and living together with their 10-month-old son. The circuit court judge took an unusual line. He wondered aloud why the girl was being referred to as an 'injured party' and enquired of a senior *Garda* giving evidence why advice had not been sought from the DPP to prosecute her for 'conspiracy to commit an indictable crime'. He had little sympathy for the entreaties from the girl's mother who, to her regret, had reported the matter to the police when she realised her daughter was pregnant. Perhaps, the defendant's lawyer suggested, the law should be changed to deal with the reality of consensual sex among Irish teenagers. 'Perhaps', retorted the judge, 'it is time courts started jailing young men who behave in this fashion and maybe young ladies too'. In the final analysis he was not as tough as his rhetoric led observers to fear and he suspended the prison term (*The Irish Times*, 23 November 2005, 30 November 2005; *The Sunday Times*, 27 November 2005). Nonetheless the young man will be required to register as a sex offender and will carry this conviction for life, as there is no provision in Irish law for adult convictions to become spent.

This contrasts starkly with the situation in Spain when, in May 2005, the country's highest court ruled that there was 'nothing perverse or extravagant' about a 31-year-old teacher having sex with a 14-year-old pupil. Overturning a previous ruling, the court quashed his one-year suspended jail term, leaving him free to return to work. The part-time teacher was also a member of the town's police force. The girl later sought psychiatric treatment but the court noted that: 'While the girl had shown signs of "serious alterations" in her personality and a "marked fall" in her schoolwork, it could not be said that her relationship with the teacher would produce significant problems in her future sex life. The anxiety she had shown ... could just as well have been caused by her parents' reaction to finding out about the relationship as by the fact that she had sex with her teacher' (*The Guardian*, 5 May 2005). Raised from 12 in 1999, the legal age of consent in Spain is 13, one of the lowest in the world. Spaniards are able to marry at 14 with parental consent (*The Sunday Times*, 27 November 2005). In response to the judgment, Carmen González of the Madrid regional government's children's ombudsman's office said: 'We see the age of consent as very low. We think it should probably go up to 14' (*The Guardian*, 5 May 2005).

These may be extreme judgments but they illustrate the range of views found in two EU countries and highlight the practical difficulties around harmonisation of laws in the sexual sphere when there is such divergence of attitude.

The fear factor

In his book *Paranoid Parenting*, Frank Furedi (2002) teases out the implications for children of excessive parental caution. In his view good parenting is no longer about nurturing, stimulating and socialising children. Rather it is about monitoring their activities and shielding them from risks, however minor or remote. He gives the example of an advertisement from a 1950 edition of *Life* magazine. It shows babies sitting in their buggies *outside* a supermarket while their mothers do the shopping. The caption states: 'It's a pretty good sign, when you see a pram parade lined up outside a store, that mothers are inside doing a smart bit of shopping' (p. 23). Any parent who left their baby unattended outside a big supermarket today, while they went inside to cruise the aisles, would be considered criminally negligent.

Over the course of half a century a belief that the world was a safe place and that other adults could be relied upon has been sundered. In its place has grown an attitude of generalised mistrust accompanied by an ingrained tendency to overestimate the dangers of childhood. This combination of undifferentiated fear and risk aversion extends widely. It seems as if adults have lost the ability to discriminate between degrees of danger. Even mundane situations have become potentially hazardous and innocence is under constant threat. Instances of this new preoccupation can be found in many spheres of life.

It is difficult to imagine that a generation ago the principal of a primary school would have protested against the construction of new apartments on an adjacent site on the basis that 'strangers' could observe pupils playing in the yard. Yet this is precisely what happened in a town in rural Ireland in 2006. The substance of the objection was that:

Young children use the school and yard for play and recreation during the day and evening and we believe that it would not be appropriate to have tenants, who would be unknown to school management, able to observe pupils. The board of management believes that this may constitute a risk to pupils and should be avoided.

In response, the developers revised their plans to ensure that there were no rear windows at first floor level (*The Irish Times*, 24 October 2006). It is a similar anxiety that leads to the prohibition of photography at swimming pools and leisure centres.

A final example of how deeply this fear penetrates is captured by a newspaper advertisement for an 'Amazing Super-Loud Child Safety Watch' under the headline 'Protect your Children'. The watches are produced by a US charity called the AmberWatch Foundation, which is dedicated to the prevention of child abduction and molestation. If the child presses two buttons on the side of the watch simultaneously or it is forcefully pulled from their wrist an alarm of 115 decibels is sounded. This we are told is 'more than four times louder than a child's scream'. They come in two colours, Ice Petal Pink and Sharks (blue) and are priced at €45.95 (*The Irish Times*, 31 July 2006). On the day that this advertisement appeared, the front page of the same newspaper carried a story about a Department of Education survey that found an increase in the number of children meeting up with people who they first encountered on the Internet. A small proportion of these meetings led to physical threats and abuse but in each one of these the abusive party, who had introduced himself or herself as a child, turned out to be an adult. The combined effect of the publicity for the anti-molestation watch and the story about innocent encounters turning sour must have caused some parents to despair.

The extent to which society has reorganised itself around the perceived threat to children and the way that law enforcement has adopted the paedophile's gaze are not the only unintended harmful consequences of the expressed desire to protect children and punish those who enjoy viewing their abuse. Another negative side effect is the extent to which a desire to eradicate this activity may infringe civil liberties. While not addressing child pornography specifically, White (2006) strongly made the point that regulation of the Internet is difficult, inevitably imperfect and anyway undesirable. She argued that the associated gains are more than outweighed by two considerations. First, the value of sexually explicit material to those who seek it out. Second, the threat posed to the Internet more generally of restrictions on content which will inevitably stray beyond the initial targets to embrace material deemed to be offensive or corrupting by those with power to make the rules. This has implications for promoting art, providing information about human sexuality in all its diversity, and encouraging the expression of difference. The danger is that the search for more stringent controls will lead to self-censorship and a general curtailment of liberty. In White's view this is too great a price to pay for the partial removal of sexually explicit material. Only by resisting the State's attempts to control the Internet will important freedoms be protected.

Against a background of increased Internet use but declining police investigations (in Ireland at any rate) the option of allowing the cyber-environment to grow unchecked and uncensored deserves more serious attention than it has received to date. This is particularly true in light of the likely ineffectiveness of attempts to impose order on a system where decentred, even anarchic, arrangements are part of the design.

Under the guise of public protection, private electronic communications and what they might reveal about citizens' fantasy lives as well as their involvement in criminal activity are being monitored, controlled and made amenable to punishment. Mass surveillance became a reality in the European Union with the introduction of the Data Retention Directive in February 2006. This requires telephone companies to retain details of customers' calls and Internet Service Providers to record online behaviour. The date, duration and destination of communications will be stored for up to two years, but not the content. Because such surveillance takes place in the background it has generated little debate but this development is likely to have a chilling effect on freedom of expression and to impede the exchange of views that is essential to healthy democracy. While such powers will no doubt make trawling for child pornographers, terrorists and other offenders more straightforward, the implications for society more generally are not to be underestimated. A world where every movement and exchange of information are treated as potentially criminal is one where the trust required for successful interaction has been violated. The likely effects on spontaneity, risky thinking, contestation, crime prevention and vigorous political dialogue remain to be seen.

Danay (2005: 172) argued that the *Ferber* case (see Chapter 1) began an 'unsettling trend' in America whereby, without constitutional protection, the laws regulating child pornography began to erode expressive freedoms more generally. In the same vein, Adler (2001b: 921) described child pornography law as the contemporary concern, 'where popular pressure on courts and legislatures exerts itself most ferociously; it is where the greatest encroachments on free expression are now accepted'. Notwithstanding the qualms of a small number of academic commentators the calls for tougher regulation show no signs of abating.

And finally ...

We have seen that the criminal justice response to child pornography exacerbates the problem that it is intended to address by adopting the 'paedophile's gaze' and transforming innocent images of children into opportunities for perverse delight. It foists upon us a view of children as sexual objects and causes an overestimation of the risks faced by children with all of the attendant anxiety for parents and carers. In a very real way it affects how we look at, and interact with, young people. It has adverse implications for art, photography, research and freedom of expression more generally. It draws attention away from arguably more fundamental matters that make children vulnerable to abuse, such as poverty and social isolation. It criminalises possession of materials the production of which involved harm to no children (for example, text or pseudo-photographs). Finally, it allows the state to extend its surveillance of electronic communications under the guise of child protection. In these ways we are all diminished and our liberties are curtailed. This is a significant price to pay for what is essentially an indirect, and severely limited, attack on child abuse.

In his book, *Erotic Innocence: The Culture of Child Molesting*, James Kincaid (1998) makes the point that child abuse narratives serve a social purpose; while we might express abhorrence we are also excited. The high levels of denunciation and indignation betray a deep fascination with childhood sexuality. Quite simply these are stories that we like to tell, over and over again. Kincaid argues that 'our culture has enthusiastically sexualized the child while denying just as enthusiastically that it was doing any such thing. We have become so engaged with tales of childhood eroticism (molestation, incest, abduction, pornography) that we have come to take for granted the irrepressible allure of children' (p. 13). His view is that by simultaneously fetishising and denying the sensuousness of childhood we are creating a dangerous social fault-line. His recommendation is as profound as it is contentious: to accept that most adults feel some measure of erotic attraction to children and the childlike and to recognise that such acceptance will not compel them to rush out and have sex with children.

The modern tendency to deny that children are sexual beings is the source of much of the current difficulty. We noted in Chapter 1 how Allen Ginsberg explained his decision to join NAMBLA as a demonstration of solidarity with a group whose freedom of speech was under threat. He further elaborated that: 'A dash of humor, common sense humanity and historical perspective would help discussion of NAMBLA's role'. These ingredients are spectacularly absent from the debate about child pornography. While there are serious issues at stake here, as set out in the preceding chapters, there is certainly scope for a more even-handed debate. This will require acceptance of a number of truths: that many adults appreciate the erotic dimension of youth and that this does not necessarily make them menaces; that the genre of storytelling and news reporting that involves child sex has been given a lease of life by the Internet that makes it impossible to extinguish, even if we wanted to; that the sincere desire to protect children and preserve their innocence is not best served by an increasingly harsh and blinkered criminal justice response; and that on the global scale of threats faced by children, participation in child pornography comes way behind poverty, disease and neglect.

This is not to trivialise the problem, which as we have shown throughout this book can have savage consequences, but rather to attempt to shift how it is perceived. As we have seen there is plenty of evidence that young lives are destroyed to cater for the pleasures of those who should know better. And there can be no doubt that the producers, distributors and collectors of images of child abuse are breaking the law and should face the consequences. But the definition of what constitutes child pornography has become increasingly elastic and the criminal justice response is inevitably limited. In this context the adverse social consequences become a legitimate cause of concern.

Freud memorably described the therapeutic process as an attempt to transform neurotic misery into ordinary unhappiness. Similarly, it would be to our collective advantage to shape a society where the threat to children's sexual integrity is acknowledged as real but manageable rather than as a cause of crippling anxiety. This would constitute a major leap forward.

References

Adler, A. (2001a) 'The perverse law of child pornography', *Columbia Law Review*, 101(2): 209–73.

Adler, A. (2001b) 'Inverting the First Amendment', *University of Pennsylvania Law Review*, 149(4): 921–1003.

Akdeniz, Y. (1999) *Sex on the Net: The Dilemma of Policing Cyberspace*. Reading: South Street Press.

Akdeniz, Y. (2001) 'Governing pornography and child pornography on the Internet: The UK approach', *University of West Los Angeles Law Review*, 32: 247–75.

Akdeniz, Y. (2002) *Response to the Sentencing of Offences Involving Child Pornography Consultation Paper*. Submitted to Professor Martin Wasik, Chairman of the Sentencing Advisory Panel, 9 April 2002. (Forwarded to authors upon request.)

Alexander, M. (2002) 'The First Amendment and problems of political viability: The case of internet pornography', *Harvard Journal of Law and Public Policy*, 25(3): 977–1030.

Alexy, E.M., Burgess, A.W. and Baker, T. (2005) 'Internet offenders: Traders, travelers, and combination traders-travelers', *Journal of Interpersonal Violence*, 20(7): 804–12.

American Psychiatric Association (2000) *Diagnostic and Statistical Manual of Mental Disorders* (4th edn, text revision) (DSM-IV-TR). Washington, DC: American Psychiatric Association.

An Garda Síochána (2002) *Annual Report 2000*. Dublin: Stationery Office.

Anglin, H. (2002) 'The potential liability of federal law-enforcement agents engaged in undercover child pornography investigations', *New York University Law Review*, 77: 1090–18.

Anon (1975) *The Discreet Gentleman's Guide to the Pleasures of Europe*. New York: Bantam Books.

Ariès, P. (1962) *Centuries of Childhood: A Social History of Family Life.* New York: Vintage.

Association of Chief Police Officers (2006) *Good Practice Guide for Computer based Electronic Evidence,* Version 3.0 (retrieved 21 June 2006, from http://www.acpo.police.uk/policies.asp).

Astrowsky, B.H. (2000) 'Hidden images: A new challenge in the fight against child porn. *UPDATE,* 13(2). Alexandria, VA: American Prosecutors Research Institute (retrieved 20 July 2006, from http://www.ndaa-apri.org/publications/newsletters/update_volume_13_number_2_2000.html).

Attorney General's Commission on Pornography (1986) *The Meese Report.* Washington, DC: US Department of Justice.

Bender, G. (1998) 'Bavaria v Felix Somm: The pornography conviction of the former CompuServe manager', *International Journal of Communications Law and Policy,* Issue 1, Summer.

Bhreatnach, A. (2006) *Becoming Conspicuous: Irish Travellers, Society and the State, 1922–1970.* Dublin: University College Dublin Press.

Bonner, R.C. (2002) Remarks of US Customs Commissioner Robert C. Bonner at Press Conference on Operation Hamlet. US Customs and Border Protection, 9 August (retrieved 20 July 2006, from http://www.cbp.gov).

Bowker, A. and Gray, M. (2004) 'An introduction to the supervision of the cybersex offender', *Federal Probation,* 68(3): 3–8.

Breen, M.J. (2007) 'Through the looking glass: How the mass media represent, reflect and refract sexual crime in Ireland', *Irish Communications Review,* 10: 5–22.

Brenner, S.W. (2004) 'Distributed security: A new model of law enforcement', *Journal of Internet Law,* 8(5): 1 and 8–25.

Brenner, S.W., Carrier, B. and Henninger, J. (2004) 'The Trojan Horse defense in cybercrime cases', *Santa Clara Computer and High Technology Law Journal,* 21(1): 1–53.

Brown, A. and Barrett, D. (2002) *Knowledge of Evil: Child Prostitution and Child Sexual Abuse in Twentieth-Century England.* Cullompton, Devon: Willan.

Burke, A., Sowerbutts, S., Blundell, B. and Sherry, M. (2002) 'Child pornography and the Internet: Policing and treatment issues', *Psychiatry, Psychology and Law,* 9(1): 79–84.

Campbell, D. (2005) 'Operation Ore exposed', *PC Pro Magazine,* July No. 130.

Carr, J. (2001) 'Child Pornography.' Theme paper at the Second World Congress Against Commercial Sexual Exploitation of Children, Yokohama, Japan (retrieved 20 July 2006, from http://www.ecpat.net/eng/Ecpat_inter/projects/monitoring/wc2/wc2_resources.asp#2).

Carr, J. (2003) *Child Abuse, Child Pornography and the Internet.* London: NCH.

Censorship of Publications Board (2004) *Register of Prohibited Publications.* Dublin: Stationery Office.

Central Statistics Office (2006) *Information Society and Telecommunications 2005.* Dublin: Stationery Office.

Chin, G.J. (2006) 'The story of Jacobson v. United States: Catching criminals or creating crime?', Arizona Legal Studies, Discussion Paper No. 06-12. University of Arizona: James E. Rogers College of Law.

Cleland, J. (1749/2005) *Fanny Hill or, Memoirs of a Woman of Pleasure.* London: Penguin Classics.

ClickZ Stats (2006) *Population Explosion! Internet* (retrieved 20 July 2006, from http://www.clickz.com/showPage.html?page=3605776).

Council of Europe (1991) *Explanatory Memorandum to Recommendation No. R (91) 11 of the Committee of Ministers to Member States concerning Sexual Exploitation, Pornography and Prostitution of, and Trafficking in, Children and Young Adults.* Strasbourg: Council of Europe.

Crewdson, J. (1988) *By Silence Betrayed: Sexual Abuse of Children in America.* Boston: Little, Brown.

Cross, S. (2005) 'Paedophiles in the community: Inter-agency conflict, news leaks and the local press', *Crime, Media, Culture,* 1: 284–300.

Danay, R.J. (2005) 'The danger of fighting monsters: Addressing the harms of child pornography law', *Review of Constitutional Studies,* 11(1): 151–91.

Dardenne, S. (2004) *I Choose to Live.* London: Virago Press.

Darlington, R. (2004) *Sex on the Net* (retrieved 25 February 2005, from http://www.rogerdarlington.co.uk/sexonnet.html).

Davis, R.A. (2001) 'A cognitive-behavioral model of pathological Internet use', *Computers in Human Behavior,* 17: 187–95.

Demetriou, C. and Silke, A. (2003) 'A criminological Internet "sting": Experimental evidence of illegal and deviant visits to a website trap', *British Journal of Criminology,* 43: 213–22.

Department of Health (1983) *Non-Accidental Injury to Children: Guidelines on Procedures for the Identification and Management of Non-Accidental Injury to Children.* Dublin: Department of Health.

Department of Health (1987) *Child Abuse Guidelines: Guidelines on Procedures for the Identification, Investigation and Management of Child Abuse.* Dublin: Department of Health.

Department of Health (1996) *Report on the Inquiry into the Operation of Madonna House.* Dublin: Stationery Office.

Department of Justice, Equality and Law Reform (1998a) *First Report of The Working Group on Illegal and Harmful Use of the Internet.* Dublin: Stationery Office.

Department of Justice, Equality and Law Reform (1998b) *The Law on Sexual Offences: A Discussion Paper.* Dublin: Stationery Office.

DeYoung, M. (1989) 'The world according to NAMBLA: Accounting for deviance', *Journal of Sociology and Social Welfare,* 16(1): 111–26.

Director of Public Prosecutions (2001) *Statement of General Guidelines for Prosecutors.* Dublin: Office of the DPP.

Director of Public Prosecutions (2005) *Annual Report 2004*. Dublin: Office of the DPP.

Douglas, J. and Singular, S. (2004) *Anyone You Want Me To Be: A Shocking True Story of Sex and Death on the Internet*. London: Simon and Schuster.

Dover, K.J. (1978) *Greek Homosexuality*. London: Duckworth.

Durkin, K.F. (1997) 'Misuse of the Internet by paedophiles: Implications for law enforcement and probation practice', *Federal Probation*, 61(3): 14–18.

Durkin, K.F. and Bryant, C.D. (1999) 'Propagandising pederasty: A thematic analysis of the on-line exculpatory accounts of unrepentant pedophiles', *Deviant Behavior*, 20(2): 103–27.

Edwards, S. (1994) 'Pretty babies: Art, erotica or kiddie porn?', *History of Photography*, 18(1): 34–6.

Edwards, S.S.M. (2000) 'Prosecuting "child pornography": Possession and taking of indecent photographs of children', *Journal of Social Welfare and Family Law*, 22(1): 1–21.

Elias, N. (1939/2000) *The Civilizing Process: Sociogenetic and Psychogenetic Investigations* (Revised Edition). Oxford: Blackwell.

Elliott, M. (1992) 'Images of children in the media: "Soft kiddie porn"', in C. Itzin (ed.), *Pornography: Women, Violence and Civil Liberties – A Radical New View*. Oxford: Oxford University Press, pp. 217–21.

Fahey, T., Russell, H. and Whelan, C.T. (eds) (2007) *Best of Times? The Social Impact of the Celtic Tiger*. Dublin: Institute of Public Administration.

Ferguson, H. (1996) 'Protecting Irish children in time: Child abuse as a social problem and the development of the child protection system in the Republic of Ireland', *Administration*, 44(2): 5–36.

Ferraro, M.M. and Casey, E. (2005) *Investigating Child Exploitation and Pornography: The Internet, the Law and Forensic Science*. Amsterdam: Elsevier.

Ferriter, D. (2004) *The Transformation of Ireland, 1900–2000*. London: Profile.

Finkelhor, D., Mitchell, K. and Wolak, J. (2001) *Highlights of the Youth Internet Safety Survey*. Office of Juvenile Justice and Delinquency Prevention Fact Sheet No. 4. Washington, DC: US Department of Justice.

Forde, P. and Patterson, A. (1998) 'Paedophile Internet Activity', *Trends and Issues in Crime and Criminal Justice*, November, No. 97. Canberra: Australian Institute of Criminology.

Frazier, P., Conlon, A. and Glaser, T. (2001) 'Positive and negative life changes following sexual assault', *Journal of Consulting and Clinical Psychology*, 69: 1048–55.

Frei, A., Erenay, N., Dittmann, V. and Graf, M. (2005) 'Paedophilia on the Internet: A study of 33 convicted offenders in the Canton of Lucerne', *Swiss Medical Weekly*, 135: 488–94.

Friendship, C. and Thornton, D. (2001) 'Sexual reconviction for sex offenders released from prison in England and Wales: Implications for evaluating treatment', *British Journal of Criminology*, 41: 285–92.

Furedi, F. (2002) *Paranoid Parenting: Why Ignoring the Experts May be Best for your Child*. Chicago: Chicago Review Press.

Furedi, F. (2005) *Culture of Fear: Risk-taking and the Morality of Low Expectation.* Revised Edition. London: Continuum.

Gillespie, A. (2002) 'Child protection on the Internet: Challenges for criminal law', *Child and Family Law Quarterly*, 14(4): 411–25.

Gillespie, A. (2003) 'Sentences for offences involving child pornography', *Criminal Law Review*, February, 81–93.

Gillespie, A. (2004) 'The Sexual Offences Act 2003: Tinkering with child pornography', *Criminal Law Review*, May, 361–68.

Gillespie, A. (2005) 'Indecent images of children: The ever-changing law', *Child Abuse Review*, 14(6): 430–43.

Ginsberg, A. (2000) *Deliberate Prose: Selected Essays 1952–1995* (edited by Bill Morgan). New York: HarperCollins.

Glosserman, B. (2000) 'Reversal of fortune', *Index on Censorship*, 29(3): 132–35.

Goode, H., McGee, H. and O'Boyle, C. (2003) *Time to Listen: Confronting Child Sexual Abuse by Catholic Clergy in Ireland*. Dublin: The Liffey Press.

Graham, W.R. (2000) 'Uncovering and eliminating child pornography rings on the Internet: Issues regarding and avenues facilitating law enforcement's access to "Wønderland"', *Law Review M.S.U.–D.C.L*, 2: 457–84.

Grant, A., David, F. and Grabosky, P. (1997) 'Child pornography in the digital age', *Transnational Organised Crime*, 3(4): 171–88.

Greer, C. (2003) *Sex Crime and the Media: Sex Offending and the Press in a Divided Society.* Cullompton, Devon: Willan.

Hacking, I. (1991) 'The making and molding of child abuse', *Critical Inquiry*, 17(2): 253–88.

Hacking, I. (1995) *Rewriting the Soul: Multiple Personality and the Sciences of Memory*. Princeton: Princeton University Press.

Hamilton, J. (2004) 'The summary trial of indictable offences', *Judicial Studies Institute Journal*, 4(2): 154–81.

Harmon, D. and Boeringer, S.B. (1997) 'A content analysis of Internet-accessible written pornographic depictions', *Electronic Journal of Sociology*, 3(1): September.

Healy, M. (1996) *Child Pornography: An International Perspective*. Prepared as a working document for the First World Congress Against Commercial Sexual Exploitation of Children (retrieved 20 July 2006, from http://www.usemb.se/children/csec/child_pornography.html).

Hebditch, D. and Anning, N. (1988) *Porn Gold: Inside the Pornography Business.* London: Faber and Faber.

Holland, G. (2004) 'Identifying victims of child abuse images: An analysis of successful identifications', *Proceedings of the Fifth COPINE Conference*. Cork: University College Cork.

Home Office (2006) *Investigation of Protected Electronic Information: A Public Consultation*. London: Home Office.

Hose, K. (1976) *PIE Chairperson's Annual Report, 1975–1976*. London: Paedophile Information Exchange (retrieved 20 July 2006, from http:// en.wikipedia.org/wiki/Paedophile_Information_Exchange).

Hotline (2004) *Second Annual Report* (available at: http://www.hotline.ie).

Hotline (2006) *Third Annual Report* (available at: http://www.hotline.ie).

Howard, T. (2004) 'Don't cache out your case: Prosecuting child pornography possession laws based on images located in temporary Internet files', *Berkeley Technology Law Journal*, 19: 1227–73.

Howitt, D. (1995) 'Pornography and the paedophile: Is it criminogenic?', *British Journal of Medical Psychology*, 68: 15–27.

Huda, S. (2005) 'ICTs and trafficking of children for sexual exploitation'. Panel Presentation: WSIS Conference, Tunis, 15 November.

Hudson, K. (2005) *Offending Identities: Sex Offenders' Perspectives on their Treatment and Management*. Cullompton, Devon: Willan.

INHOPE (2004) *INHOPE Internet Hotline Providers Second Report* (retrieved 20 July 2006, from http://www.inhope.org).

Interpol (2005) *Media Releases* (retrieved 20 July 2006, from http://www. interpol.org).

Irish Council for Civil Liberties: Working Party on Child Sexual Abuse (1988) *Report of the ICCL Working Party on Child Sexual Abuse*. Dublin: ICCL.

Itzin, C. (1992) 'Legislating against pornography without censorship', in C. Itzin (ed.), *Pornography: Women, Violence and Civil Liberties, A Radical New View*. Oxford: University Press, pp. 401–34.

Jenkins, P. (2001) *Beyond Tolerance: Child Pornography on the Internet*. New York: New York University Press.

Jewkes, Y. (2003) 'Policing cybercrime', in T. Newburn (ed.), *Handbook of Policing*. Cullompton, Devon: Willan, pp. 501–24.

Jewkes, Y. and Andrews, C. (2005) 'Policing the filth: the problems of investigating online child pornography in England and Wales', *Policing and Society*, 15(1): 42–62.

Jones, V. and Skogrand, E. (2005) *Position Paper Regarding Online Images of Sexual Abuse and Other Internet-Related Sexual Exploitation of Children*. Copenhagen: Save the Children.

Kelly, K. (2005) 'We are the Web', *Wired Magazine*, 13(8) (retrieved 20 July 2006, from http://www.wired.com/wired/archive/13.08).

Kelly, L. (1992) 'Pornography and child sexual abuse', in C. Itzin (ed.),

Pornography: Women, Violence and Civil Liberties – A Radical New View. Oxford: Oxford University Press, pp. 113–23.

Kelly, L. and Regan, L. (2000) 'Sexual exploitation of children in Europe: Child pornography', *The Journal of Sexual Aggression*, 6(1/2): 6–28.

Kelly, L., Wingfield, R., Burton, S. and Regan, L. (1995) *Splintered Lives: Sexual Exploitation of Children in the Context of Children's Rights and Child Protection.* London: Barnardos.

Kennedy, F. (2000) 'The suppression of the Carrigan Report: A historical perspective on child abuse', *Studies: An Irish Quarterly Review*, 89(359): 354–63.

Kennedy, J. (2000) 'Monstrous offenders and the search for solidarity through modern punishment', *Hastings Law Journal*, 51: 829–908.

Khan, K. (1999) 'Child pornography', *Computer and Telecommunications Law Review*, 5(7): 203–07.

Kincaid, J.R. (1998) *Erotic Innocence: The Culture of Child Molesting.* Durham, NC: Duke University Press.

Kinsey, A.C., Pomeroy, W.B. and Martin, C.E. (1948) *Sexual Behavior in the Human Male.* Philadelphia: W.B. Saunders.

Krone, T. (2004) 'A typology of online child pornography offending', *Trends and Issues in Crime and Criminal Justice*, July, No. 279. Canberra: Australian Institute of Criminology.

Krone, T. (2005a) 'International police operations against online child pornography', *Trends and Issues in Crime and Criminal Justice*, April, No. 296. Canberra: Australian Institute of Criminology.

Krone, T. (2005b) 'Child pornography sentencing in NSW', *High Tech Crime Brief*, 08. Canberra: Australian Institute of Criminology.

La Fontaine, J. (1998) *Speak of the Devil: Tales of Satanic Abuse in Contemporary England.* Cambridge University Press.

Lalor, K. (2001) 'Child sexual abuse in Ireland: A brief history', in K. Lalor (ed.), *The End of Innocence. Child Sexual Abuse in Ireland.* Cork: Oak Tree Press, pp. 1–26.

Lamb, M. (1998) 'Cybersex: Research notes on the characteristics of the visitors to online chat rooms', *Deviant Behavior*, 19(2): 121–35.

Lane, F.S. (2001) *Obscene Profits: The Entrepreneurs of Pornography in the Cyber Age.* London: Routledge.

Langevin, R. and Curnoe, S. (2002) 'The use of pornography during the commission of sexual offences'. Paper presented at the Seventh Biennial Conference of the International Association for the Treatment of Sexual Offenders (IATSO), Vienna, Austria, 11–14 September.

Lanning, K.V. (2001) *Child Molesters: A Behavioral Analysis* (4th edn). Alexandria, VA: National Center for Missing and Exploited Children.

Lanning, K.V. and Burgess, A.W. (1989) 'Child pornography and sex rings', in D. Zillmann and J. Bryant (eds), *Pornography: Research Advancesand Policy Considerations.* Hillsdale, NJ: Lawrence Erlbaum Associates, pp. 235–55.

Lee, C.J.P. (2005) *Pervasive Perversions: Paedophilia and Child Sexual Abuse in Media/Culture*. London: Free Association Books.

Lehman, P. (ed.) (2006) *Pornography: Film and Culture*. New Brunswick, NJ: Rutgers University Press.

Lloyd, R. (1976) *For Money or Love: Boy Prostitution in America*. New York: Vanguard Press.

Lopez, A.D. (2000) 'Reducing child mortality', *Bulletin of the World Health Organisation*, 78(10): 1173.

Malone, S. (2006) 'Child porn sites targeted by financial institutions'. *PCPro*, 17 March 2006 (retrieved 20 July 2006, from http://www.pcpro.co.uk/news/archive).

Mankoff, A.H. (1973) *Mankoff's Lusty Europe: The First All-Purpose European Guide to Sex, Love and Romance*. New York: Viking Press.

Marshall, D., Bailey, T., Van Teijlingen, D. and Den Breejen, O. (1999) 'The work of the OCG Paedophile Unit with regard to cross-border paedophile activity – a case study "Operation Mansard" involving cooperation between British and Dutch police', *Proceedings of the Second COPINE Conference*. Cork: University College Cork.

Mayock. P. and O'Sullivan, E. (2007) *Youth Homelessness in Dublin*. Dublin: Liffey Press.

McAlinden, A.M. (2006) "'Setting 'em up": Personal, familial and institutional grooming in the sexual abuse of children', *Social and Legal Studies*, 15(3): 339–62.

McGee, H. Garavan, R., de Barra, M., Byrne, J. and Conroy, R. (2002) *The SAVI Report: Sexual Abuse and Violence in Ireland. A National Study of Irish Experiences, Beliefs and Attitudes Concerning Sexual Violence*. Dublin: The Liffey Press in association with The Dublin Rape Crisis Centre.

McGuinness, C. (1993) *Report of the Kilkenny Incest Investigation*. Dublin: Stationery Office.

McKay, S. (1998) *Sophia's Story*. Dublin: Gill and Macmillan.

McLachlan, B. (2000) 'And what did you do on holiday? Personality, opportunity or geography. Sex offenders [sic] against children at home or abroad', *Proceedings of the Third COPINE Conference*. Cork: University College Cork.

McLaughlin, J.F. (2000) 'Cyber child sex offender typology' (retrieved 28 December 2006, from http://www.ci.keene.nh.us/police/Typology.html).

Mehta, M.D. (2001) 'Pornography in Usenet: A study of 9800 randomly selected images', *Cyberpsychology and Behavior*, 4(6): 695–703.

Mitchell, K.J., Wolak, J. and Finkelhor, D. (2005) 'Police posing as juveniles online to catch sex offenders: Is it working?', *Sexual Abuse: A Journal of Research and Treatment*, 17(3): 241–67.

Moore, C. (1995) *Betrayal of Trust: The Father Brendan Smyth Affair and the Catholic Church*. Dublin: Marino Books.

Murphy, F.D., Buckley, H. and Joyce, L. (2005) *The Ferns Report*. Dublin: Stationery Office.

Nash, M. (1999) *Police, Probation and Protecting the Public*. London: Blackstone Press.

Nathan, D. and Snedeker, M. (1995) *Satan's Silence: Ritual Abuse and the Making of a Modern American Witch Hunt*. New York: Basic Books.

Naughton, J. (2000) *A Brief History of the Future: The Origins of the Internet*. London: Phoenix.

Nolan, B., O'Connell, P. and Whelan, C.T. (eds) (2000) *Bust to Boom: The Irish Experience of Growth and Inequality*. Dublin: Institute of Public Administration.

O'Brien, B. (2006) 'Miscarriage of justice: Paul McCabe and Nora Wall', *Studies: An Irish Quarterly Review*, 95(380): 355–64.

O'Brien, S. (1983) *Child Pornography*. Dubuque, Iowa: Kendall/Hunt.

O'Carroll, T. (1980) *Paedophilia: The Radical Case*. London: Peter Owen.

O'Connell, R. (1998) 'Paedophilia networking and the Internet 2: Newsgroups', *Proceedings of the First COPINE Conference*. Cork: University College Cork.

O'Connor, A. (2000) *A Message from Heaven: The Life and Crimes of Father Sean Fortune*. Dingle: Brandon.

O'Malley, T. (1996) *Sexual Offences: Law, Policy and Punishment*. Dublin: Round Hall Sweet and Maxwell.

O'Malley, T. (2000) *Sentencing Law and Practice*. Dublin: Round Hall Sweet and Maxwell.

O'Malley, T. (2004) 'Sentencing of child pornography offences', Paper presented at the Fifth Annual Prosecutors Conference, Dublin (forwarded to authors upon request).

O'Malley, T. (2006) *Sentencing Law and Practice* (2nd edn). Dublin: Thomson Round Hall.

Orzack, M.H. and Ross, C.J. (2000) 'Should virtual sex be treated like other addictions?', *Sexual Addictions and Compulsivity*, 7: 113–25.

O'Sullivan, E. (2002) '"This otherwise delicate subject": Child sexual abuse in early twentieth-century Ireland', in P. O'Mahony (ed.), *Criminal Justice in Ireland*. Dublin: Institute of Public Administration, pp. 176–201.

Oswell, D. (2006) 'When images matter: Internet child pornography, forms of observation and an ethics of the virtual', *Journal of Information, Communication and Society*, 9(2): 244–65.

O'Toole, F. (1990) *A Mass for Jesse James: A Journey through 1980s Ireland*. Dublin: Raven Arts.

Pearsall, R. (1969) *The Worm in the Bud: The World of Victorian Sexuality*. London: Weidenfeld and Nicolson.

Point Topic (2005) *World Broadband Statistics: Q3 05*. London: Point Topic (retrieved 20 July 2006, from http://www.point-topic.com).

Prentky, R.A., Knight, R.A. and Lee, A.F.S. (1997) *Child Sexual Molestation: Research Issues*. National Institute of Justice Research Report. Washington, DC: US Department of Justice.

Quayle, E. and Taylor, M. (2001) 'Child seduction and self-representation on the Internet', *CyberPsychology and Behavior*, 5: 597–608.
Quayle, E. and Taylor, M. (2002) 'Child Pornography and the Internet: Perpetuating a cycle of abuse', *Deviant Behavior*, 23(4): 331–61.

Raftery, M. and O'Sullivan, E. (1999) *Suffer the Little Children: The Inside Story of Ireland's Industrial Schools*. Dublin: New Island.
Reisman, J. (2003) *Kinsey: Crimes and Consequences* (3rd edn). Crestwood, KY: Institute for Media Education.
Renold, E., and Creighton, S. (2003) *Images of Abuse: A Review of the Evidence on Child Pornography*. London: NSPCC.
Reynolds, J. (1998) 'Evidential issues in child pornography', *Proceedings of the First COPINE Conference*. Cork: University College Cork.
Rind, B., Tromovitch, P. and Bauserman, R. (1998) 'A meta-analytic examination of assumed properties of child sexual abuse using college samples', *Psychological Bulletin*, 124(1): 22–53.
Robbins, P. and Darlington, R. (2003) 'The role of the industry and the Internet Watch Foundation', in A. MacVean and P. Spindler (eds), *Policing Paedophiles on the Internet*. Goole: New Police Bookshop, pp. 79–86.
Ropelato, J. (2006) *Internet Pornography Statistics* (retrieved 20 July 2006, from http://www.internet-filter-review.toptenreviews.com/internet-pornography-statistics.html).
Ryder, B. (2003) 'The harms of child pornography law', *University of British Columbia Law Review*, 36: 101–35.

Sampson, A. (1994) *Acts of Abuse: Sex Offenders and the Criminal Justice System*. London: Routledge.
Sandfort, T. (1982) *The Sexual Aspect of Paedophile Relations: The Experiences of Twenty-Five Boys*. Amsterdam: Pan/Spartacus.
Schmidt, G. (2002) 'The dilemma of the male pedophile', *Archives of Sexual Behavior*, 31(6): 473–77.
Schuijer, J. and Rossen, B. (1992) 'The trade in child pornography', *Issues in Child Abuse Accusations*, 4(2): 55–107.
Sentencing Advisory Panel (2002) *Offences Involving Child Pornography*. Advice to the Court of Appeal – 10. London: SAP.
Seto, M.C. and Eke, A.W. (2005) 'The criminal histories and later offending of child pornography offenders', *Sexual Abuse: A Journal of Research and Treatment*, 17(2): 201–10.
Silbert, M.H. (1989) 'The effects on juveniles of being used for pornography and prostitution', in D. Zillmann and J. Bryant (eds), *Pornography: Research Advances and Policy Considerations*. Hillsdale, NJ: Lawrence Erlbaum Associates, pp. 215–34.

Silverman, J. and Wilson, D. (2002) *Innocence Betrayed: Paedophilia, The Media and Society*. Oxford: Blackwell.

Singular, S. (1999) *Presumed Guilty: An Investigation into the JonBenet Ramsey Case, the Media and the Culture of Pornography*. Beverly Hills, CA: New Millennium Press.

Smith, S.A. (1986) 'PIE: From 1980 until its demise in 1985', in W. Middleton (ed.) *The Betrayal of Youth: Radical Perspectives on Childhood Sexuality, Intergenerational Sex and the Social Oppression of Children and Young People*. London: CL Publications, pp. 215–45.

Sommer, P. (2002) 'Evidence in Internet paedophilia cases', *Computer and Telecommunications Law Review*, 8(7): 176–84.

Sommer, P. (2004) 'Emerging problems in digital evidence', *Criminal Justice Matters*, 58: 24–25.

Soothill, K., Francis, B. and Ackerley, E. (1998) 'Paedophilia and paedophiles', *New Law Journal*, 148: 882–83.

Stack, S., Wasserman, I. and Kern, R. (2004) 'Adult social bonds and use of Internet pornography', *Social Science Quarterly*, 85(1): 75–88.

Stewart, J. (1997) 'If this is the global community, we must be on the bad side of town: International policing of child pornography on the Internet', *Houston Journal of International Law*, 20: 205–46.

Suler, J. (2004) 'The online disinhibition effect', *CyberPsychology and Behavior*, 7(3): 321–26.

Tarbox, K. (2000) *Katie.com: My Story*. New York: Dutton.

Tate, T. (1990) *Child Pornography: An Investigation*. London: Methuen.

Tate, T. (1992) 'The child pornography industry: International trade in child sexual abuse', in C. Itzin (ed.), *Pornography: Women, Violence and Civil Liberties – A Radical New View*. Oxford: Oxford University Press, pp. 203–16.

Taylor, M. (1998) 'Paedophilia and the Internet', *Proceedings of the First COPINE Conference*. Cork: University College Cork.

Taylor, M. (1999) 'The nature and dimensions of child pornography on the Internet', Paper presented at the international conference 'Combating Child Pornography on the Internet', Vienna, Austria (retrieved 20 July 2006, from http://www.copine.ie/publications.php).

Taylor, M. and Quayle, E. (2003) *Child Pornography: An Internet Crime*. Hove, East Sussex: Brunner-Routledge.

Taylor, M., Quayle, E. and Holland, G. (2001) 'Child pornography, the Internet and offending', *ISUMA: Canadian Journal of Policy Research*, 2(2): 94–100.

Thomas, T. (2005) *Sex Crime: Sex Offending and Society*. Cullompton, Devon: Willan.

Thompson, B. and Williams, A. (2004) 'Virtual offenders: The other side of Internet allegations', in M. Calder (ed.), *Child Sexual Abuse and the Internet: Tackling the New Frontier*. Dorset: Russell House Publishing, pp. 113–32.

Tremblay, P. (2006) 'Convergence settings for non-predatory "boy lovers"', in R. Wortley and S. Smallbone (eds), *Situational Prevention of Child Sexual Abuse* (Crime Prevention Studies, Vol. 19). New York: Criminal Justice Press, pp. 145–68.

US Customs Service. (2001) 'US Customs, Moscow City Police team up against child pornography', *US Customs TODAY*, April.

US Postal Inspection Service (2001) *Annual Report of Investigations 2001.* Chicago, Illinois (retrieved 20 July 2006, from http://www.usps.com/postalinspectors).

Utting, W. (1997) *People Like Us: The Report of the Review of the Safeguards for Children Living Away from Home.* London: The Stationery Office.

Vachss, A. (1987) *Strega.* New York: Knopf.

Veyne, P. (1987) 'The Roman Empire', in P. Veyne (ed.), *A History of Private Life. Vol. 1. From Pagan Rome to Byzantium* (General Editors: P. Ariès and G. Duby). Cambridge, MA: Harvard University Press, pp. 5–234.

Walsh, P. (2004) 'Internet child abuse: Characteristics of those who download', Paper presented at the Fifth Annual National Prosecutors' Conference, Dublin (forwarded to authors upon request).

White, A. (2006) *Virtually Obscene: The Case for an Uncensored Internet.* Jefferson, NC: McFarland.

Wilding, E. (2003) 'Operation Ore: The tip of the iceberg?', *Computer Fraud and Security Bulletin*, March.

Williams, K. (2004) 'Child pornography law: Does it protect children?', *Journal of Social Welfare and Family Law*, 26(3): 245–61.

Wilson, G.D. and Cox, D.N. (1983) *The Child-Lovers: A Study of Paedophiles in Society.* London: Peter Owen.

World Health Organization (1999) *Report of the Consultation on Child Abuse Prevention, Geneva, 29–31 March 1999.* Geneva: WHO.

Wortley, R. and Smallbone, S. (2006) *Child Pornography on the Internet.* Problem-Oriented Guides for Police. Problem-Specific Guides Series No. 41. Washington, DC: US Department of Justice.

Wyre, R. (2003) 'No excuse for child porn' (retrieved 4 April 2005, from www.communitycare.co.uk).

Yar, M. (2006) *Cybercrime and Society.* London: Sage.

Zevitz, R.G. and Farkas, M.A. (2000) 'Sex offender community notification: Examining the importance of neighborhood meetings', *Behavioral Sciences and the Law*, 18: 393–408.

Index

Dodgson, Charles Lutwidge 4
domestic violence 103
drawings 19, 65, 228
Dublin 105, 107, 126
Dutroux case 15, 23–5, 117, 118, 163, 196
DVDs 89

Eastern Europe 21, 23, 56, 90
e-commerce 33
Edinburgh 217
Edith Wilkins Foundation 101
email 32, 37, 40, 41, 42, 155, 190
encryption 39, 48, 82, 161–2, 165, 171
End Child Prostitution in Asian Tourism (ECPAT) 23, 26
ephebophiles 79
Ethical Hackers Against Pedophilia 177
European Union 26–7, 117, 163
    Data Retention Directive 233
    Framework Decision on Combating the Sexual Exploitation of Children and Child Pornography 153
    harmonisation of laws 231
Europol 27, 162
evidence 69
    digital 160, 168–70
    insufficient 179
evidence elimination 48
extradition treaties 159
extraterritorial criminal laws 21

family 52, 53, 58–9, 109–11, 216
Fanny Hill 3
FBI 11, 60, 63, 80, 119, 156, 176
feminist movement 15
Ferns, diocese of 107
fetishes 34
films 190
filters 45
Fine Gael 102
fines 101, 140, 142

Finland 206
First Amendment 8, 18, 65
First World Congress against the Commercial Sexual Exploitation of Children 26, 65, 117
floppy disks 89
Fondation Nouvelle 14
For Money or Love: Boy Prostitution in America 16
Fortune, Fr. Sean 106
France 206
free speech 12, 155
Freud, Sigmund 35, 235
Furedi, Frank 231

Gadd, Paul 69, 227
Garry Glitter see Gadd, Paul
Germany 10, 13, 31, 70, 118
Gibney, George 112
Ginsberg, Allen 12, 235
Globe and Mail 55–6
Gnutella 39, 40
Google 30, 32, 34, 205
Granada Institute 83, 196
Greater Manchester Police Abusive Images Unit 50
Greece 197, 206
Greeks, ancient 3
grooming 42, 43, 59–60, 61, 73, 222

hacking 157, 176
hard drives 89
Hayler, Henry 4
Health and Efficiency 4–5
hebephiles 79
Hefner, Hugh 7
Hindley, Myra 213
History of Photography 67
Hose, Keith 9
hotline 171–3

I Choose To Live 24
identity theft 157
images
    anatomical focus 189

lawyers 84
LeCraw, James 211
Lejeune, Julie 23, 24
Lelièvre, Michel 24, 25
Lenihan, Brian 105
Lithuania 31
Lloyd, Robin 16
Lolita magazine 7, 28, 71
Lolita series 6, 18, 71
Lolita Slavinder 19
Los Angeles 8, 35
Louis XIII 206
Lovett, Ann 103
Lucerne 85

Macmillan publishers 67
magazines 5–6, 8–9, 17, 18, 19–20,
    21, 28, 88
  barely legal 189
  collecting 83
  criminalise sale of 114–15
  decline of sex-related 34
  underground 9
Magdalene laundries 104–5
Maine 217
Malcolm in the Middle 90
malls 45
manga 66
Manila 21
Mankoff's Lusty Europe 21
Mann, Sally 67, 225
Mapplethorpe, Robert 67, 225–6
Marchal, An 23
marriage 83–4, 127
masturbation 70, 83, 93, 94, 95, 111,
    123, 209, 223, 224, 227–8
McCabe, Pablo 108
McColgan, Joseph 110–11
McGennis, Fr. Paul 113
McGuinness report 110
McQuaid, Archbishop John Charles
    113
media, the
  amount of coverage 64, 118
  campaign in America 17–18

discovered paedophile 208–9
and Dutroux case 25
gagging orders 139, 203
get it wrong 202
interest in Ireland 100–3, 106,
    108, 117, 118, 120–1, 135, 139
intrusion 225
mixed messages 216–17
Operation Ore and 169–70
public perception 201–3
publishing names 211–12
sensational reports 201
tabloid newspapers 120–1, 203,
    212, 216
Members of Parliament 84
Mexico 9
Microsoft 119, 174
Millbank, Joseph 73
Miller, Marvin 7–8
Miller test 8, 18
miscarriages of justice 170
mobile phones 63,
    3G 175
modems 36, 57
money-laundering 62
morphed images 28, 66, 91–2 *see
    also* computer-generated images
Moscow 37
MySpace 44

Namibia 66
Napster 39
National Center for Missing and
    Exploited Children (NCMEC) 176
National Centre for Technology in
    Education 41
National Crime Squad (NCS) 39
naturist magazines 4
Naughton, Fr. Thomas 107
Netherlands 7, 13, 14, 18, 19, 37,
    39, 73, 126, 206
  access to Internet 31
New Hampshire 85
New Jersey 62, 217
New South Wales 198

appropriate 192–201
maximum 137, 147
nature of material central to 196
Penthouse 34
Philippines 52, 89, 156, 207
photographers 78
photographs
books containing 67
collecting 87
compared 229
computers and 36, 89
family 188, 225
Internet and 57, 63
naturist 5
pseudo 66, 192, 228, 234
readers' 6
Victorian England 4
Playboy 7, 34, 35, 219
police
amateurism of 25
conspiracy of silence and inaction 107
Irish investigations 121–4
presence on Internet 81, 158–9
police officers 84
investigating cybercrime 162–3
policing 153–78
balancing act 173
difficulties in 155–62
resources needed 160–1, 165
sting operations 155
target groups 154–5
threats to investigators 163
political debates 112, 117
pornography
adult 4, 165–6, 178
amount on Internet 54
change from commercial to homemade 17
decriminalising 5
differing definitions 35
hardcore 54
link to sexual misconduct 15
printing 3
postal services 88

poverty 52, 159, 226, 234, 235
premium rate numbers 217–18
priests 103, 105
probation 142–3
Probation and Welfare officers 139
profit 78, 87
Project Snowball 211
prosecutions 127–8
challenges to 186–90
failed 180–6
prostitutes 84, 207
prostitution 15, 16, 21–3, 26, 27, 65, 66, 72, 103, 113
Protection of Children Against Sexual Exploitation Act 1977 (USA) 17
psychiatric disorder 79
Psychological Bulletin 47
psychological perspective 93–4
Pumbroek, Thea 96, 222, 228
punishment 103, 179–204
conviction as 212–13
eroding disparities 201–3
totality of 198–201
variation in USA 197–8
Punishment of Incest Act 1908 (Ireland) 109–10

Rädda Barnen 53
radical politics 9
Rage 92
Ramsey, JonBenet 93, 219–20
rape 103, 127
Read, 'Chopper' 213
recidivism 76, 210
recreational areas 45
Reedy, Thomas and Janice 119–20
Register of Prohibited Publications 115
Regpay Co. Ltd. 62
Regulation of Investigatory Powers Act 2000 (UK) 162
religion 84
remorse 138, 194
Rene Guyon Society 11
researchers 49–50 *see also* academics